Teaching Reading in the Middle Grades

Understanding and Supporting Literacy Development

James A. Rycik

Ashland University

Judith L. Irvin

Florida State University

PEARSON

Boston • New York • San Francisco
Mexico City • Montreal • Toronto • London • Madrid • Munich • Paris
Hong Kong • Singapore • Tokyo • Cape Town • Sydney

Senior Editor: *Aurora Martinez*
Editorial Assistant: *Kevin Shannon*
Marketing Manager: *Amy Cronin Jordan*
Production Editor: *Greg Erb*
Editorial-Production Service: *Walsh & Associates, Inc.*
Composition and Prepress Buyer: *Linda Cox*
Manufacturing Buyer: *Andrew Turso*
Electronic Composition: *Publishers' Design and Production Services, Inc.*
Cover Administrator: *Kristina Mose-Libon*

For related titles and support materials, visit our online catalog at www.ablongman.com.

Between the time Web site information is gathered and published, some sites may have closed. The publisher would appreciate notification where these errors occur so that they may be corrected in subsequent editions.

Disclaimer

This book offers expert and reliable information regarding the exams and content that it covers. It is sold with the understanding that the purchaser/user will verify all of the information about these exams since said information is subject to change. The purchaser/user also recognizes that no promise of success can reasonably accompany the purchase/use of this book. All information about the exams addressed in this text is taken from publicly available materials and materials available as a matter of the public record. The author and publisher specifically disclaim any liability that is incurred from any and all types of use/misuse and/or application/misapplication of the contents herein.

Library of Congress Cataloging-in-Publication Data

Rycik, James A.
    Teaching reading in the middle grades : understanding and supporting literacy development /
by James A. Rycik and Judith L. Irvin.
        p.   cm.
    Includes bibliographical references and index.
    ISBN 0-205-37322-4
    1. Reading (Middle school)   I. Irvin, Judith L., 1947–   II. Title.

LB1632.R93 2004
428.4'017'2—dc22   2004051041

Printed in the United States of America

10 9 8 7 6 5 4 3 2 1   09 08 07 06 05 04

Contents

3   *Reading the Words: Word Identification and Vocabulary Development*   **36**

4   *Mastering Messages: Learning the Purposes and Forms of Written Language*   **53**

5 *Engaging with Texts: Motivation and Personal Reasons to Read   67*

PART TWO • *Supporting the Literacy Development of All Students   83*

6 *Environments for Diverse Learners: Scaffolds and Literacy Routines   85*

8   *Guided Reading: Planning Students' Engagements with Texts*   *120*

9   *Guided Literature Study*   *135*

Preface

Teaching reading has become a high-pressure endeavor in recent years. Every day it becomes more apparent that literacy is crucial in determining the quality of life for the students. Efforts to set standards and measure performance both reflect and add to the pressure. We wrote this book to support the efforts of teachers and students working to achieve new and higher standards of reading proficiency in grades 4–8.

Throughout this book, you will find references to recent documents that articulate standards for proficient reading performance and for effective instruction. These documents have been developed by professional organizations, researchers, and government agencies, including the National Council of Teachers of English, the International Reading Association, and the National Reading Panel. We believe that these standards provide a useful synthesis of current research and practice about teaching methods, but we are also aware that research shows that the crucial factor in student achievement is the teacher, not only the method.

Students in grades 4–8 receive their reading instruction in a variety of settings from self-contained classrooms in an elementary school; to language arts classrooms; to science, social studies, or other content area classrooms; to separate reading classes. Instruction may be delivered by a teacher who has prepared to teach all subjects, by a specially prepared reading specialist, by a language arts teacher, or by a teacher who has had no preparation at all. We have tried to meet the specific needs of all the teachers who have been given responsibility for developing the proficiency of readers in the middle grades.

For language arts teachers, who are often concerned with smoothing the transition to high school, we have included chapters on scaffolding the comprehension of literature as well as ways of integrating reading with the other language arts. Teachers working in self-contained classrooms may find the chapter on planning units particularly useful. Administrators, reading teachers, and reading specialists will find the chapters on classroom routines and designing interventions particularly useful. We intend, however, that every chapter will add its unique perspective on proficient reading and the environments that support improved literacy learning of young adolescents.

Assessment and vocabulary development are essential topics in any literacy discussion. Rather than write separate chapters on these important topics, we chose to infuse them throughout the book when they naturally connect to instruction. The book is divided into two parts: (1) a general presentation of issues important to middle grades literacy, including meeting the needs of struggling readers and English language learners; and (2) routines, strategies, and assessment within the language arts and reading classroom.

Within each chapter, you will find an activity to activate your prior knowledge on the topic and to generate questions you may have about the literacy issue. At the end of the chapter, you will find an activity to help you check your comprehension or to organize your knowledge. In addition, you will find *A Case to Consider*, which will help you apply your new knowledge to a "real life" situation. *Beyond the Book* is designed to assist you in exploring the topic further through additional reading and Internet sites.

We have both spent our careers assisting young adolescents to read and write well, and we work with teachers every day. We hope that this book becomes a resource to you as you work toward improving the literacy performance of your students.

Finally, we would like to thank the reviewers of this book for their valuable feedback during the writing process: Lee A. Dubert, Boise State University; Lois E. Huffman, North Carolina State University; Paul L. Markham, University of Kansas; and Mary-Kate Sableski, University of Dayton.

James A. Rycik

Judith L. Irvin

I

Literacy in the Middle Grades

1

What Middle Grades Readers Need and What Their Teachers Need to Understand

Activating Prior Knowledge and Generating Questions

A group of students in Ms. Wolfowitz's sixth-grade class gathered around a computer. They had just finished reading Jerry Spinelli's (1997) book *Wringer,* which described a town that held an annual pigeon shoot in which hundreds of birds were shot for sport. They had already found information about a town in Pennsylvania where such a yearly event actually occurred until protests from outside activists stopped it. Now they were searching the Web for information that they could use in a debate about whether humans had the right to kill animals that they considered to be "pests."

Ms. Wolfowitz suggested issues such as thinning the population of deer herds and releasing wolves into areas of the west where they might kill cattle, and the group decided to begin their search by typing "reintroducing wolves" into a browser. As they searched, they built and saved a file of relevant pages and highlighted particular facts and quotes. Mrs. Wolfowitz stopped by and talked with them about ways they could keep track of the sources of their information. They discussed the meaning of several words, and she reminded them that there was a link on the menu that would take them to an online dictionary.

The debate was lively since there were several students in the class who were weekend hunters and objected strongly to the assertion made by some of their classmates that "killing animals is always wrong." Eventually, the students would write letters to newspapers or to appropriate government agencies in an effort to persuade others of their opinions or to stir them to action.

Before you go on with this chapter, consider these three questions:
1. How do these students show that they are proficient readers and writers?
2. How does this activity allow students to expand their understanding of language, of themselves, and of the world?
3. How does the teacher in this classroom support students as they move from the known to the unknown?

What Young Adolescent Readers Need

In many schools around the country, teachers and administrators working in the middle grades are struggling to address demands that they be more accountable for the reading proficiency of all students. Often, these demands are framed in terms of improving students' performance on state mandated tests, but there is also a growing realization that preparing young adolescents for the future requires preparing them for a more literate world. In *Adolescent Literacy: A Position Statement* (Moore, Bean, Birdyshaw, & Rycik, 1999), the International Reading Association's (IRA) Commission on Adolescent Literacy assert that

> Adolescents entering the adult world in the 21st century will read and write more than at any other time in human history. They will need advanced levels of literacy to perform their jobs, run their households, act as citizens, and conduct their personal lives. They will need literacy to cope with the flood of information they will find everywhere they turn. They will need literacy to feed their imaginations so they can create the world of the future. In a complex, and sometimes even dangerous world, their ability to read will be crucial. (p.3)

The position statement calls for a commitment by educators, parents, policy makers, and communities to give adolescent literacy as much attention as has traditionally been given to beginning readers. The need for that level of commitment may seem obvious, but the general public, and even some educators, have too often believed either that students in the middle grades have learned all there is to know about reading or that it is too late for them to learn.

The Need for Continued Instruction

The need for reading instruction during the middle grades is not the result of any failure on the part of elementary teachers. Students need additional reading instruction for the same reason that they need additional math instruction: to support further growth and development. Students in the middle grades must continually extend what they learned in the elementary grades as they encounter new kinds of text and read about topics that may be far removed from their personal experience.

Reading instruction in the middle grades is not just for students who struggle. Nevertheless, it is important to acknowledge that many students in the middle grades do struggle. A study by Showers, Joyce, Scanlon, and Schnaubelt (1998) found that approximately

30 percent of the students leaving the primary grades lacked basic reading skills. In that same year, the *Reading Report Card* issued by the National Assessment of Educational Progress (NAEP) indicated that 38 percent of fourth-grade students had failed to achieve even the "basic" level of performance, and only 31 percent were reading at or above the "proficient" level (Donahue, Voekl, Campbell, & Mazzeo, 1999).

NAEP findings for eighth graders suggested that students were not achieving dramatic improvements during the middle grades. The number of eighth-grade students below the basic level fell to 26 percent, but the percentage of students scoring at the "advanced" level was actually *smaller* for eighth graders (only 3 percent) than it was for fourth grade (7 percent).

To become proficient (let alone advanced), middle grade readers require steady guidance. Humphrey (2002) points out that,

> Because reading achievement is the crucial link between middle school students and their future success, it is vital that middle schools provide the personnel, time, and resources needed to produce successful readers. Middle school students should have the support of reading teachers every day, just as they are engaged each day with teachers of English, mathematics, science, and social studies. Moreover, special attention from reading teachers should be given to those students who read two or more grade levels below their expected level. (p. 754)

During the middle grades, students experience dramatic changes in both the amount and the kind of reading they are expected to do. In their content area classes, they are often confronted with informational texts that are complex, detailed, and filled with difficult vocabulary. They need instruction during these years that will help them to cope with these new demands. They also need guidance to become increasingly independent in using what they have already learned. Finally, they need continued instruction that acknowledges and builds upon their unique developmental needs.

The Need for Developmentally Appropriate Experiences

The reading development of young adolescents is best understood in relation to their overall development as individuals. In many ways, early adolescence is a time of paradoxes, "a period of both enormous opportunities and enormous risks" (Carnegie Council on Adolescent Development, 1989, p. 20). As Figure 1.1 illustrates, the reading of young adolescents is entangled with all of the chaotic relationships, feelings, and explorations of that period in their lives. Treating growth in reading as unconnected from growth in every other part of life would be disastrous; it is probably not even possible.

Irvin and Strauss (2000) note that the series of swift and dramatic physical changes that begin at the onset of puberty are accompanied by changes in intellectual capacity and emotional stability as well as moral development.

> Many students develop the ability to think abstractly. Well-known to most middle grades teachers is that emotions tend to run high at this age and are often unpredictable. This pe-

Kate —

I can't believe this woman actually expects us to read this stuff! She should know us better than that by now. God, I hate where I sit. Are you doing anything Saturday? Do you want to go to the Dance? Will your mom let you if your answers are No, Yes, Yes, Read the next question. Do you think I could spend the night with you and your mom could take us. But, if you don't want to that's OK. It was just an idea. Mrs. Hillert just started talking again. Why can't she leave us be. I don't wanna listen to her lectures. If you do want to go I would ask my mom to take us but I'm not allowed to go. What a bunch of rejects?! Call me when you get home and tell me.
                                        Gotta go.
                                            Love,
                                            Anna

FIGURE 1.1 *Anna's Note*

riod of life is also characterized by a new sense of social awareness in which students move from the security of the family to an added dependence on their relationships with their peers. Coping with and adapting to all these new experiences is often difficult for young adolescents. (p. 118)

Literacy experiences are developmentally appropriate when they can accommodate all of the changes and stresses in students' lives while allowing them to use their new understandings of language, themselves, and the world. Consider, for example, how students' developmental needs are addressed in the scenario at the beginning of this chapter.

- The freedom to move around the room from computers to various reference books accommodates the difficulty that many young adolescents have in sitting still for extended periods of time.

- Students are asked to move gradually from reacting to the concrete example depicted in the novel to framing logical arguments based on abstract principles.
- Working in small groups allows social interaction with peers but also develops skills of negotiating and compromising in order to complete the task.
- Students have opportunities to explore and affirm their own moral principles while considering "gray areas" where positive values may conflict with each other. They can also learn to interact respectfully with individuals whose values differ from their own.
- The support provided by the teacher and by peers makes success likely, and success builds the confidence that leads to emotional stability and a feeling of self-worth.

Young adolescents need the opportunity to *learn* literacy through experiences that provide both challenge and security. They also need to *use* literacy in ways that are meaningful in the context of their dramatically changing life experiences.

Diversity of Needs

All young adolescents are coping with dramatic physical, social, and psychological changes in their lives, and most are facing the challenges of increasing academic demands. It would be a mistake, however, to think that all middle grades students are alike. Teachers in the middle grades, like their colleagues at other levels, are challenged to respond to the needs of a population that is increasingly diverse in language, experience, values, and abilities. In this book, we will focus especially on the needs of students in middle grades who are in the process of learning English.

In some states, more than one in three students speaks a language other than English. English language learners may be at varying ends of a spectrum. Some may be newcomers to the United States, speaking little to no English. Others may have been in the country since kindergarten, without becoming proficient readers or without learning the academic language necessary to be productive in school. As a result, our public school system faces enriching opportunities, as well as enormous challenges, to ensure that English language learners (ELL) receive the education that they deserve.

What Teachers Need to Understand

Literacy teachers in the middle grades might be excused if they experienced a bit of panic when they consider the many needs of their students. Bintz (1997) found that many teachers in the middle grades—including English teachers—experienced "reading nightmares." They could see that their students were often unable or unwilling to meet the reading demands of the curriculum, but they felt powerless to correct the problem.

Humphrey (2002) points out that many middle school teachers were prepared for subject-matter disciplines and may have had only one course dealing with reading. Even those middle school teachers who completed a program in elementary education may have limited preparation for reading development in middle grades because that program may have placed a heavy emphasis on beginning reading instruction.

We believe that teachers can fight nightmares with knowledge. Basic knowledge about reading and readers provides a map that they can use to guide students' literacy journeys. Specifically, teachers in the middle grades need (1) an understanding of proficient reading and writing, a clear vision of the destination; (2) an understanding of literacy development so that they recognize important milestones along the way; and (3) some basic principles for creating environments that support students during the journey.

Understanding Proficiency in Literacy

Imagine that an alien scouting party observed you reading this chapter. They see you looking at an object in your hands, moving your eyes back and forth, and occasionally turning pages. Suppose they asked you to explain. How would you answer the following questions?

- Why do you sometimes pause and look off into space or shift your gaze back to a part of the page you have previously examined?
- How do you know the meaning of all of the words on the page, and how do you know that you have received the message successfully?
- Do all of the people of your planet read such books, or only the most powerful and important people?

The alien visitors could carefully observe the outward behaviors of reading and writing and yet be totally unable to understand the significance of what they were seeing. That would be understandable for aliens, but even people from highly literate societies may find that the apparently simple and ordinary activity of reading becomes complex and mysterious when they are asked to explain it.

Attempting to explain reading is like the story of the blind men trying to describe an elephant. Each man came to the conclusion that the elephant was like a rope, a snake, or something else depending on whether he was examining the tail, the trunk, or some other part of the body. Different researchers and educators have tended to focus on different parts of reading because the whole is too large and too complex to be easily understood. Tompkins (2003) compared theories of reading to pieces in a jigsaw puzzle that each contribute to an understanding of the whole picture. The blind men came to some understanding of elephants when they combined their individual impressions, and teachers can better understand reading when they use a model that includes more than one perspective.

Recent models of literacy have tried to show that reading involves a number of different components that can be considered separately but that work together during actual reading and writing events. Luke and Freebody (1999), for instance, identify "a family of literacy practices" that include breaking the code of written texts, understanding and composing meaningful texts, using texts for functional purposes inside and outside school, and critically analyzing the ways in which written material represents social and cultural viewpoints. Similarly, Greenleaf, Schoenbach, Cziko, and Mueller (2001) identify four "dimensions" of literacy that could be combined in order to "apprentice" adolescent readers.

Table 1.1 combines insights from these and other models in order to depict four components of proficient reading. Understanding these components may help you to understand the reading process and to assess and guide the reading of your students.

TABLE 1.1

Reading the Words	*Making Meaning*
• Integrating cues	• Using and building schemas
• Letters and sounds	• Strategic reading
• Syntax clues	• Monitoring
• Using context	• Using text structure
• Morphology	• Reader response
Mastering Messages	*Engaging with Text*
• Communication competence	• Confidence and competence
• Purposes and effects of language	• Identity development
• Critical literacy	• Attitudes and values
• Media literacy	• Motivation
• Genre knowledge	• Ownership

Reading the Words.   This component corresponds to the "code-breaking" practices identified by Luke and Freebody (1999). This aspect of proficiency involves smoothly and easily recognizing the words on the page. Word identification certainly includes an understanding of the relationship between letters and sounds, but it involves much more. Readers recognize words by using different kinds of "cues," both sound (phonics) and sense (context). We will examine that process in Chapter 3.

Mastering Messages.   The ability to identify words and to understand the ideas in texts are certainly crucial to reading proficiency. Readers are not proficient, however, if they do not see the uses of reading and writing. Literacy is, to a great extent, a matter of learning why people send and receive messages and the forms those messages can take. The IRA/NCTE *Standards for the English/Language Arts* (IRA, 1996) point out that although reading and writing are often thought of as solitary activities, the use of reading and writing is intertwined with relationships to other people.

> All of us draw on our own sets of experiences and strategies as we use language to construct meanings from what we read, write, hear, say, observe, and represent. These specific meanings are individual and personal. Yet the range of possible meanings that we can discover and know is, to a great extent, socially determined. What we can know is much influenced by what those in our language community know and by our shared experiences and shared texts. (p 22)

Proficient readers and writers know that written language can be directed toward a wide range of audiences for many different purposes, and they draw on that knowledge when interpreting or creating texts. Chapter 4 emphasizes that students can learn about the uses of language through reading, through writing, or, perhaps most powerfully, through experiences in which reading and writing are combined.

Making Meaning.   Making meaning, or reading comprehension, can be thought of as the cognitive or thinking dimension of reading (Greenleaf, Schoenbach, Cziko, & Mueller, 2001). When reading proficiently, individuals are able to see beyond individual words and to create connections among text ideas. They also create connections between the ideas in the text and their own background knowledge and experience. In this way, reading both requires and builds knowledge of the world.

Engaging with Text.   An understanding of proficiency must include the attitudes and beliefs of readers as well as their knowledge and skill. Proficient reading is most likely to occur when readers have a high level of engagement with a reading task (Guthrie & Wigfield, 1997). When readers show a high level of engagement, they have an inclination to *find* interest in what they read, and they feel confident that they can make sense of even a difficult text.

The engagement component of reading includes the notion of developing a reader identity (Greenleaf, Schoenbach, Cziko, & Mueller, 2001). The way that people see themselves as readers and writers is closely connected with the way they see themselves as individuals and as members of society. Atwell (1998), for instance, provides a picture of a reader that would be very much at odds with the way most young adolescents would like to see themselves.

> Ensconced in a leather wing chair in his book-lined study, he's pedantic and dispassionate. He keeps his encounters with books free of messy personal associations and biases: instead he brings to bear a received body of literary theory and history. The good reader reads no text more contemporary than Hemingway. He finishes every book he starts. He reads every single word. He looks up any word he's not certain of, but only after applying his extensive knowledge of Greek and Latin roots, prefixes, and suffixes. He is *not* us. (p 30)

In contrast to this mythical reader, most middle school students do not read and write to demonstrate superiority or to show respect for literary tradition. They read because they have had frequent opportunities to engage successfully with meaningful texts.

The concepts of engagement and reader identity, which will be discussed at greater length in Chapter 5, give teachers a new perspective for explaining motivation to read and for understanding reluctant and resistant readers.

Multiple Literacies.   A description of reading proficiency needs to be comprehensive enough to take in the enormous range of activity that involves making meaning from both print and nonprint texts. It also needs to include literacy activities that are not traditionally found in classrooms. Vacca and Alvermann (1998) point out that the view of proficient reading that is traditionally promoted in school—what they called "literacy with a big L"—excludes many of the nonacademic kinds of literacy that adolescents value most highly. They agree with many other current theorists and educators (e.g., Bean, Bean, & Bean, 1999; New London Group, 1996; Phelps, 1997) who have argued that it is more accurate to speak of the "multiple literacies" of adolescents. These multiple literacies include workplace and consumer literacy and, especially, the use of media and technology.

Understanding Literacy Development

Teachers need a clear vision of the literacy goals students may attain, but they also need to understand where their students have been and how the journey toward proficiency might unfold. In other words, teachers and administrators need to understand literacy development.

The development of literacy is often described in terms of grade levels. A particular student may be said to be reading "at grade level" or to have scored "at a fourth grade level" on a reading test. These expressions may provide a useful shorthand for describing students' progress, but they also tend to hide the complexity of literacy development. Students may, for instance, read "at grade level" with fiction material or with a topic of interest, but struggle with nonfiction or with material that is not obviously related to their interests.

An alternative to describing reading development in terms of grade levels is to describe the stages or phases that readers pass through on their way to proficiency. Gillet, Temple, Crawford, and Cooney (2003) identify five stages in reading development that begin well before students reach school and continue throughout a lifetime. These stages are described in Table 1.2. Note the wide age ranges identified with the last two stages,

TABLE 1.2   *Stages of Reading Development*

Stage	What Is Being Learned
Emergent Literacy (Typical at ages 2–5)	• Conventions of print (e.g., left to right, top to bottom) • That letters represent sounds • How to represent thoughts in writing and pictures • What stories sound like (their language and structure)
Beginning Reading (Typical at ages 5–6)	• Recognizing matches between specific letters and sounds • Recognizing some words at sight • Using context to predict words • Using prior knowledge to predict events • How to form text that is readable by others
Building Fluency (Typical at ages 7–8)	• Reading independently from picture story books and beginning "chapter books" • Reading faster and more easily • Readily spelling many words and figuring out many more • Using patterns from reading in writing stories
Reading for Pleasure Reading to Learn (Typical at ages 8–18)	• Finding and reading books for pleasure, often chapter books of 100 pages or more • Using reading to find information they would not get otherwise • Becoming familiar with many sentence structures and forms of written language • Writing fluently for a variety of purposes
Mature Reading (May appear at ages 8–18)	• Reading critically by "arguing back" against books and looking for hidden biases • Reading multiple sources on a subject for added perspective • Being aware of the artistry (or lack of skill) shown in a piece of writing • Seeking out more challenging books

which would take in many middle school students. This suggests a wide range of individual differences among students.

The Reading for Pleasure/Reading to Learn stage seems to be most typical of the middle grades. Young adolescents are building knowledge of the vast array of vocabulary, sentence structures, and text conventions they will need for mature reading. They also amass a priceless store of background knowledge. Reading in quantity, along with explicit instruction in the use of comprehension strategies, helps students learn that they can construct meanings from a wide variety of texts.

Gillet and Temple (1994) recommend that students in this stage have regular opportunities to read literature and to engage in response activities such as writing in journals or, especially, participating in group discussions where they can compare their responses to those of others. They should also receive explicit instruction in "reading to learn" strategies such as recognizing text structures and monitoring comprehension.

Although stage four may be most typical for middle school students, it is quite possible to find some students who function at stage one or at stage five. It is also important to remember that a particular student may struggle with some tasks from an early stage but have completed other tasks from a more advanced stage. English language learners, for instance, may struggle with word identification tasks typical of the Beginning Reading stage, but they may function at a much higher level in their primary language. Even if the young adolescent is literate in the primary language, the sounds and structures may be different in English. This needs to be taken into account when assessing literacy and planning instruction.

A large number of English language learners, as well as other students who are not typical, may be at the stage of Building Fluency. Gillet and Temple (1994) suggest that many children complete the tasks of this stage in second or third grade, but they caution that some students do not make the expected leap with ease; in addition their rate of reading and writing will need continued instruction.

> These children will be beginning to feel like failures, and that attitude itself may compound the problem. We need to keep working to build those children's abilities to recognize words, and we want to find books on their level so they can practice reading. We can't neglect reading to them either. They need to keep up their intake of written language for the information, vocabulary, and text structure it yields. Otherwise their future hurdles will loom even higher. (p. 44)

Literacy development in the middle grades is difficult to control or even to predict. Although teachers have to plan classroom activities carefully, learning does not always happen in an orderly sequence, and a great deal of variability can be found among students of the same grade level (and even within the same individual) from one situation to another (Ivey, 1998).

Hynds (1999) reflects on the complexities of literacy development that she observed during her three-year study with urban middle grades readers.

> Our stories form the essence of a much larger story—one that tells how unique and individualized and yet how socially and politically situated this process of becoming literate is. In Meg's classroom, the process never seemed to happen the same way for any two students.

Much of it was in fits and starts, and there was a lot of cycling backward before going forward. (p. 2)

Teachers of young adolescents must also be aware of the transitions students make as they enter and leave the middle grades. For some students, the shift from middle grades to high school becomes a dangerous leap. Wells (1996), for instance, describes the "literacies lost" when students experience a traumatic gap between their literacy experiences in the middle grades and the expectations of the high school.

Understanding Assessment

The International Reading Association (IRA) states that all reading professionals should be able to use a variety of assessment tools and practices to plan and evaluate effective reading instruction (IRA, 2003). Assessment should be an ongoing process that helps teachers make decisions and helps learners see that they are making progress.

Effective assessment, like effective instruction, begins with a clear notion of proficiency and an understanding of readers' development. Assessment can include evaluation—assigning grades or measuring students against criteria—but it also includes the minute-to-minute process of observing whether students are learning and deciding what they need to learn next.

Throughout this book, as we examine various theories of reading and instructional practices, we will include a discussion of related assessment procedures. This reflects our belief that assessment should serve to guide teaching and learning as well as to evaluate teachers and learners.

Understanding Environments for Literacy Learning

No "one right method" for teaching reading exists (Duffy & Hoffman, 1999), but teachers can create effective learning environments by drawing on well-established principles such as those set out by the Commission on Adolescent Literacy of the International Reading Association (Moore, Bean, Birdyshaw, & Rycik, 1999). These seven principles sum up much of what is known about how to support young adolescents' development toward proficient reading. They assert that adolescents deserve:

- Access to a wide variety of reading material that they can and want to read.
- Instruction that builds both the skill and desire to read increasingly complex materials.
- Assessment that shows them their strengths as well as their needs and that guides their teachers to design instruction that will best help them grow as readers.
- Expert teachers who model and provide explicit instruction in reading comprehension and study strategies across the curriculum.
- Reading specialists who assist individual students having difficulty learning how to read.

- Teachers who understand the complexities of individual adolescent readers, respect their differences, and respond to their characteristics.
- Homes, communities, and a nation that will support their efforts to achieve advanced levels of literacy and provide the support necessary for them to succeed.

These principles call for active instruction from teachers who understand the process of reading and the development of young adolescent readers. They contend that proficiency is a matter of both skill and will, and they acknowledge that reading is learned both inside and beyond the reading classroom.

For middle grades students, the best environments for literacy learning are likely to be highly social. This not only meshes with their natural preference for peer interaction, but it is also an important part of understanding what written language can do. In the scenario that opened this chapter, Ms. Wolfowitz's students worked together in small groups to gather information, discuss what they had read, and plan how to communicate their findings to the wider world outside their classrooms.

The scenario also illustrates the crucial balance between independence and guidance. Ms. Wolfowitz's students explore written language in self-directed activities and experiences, but she provides a structure for those activities, and she is constantly present to support students as they move outside their comfort zone to engage with more "adult" forms and purposes for using language.

The process of providing just the amount of support necessary for students to succeed is called "scaffolding." Teachers can provide a wide variety of scaffolds including modeling, questioning, and feedback on a student's performance.

In Chapters 6 through 12, we will discuss various literacy routines that support readers as they learn strategies for constructing meaning while they read. We will also show how these routines allow students to make choices and to share responsibility for their own learning.

Summary

In this chapter we have provided a brief overview of the academic and personal needs of young adolescents and the implications of those needs for their reading and writing. We have also identified some specific kinds of knowledge that teachers need in order to guide and support their students in the middle grades. This knowledge includes understanding:

- Proficient reading
- Reading development
- Uses and techniques of assessment
- Effective literacy environments

The next four chapters will examine the components of proficiency that were identified in this chapter and will suggest implications for instruction and assessment.

Responding to Reading _____

Place an *A* or a *D* on the first line before each statement to show whether you agree or disagree. Mark the second line to show whether you think the authors would agree. Be prepared to discuss your choices.

You   *Authors*

_____   _____   1. Students in middle grades need additional instruction in reading for the same reasons they need additional instruction in math.

_____   _____   2. Many current middle grades teachers feel unprepared to teach reading.

_____   _____   3. Proficiency in reading is best thought of as a set of skills that can easily be tested and practiced.

_____   _____   4. Middle-level readers need to understand reading as a thinking process and as a language process that is highly social.

_____   _____   5. When middle grades students do not have the reading skills that they need to succeed, they are unlikely to ever learn those skills.

_____   _____   6. Teaching reading in the middle grades is a matter of carefully examining the proficiency test used by the district and practicing the kinds of items that are on the test.

A Case to Consider _____

Josh is a sixth grader in a self-contained classroom in a small town. He says that he is an "ok" reader, but that he does not like to read. Josh passes tests on the stories assigned for language arts, but he rarely enjoys them, and he never chooses to read fiction on his own. He says that nothing much happens in the stories, and he loses interest. Then, when he picks up the book again, he cannot remember what has happened. He especially dislikes quizzes on words from the story.

Josh and his teacher share an interest in science. He frequently borrows copies of *Popular Science* from the classroom to read short articles about the latest gadgets. He complains about reading the science textbook, though, and his grades in science, as in other subjects, are average at best. He says his textbooks are "boring" and that he reads the assignments, but does not remember what he read. He likes to surf the web, stopping at sites such as the CIA and NASA where he can pick up unusual facts to share with his teacher and a small circle of friends.

Josh passed his school's "off-year" practice proficiency test, but just barely. He had particular trouble with the vocabulary items. He was assigned to a group that works with practice materials containing items like those on the proficiency test. He does these assignments, but he does not believe they are helping him much.

Respond to some or all of these issues related to this case:

1. Would you call Josh a proficient reader or not? What evidence of proficiency do you see? What evidence do you see that indicates that he is not proficient?

2. What further information would you want about Josh's reading if you were his teacher? How might you find out what you want to know?

3. What are some goals you would like to see Josh achieve if you were his teacher? What would you try to do to help him achieve those goals?

Key Terms to Know and Use

developmentally appropriate	literacy development	mastering messages
proficient reading	effective environments	multiple literacies
reading words	reading nightmares	assessment
engaging with text	making meaning	

Possible Sentences

Choose two or three terms in the columns above and write a sentence summarizing what you now know about "What Middle Grades Readers Need and What Their Teachers Need to Understand." Write four or five sentences using different words until you have a nice summary paragraph.

Beyond the Book

- Search the Web site of the International Reading Association at www.reading.org to locate some of the resources available on the subject of adolescent literacy. While you are there, you might want to download the complete text of *Adolescent Literacy: A Position Statement,* which is available at no cost.
- Ask some middle grades students or teachers to tell "What does a reader in the middle grades have to know or do to be considered proficient?" and list their responses. You might compare the responses given by the students in a particular class with those of their teacher. You might also want to compare the responses of students and teachers with state standards or the tasks on your local or state proficiency test.
- Reflect on your own experiences with reading in the middle grades and the following points:
  - How would you describe proficient reading in the middle grades?
  - What makes reading different in the middle grades from reading in the early grades?
  - In what kind of learning environment do you think middle grades' students learn most effectively?
- Choose one of the articles from the reference list below to read. What does the article say about what constitutes proficient reading? What does it say about effective instruction or assessment?

References

Atwell, N. (1998). *In the middle: New understandings about writing, reading, and learning.* Portsmouth, NH: Heinemann.

Bean, T. W., Bean, S. K., & Bean, K, F. (1999). Intergenerational conversations and two adolescents' multiple literacies: Implications for redefining content area literacy. *Journal of Adolescent and Adult Literacy,* 42(6), 438–448.

Bintz, W. P. (1997). Exploring the reading nightmares of middle and secondary school teachers. *Journal of Adolescent and Adult Literacy,* 41(1), 12–24.

Carnegie Council on Adolescent Development. (1989). *Turning points: Preparing American youth for the 21ˢᵗ century.* The report of the task force on education of young adolescents. New York: Author.

Donahue, P. L., Voekl, K. E., Campbell, J. R., & Mazzeo, J. (1999). *The NAEP 1998 reading report card for the nation and the states.* (NCES1999–500). Washington, DC: U. S. Department of Education, Office of Educational Research and Improvement, National Center for Educational Statistics.

Duffy, G., & Hoffman, J. V. (1999). In pursuit of an illusion: The flawed search for a perfect method. *The Reading Teacher,* 53(1), 10–16.

Gillet, J. W., & Temple, C. (1994). *Understanding reading problems: Assessment and instruction* (4th ed.). New York: HarperCollins.

Gillet, J. W., & Temple, C., Crawford, A. & Cooney, B. (2003). *Understanding reading problems: Assessment and instruction.* (5th ed.). Boston: Allyn and Bacon.

Greenleaf, C., Schoenbach, R., Cziko, C., & Mueller, F. (2001). Apprenticing adolescent readers to academic literacy. *Harvard Educational Review, 71* (1), 79–129.

Guthrie, J. T., & Wigfield, A. (Eds.). (1997). *Reading engagement: Motivating readers through integrated instruction.* Newark, DE: International Reading Association.

Humphrey, J. (2002). There is no simple way to build a middle school reading. *program. Phi Delta Kappan,* 83(10), 754.

Hynds, S. (1999). *On the brink: Negotiating literature and life with adolescents.* Newark, DE: The International Reading Association.

International Reading Association (IRA). (2003). *Standards for reading professionals,* Newark, DE: Author.

International Reading Association (IRA). (1996). *Standards for the English language arts.* Newark, DE: Author.

Irvin, J. L., & Strauss, S. E. (2000). Developmental tasks of early adolescence: the foundation of an effective literacy program. In K. D. Wood & T. S. Dickinson (Eds.), *Promoting literacy in grades 4–9: A handbook for teachers and administrators* (pp. 115–127).

Ivey, G. (1998). Discovering readers in the middle level school: A few helpful clues. *NASSP Bulletin* 82(600), 48–56.

Luke, A. & Freebody, P. (1999). Media and cultural studies in Australia. *Journal of Adolescent and Adult Literacy,* 42(8), 622–626.

Moore, D. W., Bean, T. W, Birdyshaw, D., & Rycik, A. (1999). *Adolescent literacy: A position statement.* Newark, DE: International Reading Association

New London Group (1996). A pedagogy of multiliteracies: Designing social futures. *Harvard Educational Review,* 66(1), 60–92.

Phelps, S. F. (1997). Adolescents and their multiple literacies. In D. E. Alvermann, K. A. Hinchman, D. W. Moore, S. F. Phelps, & D. R. Waffs (Eds.). *Reconceptualizing the literacies in adolescents' lives* (pp. 1–2). Mahwah, NJ: Lawrence Erlbaum.

Showers, B., Joyce, B., Scanlon, M., & Schnaubelt, C. (1998). A second chance to learn to read. *Educational Leadership,* 55(6), 27–30.

Spinelli, J. (1997). *Wringer.* New York: Harper Collins.

Tompkins, G. E. (2003). *Literacy for the 21ˢᵗ century* (3rd ed.). Upper Saddle River, NJ: Merrill/Prentice Hall.

Vacca, R. T., & Alvermann, D. E. (1998). The crisis in adolescent literacy: Is it real or imagined? *NASSP Bulletin,* 82(600), 4–9.

Wells, M. C. (1996). *Literacies lost: When students move from a progressive middle school to a traditional high school.* New York: Teachers College Press.

2

Constructing Meaning: The Process of Comprehending

Activating Prior Knowledge and Making Connections

Mr. Jimenez decided to involve his fifth graders in a little demonstration about how reading comprehension works. He gave them the following text and asked them to answer the questions without discussing them.

The man stood under the bright lights trying to decide. He had run three-quarters of the way, but now he had to be careful. Everything depended on his decision. He knew he was being watched. Would he be safe if he went home, or would the man in the mask be waiting for him? Home was in sight, but he was hesitating. If he made the wrong move, it was all over. He peered into the night hoping to see some sign that would help him know what to do. He thought about the man in the mask. He'd love to even that score. He took a few hesitant steps. Nothing happened. His mind was made up. He would chance it. He ran as fast as he could for home.

1. Where was the man standing?
2. Who was the man in the mask?
3. Why was he afraid to go home?

There was some giggling and some grumbling as the students attempted to complete this task. When they had finished, Mr. Jimenez asked them to share their answers. Many students answered question one, "under the bright lights." But when Mr. Jimenez questioned them, they admitted that they had no idea what the story was about. Some students answered, "on third base." They explained that they had decided that the story was about a baseball game and that the runner was trying to decide whether to steal home. A few students had answers such as "on a street corner under a street light." These students explained that the story reminded them of a movie in which someone was being followed by a killer. Mr. Jimenez led the class in a spirited discussion about which interpretation made more sense and why they could not agree.

The class agreed that the problem was in what the story did not say rather than the words or what it did say. Over the next few weeks, Mr. Jimenez reminded his students of this experiment as he talked with them about what makes a reading task difficult and how they could overcome those difficulties.

Before you continue reading this chapter, consider the following questions:
1. What made the "Man in the Mask" story difficult to comprehend?
2. What kinds of thinking did the students do in completing the task and in the discussion that followed?
3. How was this experience like or different from the usual reading assignment?

Thinking has always been recognized as a crucial part of reading, but until recently reading comprehension, like thinking in general, was considered to be a mysterious process that took place in a kind of "black box" where it could not be observed or explained. In this chapter, we examine two major theories that have been particularly helpful in helping teachers to understand the role of thinking in reading. *Schema theory* describes proficient reading by showing how readers actively interpret, organize, and recall ideas they encounter while reading. *Metacognition* describes how readers direct and evaluate their own thinking. These two theories will be applied to suggest specific practices for assessing and supporting the process of comprehending in the middle grades.

Comprehending

In what has become a landmark study, Dolores Durkin (1978–1979) went looking for reading comprehension instruction. She did not find it. After observing the reading instruction in dozens of classrooms, Durkin concluded that comprehension was being practiced in workbooks and tested by questions at the end of a story but that it was not being taught. Durkin's study highlights the crucial distinction between *comprehension* and *comprehending.* At first, this distinction may seem like splitting hairs, but it says a great deal about the progress that has been made in understanding reading over the past two decades.

At the time Durkin's study was done, comprehension was viewed as something a reader *has,* as in "Susan has good comprehension of that story." It was the product that resulted from good reading much like gold nuggets are the result of panning in a stream. Given that view, it made sense for teachers to examine readers' efforts by checking for "nuggets," the correct answers. By contrast, comprehending is now regarded as an action, something a reader *does.* The focus for instruction and assessment is on the panning, so to speak, rather than the pan, and teachers model and support techniques that students can use for effective comprehending.

This change in perspective about reading is part of a larger shift toward constructivism (Brooks & Brooks, 1999), which is the belief that knowledge is actively constructed by the learner rather than passively received. In a constructivist view, readers need to learn how to use what they already know in order to understand new information, and they need to take active control of the process.

Teachers in the middle grades need methods that will guide students to become independent in understanding the material they read in and outside of school. Effective instruction in comprehending helps all students, including English language learners, to adopt habits of thought that are necessary for constructing meanings when no teacher is present. The concept of scaffolding, which will be fully discussed in Chapter 6, is especially important because it involves both supporting students' interaction with a present text and preparing them to do the next task with less help.

For English language learners, comprehending will be limited by the level of English proficiency. Teachers may need to provide additional preparation for reading or specific instruction related to vocabulary and language patterns presented in the text. All students in the middle grades will benefit from experiences that build their ability to use their prior knowledge and direct their own thinking. Some students, including some English language learners, may need to use additional scaffolds to address cultural differences in knowledge and values.

Using and Building Knowledge While Comprehending

Tasks similar to the "Man in the Mask" story that Mr. Jimenez used in the opening scenario have been used in experiments designed to explore the nature of comprehending in reading (Bransford & Johnson, 1972; Chiesi, Spilich, & Voss, 1979; Prichert & Anderson, 1977). The insights gained from these and other experiments have been combined in a theory called *schema theory* that describes how readers use what they already know in the process of comprehending and remembering new information.

Schema theory begins with the idea that knowledge is contained in clusters of related memories and concepts (Anderson & Pearson, 1984) called schemas (or schemata). These clusters are connected to each other like strands in a spider web of memories that is woven from every experience a person has ever had. Schemas have been called the building blocks of cognition (Rumelhart, 1981). They are difficult to define precisely, so their role in comprehending can best be understood through analogies such as the one found in Table 2.1, which compares the process of comprehending to the process of storing and retrieving information in filing cabinets.

Notice that this analogy emphasizes that comprehending both requires and builds a reader's knowledge. Information is handled most easily when a file folder full of similar information is already close at hand. Since English language learners may not have the same prior experiences as English-only students, they may requiring preteaching in essential vocabulary, background information, and language patterns.

TABLE 2.1 *Filing Cabinet Analogy*

Filing Cabinet	Schemata
• To keep a new page, we need to find a file folder to put it in.	• To understand a new idea, we need to have some related prior knowledge.
• We put each "page" in a folder with similar facts.	• We associate new facts or concepts with previous ideas.
• Most pages are cross-referenced (i.e., copies are filed in several folders)	• We may connect a new fact with several different previous ideas.
• When a file folder gets too thick, we may reorganize it by dividing it into more than one category.	• As we learn, we may just add a fact to a previous topic, or we may create new mental categories for information.
• Similar folders are placed together in the same drawer.	• Each schema (e.g., dogs) is part of a larger schema (e.g., pets).
• A particular page is located by going to the appropriate drawer and searching through the likely folders.	• We remember by selecting a schema and systematically searching our related memories.
• Pages that are left lying around are thrown away.	• Facts or ideas that cannot be related to any prior knowledge are soon forgotten.

A Schema-Based Description of Proficient Reading

We will describe proficient reading from the perspective of Mr. Jimenez and the demonstration he conducted in the opening scenario of this chapter. The demonstration illustrates five principles about the process of comprehending.

- **Readers select which schema will be useful to understand the text.** The "Man in the Mask" story is difficult to read because it does not provide enough cues for a reader to select the appropriate schema. If it is given the title "Baseball," or even if words such as "field" or "catcher" are added, it becomes much easier to read—at least for those with some knowledge of baseball.
- **Readers use a schema to decide what is important in the text.** Once readers have decided that the story is about baseball, some facts become more important than others. The score and the inning, for instance, are important information in any baseball game. The bright lights are less important. One of the main functions of schemata is to help readers see the *significance* of the information in a text (Anderson, 1985). A schema acts as a sort of a filter that screens out what is unimportant and collects what is most relevant.
- **Readers use their schema to infer information that is not directly stated in the text.** Readers who have selected a baseball schema are able to answer questions such as "What inning is it?" or "How many outs are there?" by drawing on their prior knowledge about baseball. The more they know, the more inferences they can make. Very knowledgeable readers can even use their knowledge of baseball strategy to

answer questions such as "How deep are the outfielders playing?" with some degree of confidence.

- **Readers connect ideas to each other and to prior knowledge.** In proficient reading, information from the text is stored by connecting it to the selected schema, such as baseball. The reader considers how each new piece of information is related to the other pieces by using the schema. If it cannot be connected, it will probably be forgotten. Connecting new information to prior knowledge may also cause the reader to expand or revise the previous schema.

- **Readers remember information by recalling the schema.** To remember a text, a reader calls up the schema and uses it to direct a memory search. The reader might, for instance, remember that the runner was on third base by retrieving a baseball schema and using it to "reconstruct" the details. Anderson and Pearson (1984) note that readers may distort the text during this process by omitting or slightly changing details to fit their schemas. A baseball fan's schema might, for example, lead to "remembering" that the crowd was cheering even if the text says it was silent.

Some Implications of Schema Theory for the Classroom

Schema theory helps teachers understand why a student does or does not comprehend when reading a particular text (Rumelhart, 1984). If a group of students reads the "Man in the Mask" story, and only a few of them give the expected answers about baseball, a teacher might conclude that the others did not try hard enough or that the words were too difficult. Understanding the process of using and remembering information, however, leads to some very different explanations. Schema theory would guide teachers to consider the assumptions the author has made about the background knowledge, beliefs, and values of the readers. Looking at reading tasks in this way provides a basis for predicting the difficulties students may face and the kinds of scaffolds that may help them to overcome those difficulties.

Schema theory emphasizes that comprehending is influenced by the reader's "theory of the world," the unique network of knowledge and associations that a person has built up from experience. Since people from different cultures generally have had different experiences, it is reasonable to assume that they will tend to remember and interpret new information differently. Anderson (1985) describes an experiment in which black and white male teenagers read a passage involving "sounding," an activity in which participants try to outdo each other in an exchange of insults. African American males remembered the incident as involving friendly give-and-take, but white males tended to see it as an angry confrontation. Anderson concluded that "a critical issue is whether cultural variation within the United States could be a factor in differential reading comprehension. Minority children could have a handicap if stories, texts, and test items presuppose a cultural perspective that the children do not share" (p. 380).

It is important to remember that background knowledge includes not only information but also the associations and feelings that accompany that information. Culturally different experiences can mean differences in what readers perceive to be interesting or offensive.

Classroom Applications for Assessment

A PreReading Plan   Since schema theory emphasizes the importance of a reader's background knowledge, it is important that teachers assess students' relevant background knowledge before they read. Langer (1981) suggests a PreReading Plan (PreP) that begins with eliciting students' initial associations with an important concept from the reading. Students are encouraged to explain their associations and to discuss the ways in which their thinking changed after hearing the ideas of their peers. The teacher might begin by asking an "open-ended" question such as "What comes to mind when you hear the word *survival?*" and then record the students' responses. Occasional questions, such as "What made you think of a shipwreck?" can be interjected.

Teachers can judge how well prepared students are for reading by noting whether the associations that they made first and elaborated most are the ones most relevant to the material. If not, the teacher can plan to build or activate the appropriate schema before they read. Students can also write about their knowledge of the topic by using a list of ideas written on the chalkboard. They might, for instance, be asked to explain which items they know the most about, which were new, and which they think are most important. They could also be asked to assess their own readiness to read about the topic.

Assessing prior knowledge through brainstorming activities like PreP may be particularly appropriate for classrooms where there are a variety of language levels. In brainstorming, responses are accepted without any attempt to evaluate them, so the risk for English language learners is low. If a particular student is unable to make a connection with the concept, the teacher can provide an immediate explanation. Moreover, teachers can modify lessons according to the students' demonstrated familiarity with the concepts and language contained in the text.

Testing Comprehension   Schema theory raises questions about some traditional forms of postreading assessment. Bransford (1985) suggests that students who understand what they have read may still answer comprehension questions incorrectly because the schema they have used to understand the story differs slightly from that of the teacher. As a result, the cue or the question may evoke no response or a totally unexpected response. The "Man in the Mask" story provides an extreme example of this. If the teacher sees a baseball story, but the reader constructs a (perfectly sensible) interpretation involving a masked murderer, the student's answers will all be marked wrong. These "mismatches" between the teacher's understanding of a text and those of the students may be more likely to occur in culturally diverse classrooms.

Normal texts are not as open to interpretation as the "Mask" story, but teachers may want to consider whether some traditional assessments such as multiple choice questions are accurate reflections of reading success. A student might answer incorrectly because the question prompt simply does not "ring a bell" as it does for the teacher, or at least not the same bell. For English language learners, multiple choice questions can be difficult if the student is not familiar with the vocabulary in the question. Open-ended questions allow these students to choose familiar vocabulary and to show the teacher what they know. Students may also be asked to represent their knowledge in a graphic form that requires them to identify important concepts from the text and to show the connections between those ideas.

TABLE 2.2

Types of Questions				
Comprehension Level	*Required Responses*	*Source for Answers*	*Kinds of Interaction*	*Question–Answer Relationship*
Literal Level (text-based)	Correct answers	Reading the lines	Lead to recitation	Answers found "Right there"
Interpretive Level (text- and experience-based)	Defendable answers	Reading between the lines	Lead to convergent discussion	"Think and search" or "Author and me"
Applied Level (experience-based)	Explainable answers	Reading beyond the lines	Lead to divergent discussion	"On my own"

Schema theory suggests that comprehending is a process of not only recognizing information but also of making connections to ideas in the reader's background knowledge and to other ideas in the text. The questions that teachers ask to assess comprehension should elicit information about how they are making those connections. Table 2.2 shows the different types of questions that should be used in assessing how well students are comprehending, and includes question–answering relationships (Raphael, 1982).

Classroom Applications for Instruction

Table 2.2 shows questions that are appropriate for three different levels of comprehension: literal, inferential, and applied. Schema theory leads to the belief that instruction is effective when it helps students to combine new information with what they already know, to seek out the relationships between the various ideas in texts, and to expect reading to make sense. Specifically, schema-based instruction includes building, activating, and organizing background knowledge.

Building Relevant Background Knowledge

Using media.   If students have little knowledge experience related to the material they are about to read, the teacher will need to need to build knowledge that is relevant to the text. Often media are useful in this regard. For example, a middle school English class was about to read Irene Hunt's (1970) *No Promises in the Wind,* which is a book about two boys wandering the country during the Great Depression. The teacher realized that most students had a limited knowledge of that era and decided to prepare for the reading by showing an excerpt from the film *Paper Moon,* which also depicts two characters roaming the country during the Depression. Teachers may also want to relate the event to a similar event in a different country that represents the students in the class. This cultural validation helps English language learners connect with the concept that is being taught.

Using analogies. Vacca and Vacca (1999) recommend that teachers create such analogies for students to read and discuss before they read a difficult text. They emphasize that the analogy must focus on major ideas in the text and that the new ideas must be compared to an experience or an object that is familiar to the student. They also suggest adding a question or two at the end of the analogy to direct the readers' thinking about the text to be read.

Activating Background Knowledge

Brainstorming activities. The PreP procedure previously described is one example of helping students activate the knowledge that is relevant for reading. PreP is not only a guide for planning prereading instruction, it *is* prereading instruction. As students share their associations with the key concept, they are building each other's background knowledge and sorting out different strands of ideas related to the concept. The teacher can easily extend learning by simply pointing out which of the elements students have mentioned are most important to the reading, thereby activating the most relevant information they have. Many other instructional activities have been devised that involve the use of brainstorming to activate background knowledge before reading.

All brainstorming activities share a number of desirable features. They allow a high degree of participation because there are no "wrong" answers. They build confidence by showing students that they already know something about the topic of their reading, and they arouse curiosity about how various ideas will appear in the text. If students are encouraged to re-examine their initial associations after they have finished reading (as they do in a strategy such as KWL), they can experience the satisfaction of seeing that they know more after reading than before. During a strategy such as KWL (Ogle, 1986), teachers may want to invite the English language learners to respond first (the teacher may show the beginning or intermediate level ELL student a picture, help him or her write the word on the board, and then read the answer). This allows the ELL student to participate and to learn a new concept, all with differentiated instruction.

Helping Students to Connect and
Organize Ideas

Graphic Organizers. Schema theory suggests that comprehending and remembering require readers to *see* the relationships among ideas. Graphic organizers provide a means of helping readers distinguish main ideas from their supporting details (Alvermann, 1986). Students can use these organizers to create summaries of the material they have read. Graphic organizers help English language learners because they isolate the most important concepts and connections for the students to learn. When the English words and concepts

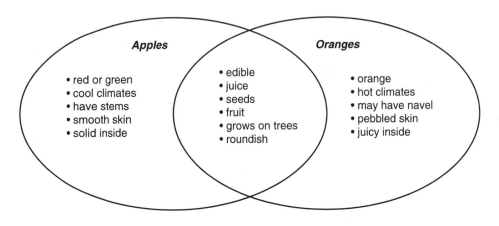

FIGURE 2.1

are new for the student, graphic organizers are invaluable in breaking down the material making it comprehensible.

Graphic organizers come in a variety of forms, but whatever form they take should reflect the underlying structure of the text. For instance, timelines can be used to reflect the structure of text in which the sequence of events is crucial, and Venn diagrams such as the one in Figure 2.1 can be used to highlight a compare and contrast organization.

Teachers can construct graphic organizers and use them to preview important ideas that will appear in the text and to help students see the connections between ideas in the material, but they are most effective when students create them after they read. The National Reading Panel (2000) reviewed the implications of research for instruction and concluded that,

> Teaching students to organize what they are reading about in a systematic, visual graph benefits the ability of the students to remember what they read and may transfer, in general, to better comprehension and achievement in social studies and science content areas. (pp. 4–5)

Metacognition and Reading

The only thing worse than not understanding is not knowing that you do no not understand. Effective readers are able to "watch" themselves reading so that they can see when they are having difficulty and can locate the obstacles to understanding. This ability to monitor comprehension is part of metacognition, which literally means thinking about thinking. Brown (1985) notes that students who are able to reflect on their own thinking processes while reading are able to take more active control of their reading.

> If children are aware of what is needed to perform effectively, then it is possible to take steps to meet the demands of a learning situation more adequately. If, however, children are not

aware of their own limitations as learners or the complexity of the task at hand, then they can hardly be expected to take preventative actions in order to anticipate or recover from problems. (p. 502)

Proficient Reading from a Metacognitive Perspective

Students often read along with little conscious attention to what they are doing. To comprehend, though, they must be purposeful, and they need to know what to do when they face difficulties. Readers are not helpless or passive. From a metacognitive perspective, the key element of proficient reading is to be strategic. Strategies are thoughtful plans that readers use to control their reading the way that a good player controls a game of tennis.

Strategic Reading: An Analogy

Strategic reading may be compared to a tennis match. Tennis players develop various shots until they are able to perform them with little conscious effort. But when they are ready to play a match, they become more deliberate. They take note of court conditions and mentally review their own strengths and weaknesses as a player and those of their opponent. They draw on this knowledge to decide whether to hit to their opponent's forehand or backhand and which shots are most likely to succeed.

Similarly, readers develop skills that allow them to read most of the time without thinking about what they are doing, but when they are faced with a more difficult task, they draw upon past experience to consider how to approach it. They decide how fast they can read, whether to preview the material, and how they will know that they are understanding.

If tennis players find themselves in difficulty during the game, they can choose from a variety of strategies such as rushing the net or hitting lob shots to turn the game around. Their muscles may be on autopilot, but their performance is directed by a very active brain. When good readers realize that they are struggling, they identify the source of the problem, perhaps a word they do not understand or a difficult new idea. Then, they take corrective action such as slowing down or stopping to summarize after every few paragraphs. In short, they do whatever is necessary to succeed.

Most current views of effective of reading instruction include directly teaching students to use strategies both for recognizing words and for comprehending what they read. An emphasis on teaching reading strategies is often contrasted with an emphasis on teaching "skills." Reading skills are generally thought of as behaviors that readers learn to perform automatically, usually through extensive practice or experience. The ability to recognize common words instantly such as *the* or *and* is an example of a skill. Middle grades readers generally recognize those words without conscious effort. Strategies, on the other hand, are used consciously, particularly when the reading is too difficult to do it automatically. In terms of metacognition, proficient reading involves conscious monitoring of comprehension.

- **Readers draw on past experience to develop a plan for reading.** A plan for reading begins with a clear understanding of the task at hand and a general strategy for how to approach the text. Choosing appropriate goals and strategies for reading becomes much easier if the reader has extensive experience with a wide range of reading tasks. Experience with reading textbook chapters in preparation for a quiz, for instance, allows a student to budget an appropriate amount of time for the task, to decide whether to take notes, to set an appropriate reading rate, and to decide on strategies such as previewing and reviewing that are often necessary when studying but not when reading for pleasure.

- **Readers consciously check their comprehending and revise the plan if necessary.** Readers who have an expectation that text will make sense stop from time to time to ask, "Am I understanding this?" They may ask themselves questions or mentally "rehearse" what they have read. Then they match their understanding to the criteria set in their original plan. If they find they have not been successful, they consider whether they need to take a different approach to reading. Sometimes readers realize that their original assumptions about the task were incorrect and revise their goals as well as their strategies.

- **Readers monitor and recognize when difficulties occur.** Comprehension monitoring is closely related to schema theory. When a reader has selected an appropriate schema and information is easily being filed away, the process goes on without much awareness by the reader. However, when information is encountered that does not fit with what is already in the file folder, the reader is alerted. Readers also have schemas for different kinds of texts. When reading a mystery, for example, readers expect the identity of the murderer to be revealed at the end of the story. If the murderer is revealed in the middle, a reader will be confused and realize that some rethinking is required.

- **Readers consciously use knowledge about reading to identify the source of difficulties.** As Brown (1985) points out, readers develop a storehouse of knowledge about texts and reading that they can state fairly explicitly. They know, for instance, that unfamiliar words are harder to read than familiar ones and that informational texts are more difficult without pictures or diagrams. They also have knowledge about their own tendencies as readers. They may know that they have a tendency to read too fast or to let their attention wander when a text does not interest them. By consciously reviewing this knowledge, they can form a hypothesis about what has gone wrong.

- **Readers use appropriate repair strategies to correct problems.** Reading proficiently from a metacognitive perspective requires readers to evaluate the outcomes of the strategies they use and to try a different one if necessary. For this reason they need a repertoire of "repair strategies" (Collins & Smith,1980). For example, rereading is often a useful strategy for coping with difficulties, but rereading the "Mask" story will not help because the key information, baseball game or murder, is not in the text. A list of repair strategies might include:
  - Reading ahead for more information that might clarify the confusion.
  - Consciously developing (or drawing) visual images of what is being read.
  - Using the glossary or other text aids.

- Verbally "reciting" what was understood up to the point of the difficulty.
- Asking whether there is a particular word or concept that is causing difficulty.
- Creating analogies to link/the information in the text to past experience.
- Seeking help by asking others questions.

Classroom Implications of Metacognition

Middle school teachers frequently agonize over their students' apparent lack of motivation. Paris, Wasik, and Turner (1991) observed that readers who have not learned to read strategically "end up devoting increasing amounts of time and energy to strategies that that are designed to stave off short-term failure in reading. As a consequence, little time is left to read or learn effective text-processing strategies" (p. 625). To protect them from a growing realization that they are ineffective, readers may:

- Avoid reading or make a minimal effort.
- Devalue reading and look for success elsewhere.
- Blame the teacher or the material.
- Try to "beat the system" through coping strategies that get around really reading.

Unfortunately, these avoidance behaviors are likely to appear during the middle grades. The increased thinking ability that comes with adolescence may result in greater metacognitive awareness, but it may also mean that readers who previously assumed they were competent become increasingly aware of their limitations.

> Dissonance increases between students' actual reading abilities and their delusions of competence, and eventually there is a humiliating collapse of confidence and self-worth that cannot be easily overcome. This typically occurs between 12 and 16 years of age, when remedial education may be difficult and time consuming. (Paris, Wasik, & Turner, 1991, p. 625)

To combat avoidance behaviors, teachers need to communicate both that it is natural to encounter difficulties when reading and that there are steps that readers can take to deal with those difficulties. They also need to use scaffolds effectively so that students can experience the difference that strategic reading makes.

Classroom Applications for Assessment

From a metacognitive perspective, proficient reading has two components: what readers know and what they are able to do. Assessment can tell teachers what students know about how reading is supposed to work and what they do to monitor or regulate their own comprehending. One way to gather this information is through the use of questionnaires. Figure 2.2 shows an inventory developed by Miholic (1994) that provides a broad range of information about students' metacognitive awareness. Administering this questionnaire early in the school year could help teachers to identify which specific strategies are least known to their students.

FIGURE 2.2 *Metacognitive Reading Awareness Inventory*

There is more than one way to cope when you run into difficulties in your reading. Which ways are best?
Under each question here, put a checkmark beside *all* the responses you think are effective.

1. What do you do if you encounter a word and you don't know what it means?
   + a. Use the words around it to figure it out.
   + b. Use an outside source, such as a dictionary or expert.
   + c. Temporarily ignore it and wait for clarification.
   − d. Sound it out.

2. What do you do if you don't know what an entire sentence means?
   + a. Read it again.
   − b. Sound out all the difficult words.
   + c. Think about the other sentences in the paragraph.
   − d. Disregard it completely.

3. If you are reading science or social studies material, what would you do to remember the important information you have read?
   − a. Skip parts you do not understand.
   + b. Ask yourself questions about the important ideas.
   + c. Realize you need to remember one point rather than another.
   + d. Relate it to something you already know.

4. Before you start to read, what kind of plans do you make to help you read better?
   − a. No specific plan is needed; just start reading toward completion of the assignment.
   + b. Think about what you know about the subject.
   + c. Think about why you are reading.
   − d. Make sure the entire reading can be finished in as short a period of time as possible.

5. Why would you go back and read an entire passage over again?
   + a. You did not understand it.
   − b. To clarify a specific or supporting idea.
   + c. It seemed important to remember.
   + d. To underline or summarize for study.

6. Knowing that you do not understand a particular sentence while reading involves understanding that
   + a. The reader may not have developed adequate links or associations for new words or concepts introduced in the sentence.
   + b. The writer may not have conveyed the ideas clearly.
   + c. Two sentences may purposely contradict each other.
   − d. Finding meaning for the sentence needlessly slows the reader.

7. As you read a textbook, which of these do you do?
   + a. Adjust your pace depending on the difficulty of the material.
   − b. Generally, read at a constant, steady pace.
   − c. Skip the parts you do not understand.
   + d. Continually make predictions about what you are reading.

8. While you read, which of these are important?
   + a. Know when you know and when you do not know key ideas.
   + b. Know what it is that you know in relation to what is being read.
   − c. Know that confusing text is common and usually can be ignored.
   + d. Know that different strategies can be used to aid understanding.

9. When you come across a part of the text that is confusing, what do you do?
   + a. Keep on reading until the text is clarified.
   + b. Read ahead and then look back if the text is still unclear.
   − c. Skip those sections completely; they are usually not important.
   + d. Check to see if the ideas expressed are consistent with one another.

10. Which sentences are the most important in the chapter?
   − a. Almost all of the sentences are important; otherwise, they would not be there.
   + b. The sentences that contain the important details or facts.
   + c. The sentences that are directly related to the main idea.
   − d. The ones that contain the most details.

(When you give this inventory to students, remember to remove the "+" and "−" marks.)

From Miholic, Vincent (1994, October). An inventory to pique students' metacognitive awareness of strategies. *Journal of Reading,*
38(2), 84–87. Reprinted with permission of Vincent Miholic and the International Reading Association. All rights reserved.

Allen (2000) used a questionnaire later in the year to assess how aware students were about some of the strategies emphasized in her language arts class. She suggested that teachers use short-answer questions about specific situations rather than general questions about students' attitudes or understandings of literacy. Her questionnaire included seven questions, such as "In what ways could making a diagram or writing a character list/map help you in reading a novel, play or short story?" (p. 206).

Assessing what students actually do to monitor and regulate their comprehension can be approached through reflection and self-reports that are made an integral part of assignments. For example, students who were assigned to read a short story and describe the main character were also asked how they decided which was the main character, how they went about finding the information they needed to complete the assignment, and how they knew they were done.

These process questions counted in the grade for the assignment just as much as the actual description, and they told the teacher whether students were using the most efficient and effective strategies for locating information and drawing conclusions.

Another way to assess strategy use is through observation. Allen (2000) suggests that when students are working on a small group reading task, their teachers can circulate with a checklist of the specific strategies that are most appropriate for the assignment and mark those that are observed in each group. Strategies such as discussing whether the group is meeting the criteria for the assignment, or deciding to seek assistance from a dictionary or other source outside the text may be fairly easy to observe. For strategies that are harder to detect, or when observing individuals, the teacher might need to stop and ask a few questions regarding how students are going about the task.

Applications for Instruction

Commercial advertising raises awareness about a product by crafting a concise message and delivering it many times. This principle may be applied to awareness of reading strategies. Teachers can communicate the message that good reading requires the use of strategies throughout the reading process by creating posters that display a list such as:

Before Reading
- Think about what you already know about this material.
- Preview or survey to predict what it is about.
- Set goals for what you will be trying to accomplish.

During Reading
- Ask yourself, "Am I understanding?"
- Stop occasionally and summarize what you just read.
- Use fix-up strategies: slow down, reread, read ahead, get help

After Reading
- Ask yourself, "How do I know I met my goals?"
- Think about what made this easy or hard to read.
- List the major ideas in your head or on paper.

Simply listing strategies will not, of course, automatically bring them to students' attention. Teachers can raise awareness of specific strategies through a procedure called a "Think-Aloud" (Davey, 1983). During a Think-Aloud, the teacher uses a challenging piece of text in order to demonstrate why, when, and how a particular strategy is used. In a Think-Aloud using the "Man in the Mask" story, for instance, the teacher might focus on the strategies of self-questioning, hypothesizing, and self-monitoring by reading aloud and commenting like this:

> *The man stood under the bright lights trying to decide.* I wonder where he is and what he's not sure about. *He had run three-quarters of the way, but now he had to be careful.* Three-quarters of the way to where? I wonder why he had to be careful. I think maybe he's in danger because he's running. Maybe he's a criminal running from the police, or maybe he's running from a criminal. *Everything depended on his decision.* I wonder why this man is so important? Maybe he's a spy or a terrorist. I'm not certain I understand this story at this point. I'm going to read on and see if some of these questions are answered.

Modeling is only the first step in using Think-Alouds. To be most effective, the teacher's demonstrations of strategies need to be deliberately connected to the reading students are about to do. If self-questioning and hypothesizing are demonstrated, for instance, the teacher needs to say something such as, "When you are reading today, make a point of stopping from time to time to ask yourself questions and predict what might be happening next." Davey (1983) recommends that students work with a partner to practice the strategies that have been demonstrated and eventually apply them independently through self-evaluation.

Greenleaf, Schoenbach, Cziko, and Mueller (2001) recommend that "metacognitive conversation" should be a central element in students' literacy learning. They note that

> These conversations about reading and reading processes *demystify* the invisible ways we read and make sense of texts. Through the metacognitive conversation, readers' knowledge, strategies, and ways of reading particular kinds of texts become an explicit part of the secondary curriculum. (p. 92)

All students can benefit from opportunities to articulate their learning strategies and to hear about those of others. English language learners should be encouraged to monitor their level of understanding and to develop strategies for seeking help when it is needed. If possible, conversations with other students who speak their primary language can help them to do so.

Summary

Supporting students' efforts at comprehending is the crucial element of reading instruction in the middle grades. To read proficiently, students need to understand that the purpose of reading is, literally, "making sense." In this chapter we have examined the insights that schema theory and metacognition provide for understanding the comprehending process. These theories suggest that effective instruction depends on making sure that students have and use the background knowledge that is relevant to their reading and that they learn to control their own learning.

Teachers will need to assess carefully both the background knowledge and related vocabulary of English language learners before they read. The use of pictures and other media as well as frequent opportunities to hear and speak about the topic of the reading can help these students to build necessary concepts and to make connections between English words and knowledge they acquired in their primary language.

A Case to Consider

Elanya is an eighth-grade student in a suburban middle school. She is the daughter of Russian Jews who emigrated to the United States when she was about 7 years old. Her mother is a doctor and her father runs a retail business. She speaks English well, but with a slight accent. She comes to her reading teacher for help with her social studies textbook. She says she has read the assigned chapter on the Constitutional Convention, but does not remember what she read.

When Elanya's teacher interviews her to find out more about the problem, she discovers that Elanya cannot describe the topic of the chapter. She is not at all sure what a convention is, although she recalls that her mother once went to a medical convention in another city. When asked what a constitution is, she answers that it is "something for the government." She can make no other associations with the word.

When asked what she did first in reading the chapter, Elanya looks puzzled and says, "I just started." When asked what she thought made the chapter difficult, she insists that "It wasn't that hard. I just don't remember it." The only suggestion she can make about how she might remember is to read it slower. The teacher asks Elanya to open the chapter, and she points out a variety of graphic aids such as diagrams and pictures. She asks which of them Elanya used. The answer is that she looked at a picture of the Founding Fathers writing the Constitution, but did not read the caption. She knows that words in bold face are important vocabulary, but she cannot say how that could help her read the chapter.

Consider Elanya's case by thinking about the following:

1. How would you explain the problem in terms of schema theory and metacognition?

2. What two or three suggestions would you give Elanya about reading the chapter? What other help could you give her?

3. What two or three suggestions could you give to the social studies to help Elanya and other students who are having similar problems?

Key Terms to Know and Use

comprehension	comprehending	prior knowledge
schema	Metacognition	PreReading Plan
literal level question	interpretive level question	
applied level question	brainstorming activities	

Possible Sentences

Use two or three terms in the columns above and write a sentence stating one idea you now know about constructing meaning. Write four or five such sentences using different words until you have a nice summary paragraph.

Beyond the Book

- Reading has often been described as "meaning construction." Try your hand at creating an analogy guide like the ones demonstrated in this chapter by comparing reading with construction. Consider, for instance, "What are the building materials?" and "What are the tools." You might also create another guide for a topic of your choice.
- Administer the Metacognitive Reading Awareness Inventory (Figure 2.2) to several students in the middle grades. Remember to remove the + and – signs before you give it to students. Examine the results to answer questions such as the following:
  1. What does the inventory tell you regarding what the students know about reading and what they do as they are reading?
  2. What does it not tell you that you would like to know?
  3. What strategies would you teach these students first?
  4. How might you teach them?
- To obtain a fuller picture of how metacognition applies to readers who struggle, read Carol Weir's (1998) article, "Using Embedded Questions to Jump-Start Metacognition in Middle School Remedial Readers." Consider what ideas in Weir's article are similar to those in this chapter. What does it say that is new? What implications does it have for teaching classes of students who are diverse in their strategy knowledge?

References

Allen, J. (2000). *Yellow brick roads: Shared and guided paths to independent reading.* Portland, ME: Stenhouse.

Alvermann, D. E. (1986). Graphic organizers: Cuing devices for comprehending and remembering main ideas, In J. F. Baumann (Ed.). *Teaching main idea/comprehension* (pp. 210–226). Newark, DE: International Reading Association.

Anderson, R. C. (1985). Role of the reader's schema in comprehension, learning and memory. In H. Singer & R. B. Ruddell (Eds.), *Theoretical models and processes of reading* (3rd ed.; pp. 372–384). Newark, DE: International Reading Association.

Anderson, R .C., & Pearson, P. D. (1984). A schema-theoretic view of reading comprehension, In P. D. Pearson (ed.), *Handbook of reading research* (pp. 255–291). New York: Longman.

Bransford, J. D. (1985). Schema activation and schema acquisition: Comments on Richard C. Anderson's remarks. In H. Singer & R. B. Ruddell (Eds.), *Theoretical models and processes of reading* (3rd ed.; pp. 385–397). Newark, DE: International Reading Association.

Bransford, J. D., & Johnson, M. K. (1972). Contextual prerequisites for understanding: Some investigation of comprehension and recall. *Journal of Verbal Learning and Verbal Behavior, 11*(6), 717–726.

Brooks, J. G., & Brooks, M. G. (1999). *In search of understanding: The case for constructivist classrooms.* Alexandria, VA: Association for Supervision and Curriculum Development.

Brown, A. L. (1985). *Teaching students to think as they read: Implications for curriculum reform* (Technical Report No. 58). Champaign, IL: Center for the Study of Reading.

Chiesi, H. L., Spilich, G. J., & Voss, J. F. (1979). Acquisition of domain-related information in relation to high and low domain knowledge. *Journal of Verbal Learning and Verbal Behavior, 18*(3), 257–273.

Collins, A., & Smith, E. (1980). *Teaching the process of reading comprehension* (Technical Report No. 182.) Urbana, IL: Center for the Study of Reading (ED 193 616).

Davey, B. (1983). Think-aloud—Modeling the cognitive processes of reading comprehension. *Journal of Reading, 27*(1), 44–47.

Durkin, D. (1978–1979), What classroom observations reveal about comprehension instruction. *Reading Research Quarterly, 14*(4), 481–533.

Greenleaf, C., Schoenbach, R., Cziko, C., & Mueller, F. (2001). Apprenticing adolescent readers to academic literacy. *Harvard Educational Review 71*(1), 79–129.

Hunt, I. (1970). *No promises in the wind.* Chicago: Follet.

Langer, J. A. (1981). From theory to practice: A prereading plan. *Journal of Reading, 25*(2), 152–156.

Miholic, V. (1994). An inventory to pique students' metacognitive awareness of reading strategies. *Journal of Reading, 38*(2), 84–86.

National Reading Panel. (2000). *Teaching children to read: An evidence-based assessment of the scientific research literature on reading and its implications for reading instruction.* Washington, DC: National Institutes of Health.

Ogle, D. M. (1986). A teaching model that develops active reading of expository text. *The Reading Teacher, 39*(6), 564–570.

Paris, S. G., Wasik, B.A., & Turner, J. C. (1991). The development of strategic readers. In R. Barr, M. L. Kamil, P. Mosenthal, & P. D. Pearson (Eds.), *Handbook of reading research,* Vol. II (pp. 609–640). New York: Longman.

Prichert, J. W., & Anderson, R. C. (1977). Taking different perspectives on a story. *Journal of Educational Psychology, 69*(4), 309–0315.

Raphael, T. E. (1982). Question–answering strategies for children. *The Reading Teacher, 36*(2), 186–191.

Rumelhart, D. E. (1981). Schemata: The building blocks of cognition. In J. T. Guthrie (Ed.), *Comprehension and teaching: Research reviews* (pp. 3–26). Newark, DE: International Reading Association.

Rumelhart, D. E. (1984). Understanding understanding. In J. Flood (Ed.), *Understanding reading comprehension* (pp. 1–20). Newark, DE: International Reading Association.

Vacca, R. T., & Vacca, J. L. (1999). *Content area reading: Literacy and learning across the curriculum* (6th ed.) New York: Longman.

Weir, C. (1998). Using embedded questions to jump-start metacognition in middle school remedial readers. *Journal of Adolescent and Adult Literacy, 41*(6), 458–467.

3

Reading the Words: Word Identification and Vocabulary Development

Activating Knowledge and Generating Questions

Mrs. Hatcher is meeting with Stacy, a student in her sixth-grade class. Stacy is reading the book *Holes* (Sachar, 1998), and she says that she wants to change books because it is "too hard." To see how well Stacy is able to recognize the words in the book, Mrs. Hatcher asks her to read the opening page aloud. She reads the passage as follows:

> There is no late at Camp Green Lake. There once was a very large late here, the largest lake in Texas. That was over a hundred years ago. Now it is just a dry, flat wasteland. There used to be a town . . . two . . . town at Green Lake as well. The town shived and died up along with the lake, and the people who lived here . . . there. During the summer, the day temperature houses around ninety-five degrees in the show shade—if you can find any shade. There is not much shade in a big dry lake. The only trees are two old oaks on the east edge of the "lake." A hammer is stuck between the two trees and a log cabin (cabin) stands behind that. The campers are forgotten to lie in the hammer. It belongs to the water. The water owns the shade. Out on the lake, rattlesnakes and scorpins find shade under rocks and in the holes dug by the campers.

Mrs. Hatcher stops Stacy at this point and jots some notes on a clipboard. She points out that Stacy has read most of the words in the passage correctly and then asks, "What do you do when you come to a word that you don't know?"

Stacy thinks for just a moment before answering. "Sound it out?"

Mrs. Hatcher nods and asks, "What else can you do?" Stacy has no other answer.

Before you continue with this chapter, take a minute to consider Stacy's reading by answering the following questions. You may want to discuss them with a classmate.
1. From this small sample, do you think Stacy has a reading problem? Why, or why not?
2. How would you explain Stacy's oral reading errors? Do you think she knows the sounds of letters?
3. What advice would you give Stacy if you were Mrs. Hatcher?

"Reading the words" in the middle grades involves identifying new words as well as recognizing old familiar ones. In this chapter, we will examine models that describe reading as a process of combining the *sounds* and the *sense* of language (the meanings of words and sentences). We will then discuss some of the implications of these "interactive" models for instruction and assessment—especially for English language learners. Finally, we will consider the place of "reading the words" within the overall literacy program.

Using Language Cues Effectively: Interactive Models of Reading

Theorists have drawn upon ideas from the fields of linguistics and psychology to develop models of the reading process that describe how readers use their knowledge of language in order to *interact* with texts. These interactive models (e.g., Ruddell, Ruddell, & Singer, 1994; Rumelhart & McClelland, 1982) show readers actively combining various kinds of language knowledge or "cues" to identify words and to construct meaning. The terms used to describe these cues may be difficult at first, but they are an important part of the language that teachers use to analyze students' reading and to design instruction.

The *graphophonemic system* is the knowledge that readers have about how the sounds of language are represented in writing. Graphophonemic cues are sometimes called sound/symbol cues or just graphic cues. Knowledge of this cueing system is usually what people mean when they use the term "phonics," but phonics is actually better thought of as an instructional approach rather than as a cueing system (Harris & Hodges, 1995).

The *syntactic system* specifies the "rules" for how sentences are put together. In English, the order of words is a key element of syntax. For example, "the yellow rose" is a common syntactic pattern, but "the rose yellow" is not. Just as "phonics" is commonly misused to describe the graphophonemic system, "grammar" is often misused to describe the syntactic system. People must use knowledge of the syntactic system to understand and create messages, but they do not need to know the formal written rules that are contained in grammar books. In reading, "our intuitive knowledge of syntax, our grammatical schema, enables us to use word endings, function words, and word order as cues to word identification" (Weaver, 1988, p. 95).

The *semantic system* is the meaning of language. People often dismiss a point in an argument as "just semantics," meaning that their opponent is cleverly using words but is not really putting forth a significant idea. Actually, the semantic system includes both words and ideas. Weaver (1988) refers to semantic cues as "the meaning relations among words and sentences in the text we are reading" (p. 95). This system of language is closely related to schema theory in the sense that the words people know about a topic reflect the extent of their background knowledge. People who have a more elaborate schema for a topic are better able to use the semantic system to identify words and to construct meaning.

Controversy has raged in recent years over which cueing system is used first and most often—particularly in beginning reading (Armbruster & Osborn, 2002). Notice the two arrows at the sides of the diagram in Figure 3.1. The arrow on the left represents a "text-based" or "bottom-up" view of reading that emphasizes recognizing individual words as the starting point for comprehending an author's message.

The view represented by the arrow on the right emphasizes how readers use knowledge about the meaning of the passage and the way sentences are put together in order to recognize words. This view is called "reader-based," or "top-down." Interactive models emphasize that proficient reading involves both reader-based and text-based processes, as Weaver (1988) explains:

> Of course, reading could not exist without the graphophonemic cues, the letters and words on the page and our intuitive knowledge of letter/sound relations and patterns. However, our reading would be both inefficient and ineffective if we relied just on graphophonemic cues. (p. 95)

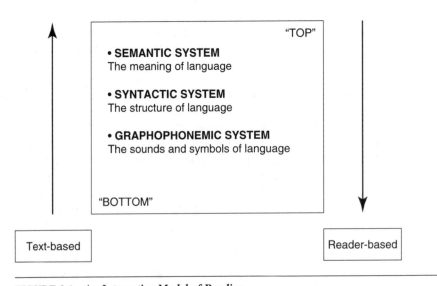

FIGURE 3.1 *An Interactive Model of Reading*

Adapted from Vacca, J. L., Vacca, R. T., Grove, M. K., Burkey, L. C., Lenhart, L. A., & McKeon, C. A. (2003). *Reading and learning to read* (6th ed.). Boston: Allyn & Bacon.

A Description of Proficient Reading

The following description of proficient reading depicts the various ways that readers use cues. Note, however, that the cues are discussed in no particular order. Interactive models generally include some notion of a "decision center" (Ruddell, Ruddell, & Singer, 1984; Rumelhart & McClelland, 1982), meaning an active intelligence that seeks out, examines, and integrates information from all kinds of cues. Different reading tasks will require different use of cues. Deciding which cues to use first or most often is part of the strategic reading or metacognition that was discussed in Chapter 2.

- **Readers use graphic information (the letters on the page) to identify some words immediately.** By the time most students reach the middle grades, they can often read with only rare stops to "sound out" words. LaBerge and Samuels (1977) propose that they have reached a stage of "automaticity" where they can recognize words rapidly without conscious effort. Many of the most common words have become "sight words" that readers recognize instantly.
- **Readers use knowledge of the relationship between sounds and letters to "decode" some words.** Decoding is a kind of letter-by-letter process of matching symbols to sounds until a word is identified or recognized as one that the reader has heard. Notice that "sounding out" words can never be completely separated from understanding their meaning. The only way for a reader to know that the "sounding out" has been successful is being able to match the sounds to a meaningful word.
- **Readers use meaning cues to anticipate what words will appear in the text.** When readers are tuned in to the overall meaning of the text, they develop an expectation for what words are coming next. This may allow them to spend less time and attention on the graphic information on the page. Goodman (1976) goes so far as to describe reading as a "guessing game" in which readers predicted which word would make sense in the context of the passage and then used the print to confirm their hypotheses. Theorists argue about how much readers rely on their expectations about words. One thing is certain, if every word in the text came as a complete surprise, reading would be slow and labored and the reader would be unlikely to comprehend or enjoy the text.
- **Readers use context to figure out unknown words.** Weaver (1988) points out that readers need to use information both *within the sentence* and *beyond the sentence* that contains an unknown word. Within the sentence, they need to use the words that come both before and after the unknown word. They also need to consider the meaning of the preceding and following sentences and the overall meaning of the passage or story.
- **Readers use the patterns of one word to identify another.** Letter-by-letter decoding should be a relatively rare event in the middle grades. Even readers who struggle have usually accumulated some store of sight words that they can use in order to identify words "by analogy" (Gaskins, Ehri, Cress, O'Hara, & Donnelly, 1997), that is, by recognizing sound/symbol elements they have in common. For example, if you encountered the word *lough* you could use your knowledge of words with similar

spelling patterns to consider pronunciations that rhyme with *rough, bough,* or *through.*

- **Making self-corrections when errors occur.** One of the surest indicators of proficient reading is that readers correct their own word recognition errors. Self-correction is so important because it is a sign of what Clay (1993) calls "cross-checking," that is confirming or correcting a word recognition by using an additional cueing system.

Implications for English Language Learners

This description of proficient word identification may help teachers to understand the many obstacles faced by students who are learning English. Beginning English language learners may struggle with use of the graphophonemic system because they lack experience with hearing and with pronouncing English sounds, particularly those sounds that are not used in their first language. A lack of experience with reading English may mean a limited sight vocabulary, which puts an even greater strain on the use of other cueing systems. Cross-checking to make sure that a word has been identified correctly is much more difficult if it is a word that the reader has never heard pronounced.

The use of the syntactic system may be hindered if the English language learner's primary language has different syntactic order than English. A limited English vocabulary makes the use of context much more challenging. Colloquial expressions and slang pose particular problems, since they may not appear in dictionaries.

English language learners can overcome these obstacles. Like many other students whose language practices and experiences are not typical, they need time, practice, and appropriate instruction that is based on careful assessment. Instruction for English language learners should be based on their assessed levels of literacy in English and their primary language, as well as their proficiency with oral English. English language proficiency progresses from the students' initial contact with formal instruction in English to the point at which their use of English compares with that of their native English-speaking peers. Because of differing academic backgrounds and ages, some students can be expected to progress more quickly and others will require more support.

Applications for Assessment: Miscue Analysis

Interactive models of reading can help teachers to understand why their students make errors in identifying words and how to help them. In an interactive view, oral reading errors are referred to as "miscues." Literally, they are the result of the reader missing one of the cues that could have led to successfully identifying the word. Consider Stacy's oral reading in the opening scenario. She makes a miscue by substituting *late* for *lake*. This might suggest that she is not using graphophonemic cues, but actually her pronunciation is very close to the letters and sounds on the page. She is not, however, using syntactic and semantic cues very effectively since the phrase *a very large late* makes no sense.

Stacy's substitution of *hammer* for *hammock* shows a similar pattern of coming close to the correct pronunciation but producing a word that makes no sense. In this instance, the problem may be that she is unfamiliar with the word *hammock* and so produced the closest word she knew. Notice that she also produces two nonwords, *shived* and *scorpins,* which also suggests that she has lost track of the meaning of the passage. Mrs. Hatcher responds to Stacy's reading by asking her about the meaning of these words. She might also demonstrate the process of cross-checking through a think-aloud.

The discussion above illustrates an assessment technique called miscue analysis. Created by Goodman (1976), miscue analysis can help teachers gain important insight into *how* their students read, not just how well. It is based on the premise that readers' miscues can provide a window on the invisible processes of reading. The procedure for miscue analysis can vary slightly (e.g., Goodman, 1976; Clay, 1983), but in general it involves listening to an individual student read orally and making a written record of miscues that shows both the word that was in the text and the word produced by the reader. Each miscue is then analyzed to determine what cueing systems the reader probably did and did not use. This involves answering three questions:

1. Did the word the reader produced look and sound similar to the word in the text? (Were graphophonemic cues probably used?)
2. Did the word the reader produced fit the syntax of the sentence in which it appeared? (Were syntactic cues probably used?)
3. Was the word the reader produced a real word that made sense in the context of the sentence and passage in which it appeared? (Were semantic cues probably used?)

Miscue analysis has been incorporated into a number of commercially available Informal Reading Inventories (Johns, 2001; Woods & Moe, 2003). These useful tools (often called IRIs) contain passages at different grade levels for students to read and a copy on which the teacher can mark miscues. Figure 3.2 shows a sample from the *Analytical Reading Inventory* (Woods & Moe, 2003). Leveled passages are important because the analysis will not be reliable if the material is too difficult. If students make more than about ten miscues in a hundred words, they become frustrated and their use of cues may become erratic. Leveled passages will enable the teacher to get an authentic assessment of the student's process for identifying words.

Miscue analysis can also be carried out using ordinary books selected by either the teacher or the student. The teacher can make a photocopy of the text and mark miscues on it. An alternative is to tape record the reading and then replay the tape in order to fill in a chart, such as the one in Figure 3.2, which shows each miscue and the word that was in the text.

The point of miscue analysis is not to classify mistakes, but rather to identify clear patterns of cue use—especially patterns that might indicate that the reader is relying too heavily on either meaning cues or graphic cues. Whenever possible, miscue analysis should be followed by brief conferences during which students can be shown their strengths as well as their weaknesses. These conferences should include discussions about how to use all of the available cues to identify words more effectively.

Goodman and Marek (1996) suggest that miscue analysis could be used to create a customized instructional program through a process called Retrospective Miscue Analysis (RMA). In essence, this procedure calls for using a miscue analysis as the basis for a con-

FORM S, LEVEL 4	Reader's Passages page 47

Prior Knowledge/Prediction

- ☐ Read the title and predict what the text is about. Comets
  - *Q: What do you know about comets?*
  - *SR: They're bright in the sky at night. They have a tail.*
- ☐ Read the first two sentences and add more to your prediction.
  - *People were scared of a comet. They thought it made an earthquake.*

Prior Knowledge
- ☐ a lot
- ☑ some
- ☐ none

	A Comet	O	I	S	A	Rp	Rv
1	got fright A long time ago/people/bacame/frightened when they saw a comet.			//			
2	even They/thought a comet was a/sign that (unpleasant) events, /(such) as an/	//		/			
3	Signs they earthquake,/would/take place. Scientists (now) k/now that these ideas are (not)	//		//			
4	comets correct.			/			
5	in parts A comet /is (a) /space (object) made up of ice particles /mixed/with dust.	//		//		/	
6	came outs stars Comets (probably) come from the far, outer/(edge) of/our/solar (system.) Comets/	///		///		/	
7	even can be seen/(only) when they are clo/se enough to the sun to /(reflect) its light.	//		/		/	
8	passed A comet has two parts: the head and the/tail. The tail is present (only)	/		/			
9	some when the /comet is heated from the sun. The tail is made of fine dust and gas.			/			

The text is continued on the next page.

Cueing Systems

LINE #	Miscue	Grapho-phonically Similar IFM (word level)	Syntactically Acceptable Unacceptable (sentence level)	Semantic Change in Meaning (CM) No Change in Meaning (NCM) (sentence level)
1	got		A	NCM
1	fright	IM	U	CM
2	even	IM	U	CM
3	signs	IM	A	CM
3	they	I	U	CM
4	comets	I	U	CM
5	in	I	U	CM
5	parts	IM	A	NCM
6	came	IF	A	NCM
6	outs	IM	U	CM
6	stars	I	U	CM
7	even	I	U	CM
8	passed	I	A	CM
9	some		A	CM
10	passes	IF	A	CM

The cueing system grid is continued on the next page.

FIGURE 3.2 ***Informal Reading Inventory***

From Woods, M. L. & Moe, A. J. (2003). *Analytical reading inventory* (6th ed.). Upper Saddle River, NJ: Merrill, pp. 73–74.

versation about how particular miscues occurred and whether they were significant, that is, whether they affected the reader's understanding of the text. This discussion would also include strategies that the reader was currently using to identify words and strategies that could be added.

Moore and Aspegren (2001) describe how a teacher used RMA with an adolescent named Dan. In a series of conferences, Dan and his teacher discussed issues such as when it is appropriate to skip a word and move on and why substituting *do not* for *don't* was a "smart" miscue that did not change the meaning of the text. Moore and Aspegren (2001) conclude that, "For Dan, RMA led to the discovery and practice of new and varied reading strategies which, through strategic conversations with [the teacher], he helped select and define" (p. 492).

Teachers may not be able to do RMA with each student, but they should reinforce the notion that "getting the words right" is important but not the ultimate goal of reading. Too much attention to accuracy in reading can be as much of a problem as too little. Especially when accompanied by a conference, Informal Reading Inventories and other oral reading assessments can be invaluable tools for understanding the needs of readers who struggle, including English language learners.

Applications for Instruction

Teachers need to be sure to do RMA with all students, but they also need to make sure that their students are aware of and use a variety of strategies to identify unknown words. The teacher can use the Think-Aloud process to demonstrate how to use a combination of sound and sense to figure out an unknown word. Students may also be involved in sharing the strategies they find effective in order to create a class list that can be posted on the wall or turned into a bookmark. One seventh-grade class developed the following "Figure It Out" procedure to use whenever their reading was by being halted by an unknown word.

When You Get Stuck, Figure It Out

- Go back to the beginning of the sentence and start again
- Read up to the word; say, "blank," and read to the end of the sentence.
- Make a guess about what the word might be.
- Look again at the word and see if your guess fits the way it looks and sounds.
- Read the whole sentence again with your guess in it. Does it make sense?

Eventually, the class condensed this procedure to:

- Back up.
- Read through.
- Make a guess.
- Check for sound.
- Check for sense.

Some educators would argue that this procedure is too "reader-driven" because it starts with sentence context rather than letters and sounds. The crucial point, however, is that readers need to have *some* strategy that guides them to integrate cues so that they can recognize words. Suggesting that students "sound it out" whenever they come to a difficult word may imply that letter sounds are the only resource they have. Stressing that they can "figure it out," on the other hand, invites them to rely on whatever cues are most useful in a particular situation. Stressing multiple cues and strategies will specifically address the needs of English learners at various developmental levels in the process of learning English.

Teachers can reinforce the use of multiple cues by using a Modified Cloze Procedure. The original cloze procedure consists of systematically replacing every fifth or seventh word with a blank. In a modified cloze, blanks are inserted in places that will allow students to draw on their semantic and syntactic knowledge to hypothesize about the missing word. If some letters are left from the original word, students can integrate the use of grapho-phonemic cues with context. Students who have a great deal of difficulty using context might also be given choices for each blank, or all the deleted words can be listed at the end of the passage (Rasinski & Padak, 2000). See if you can figure out the missing words in the passage from the first chapter that Stacy read from *Holes*.

Modified Cloze Procedure

During the summer the daytime temperature h_____s around ninety-five degrees in the shade—if you can find any _____ . There is not much shade in a big dry lake. The only trees are two old oaks on the eastern e_____e of the "lake." A h_____k is stretched between the two trees and a log cabin stands behind that. The campers are _____ to lie in the h_____k. It belongs to the warden. The _____ owns the shade. Out on the lake, rattlesnakes and _____ (snakes, scorpions, sunlight) find shade under rocks and in the holes dug by the campers.

To illustrate some of the variations of cloze, a beginning or ending letter has been left for some words. The last sentence illustrates a multiple choice cloze. In an activity such as this, when students practice with a passage from a real text that they are about to read, they also activate their prior knowledge.

Identifying Unfamiliar Words

By about third or fourth grade, students "begin to encounter an increasing number of words whose printed forms they cannot recognize immediately and whose meanings are unknown" (Harris & Sipay, 1990, p. 511). Nagy and Herman (1987) found that school-printed material in grades three through nine contained approximately 88,500 words with approximately 100,000 distinct meanings.

Anderson and Freebody (1983) indicate that average fifth graders would likely encounter almost 10,000 new words a year while completing their normal school reading assignments. To identify these new words, students need to draw upon more than their knowledge of letters and sounds. Teachers can help them to use two additional tools: structural analysis and context.

Structural Analysis

As students in the middle grades encounter more abstract concepts and sophisticated language, they also encounter longer words, many of which are constructed using pieces from other languages. That is where structural analysis, comes in. White, Power, and White (1989) speculate that "seventh-grade students may analyze successfully at least [3,000] and as many as [9,000] prefixed words a year" (p. 301). Structural analysis, also known as morphology, is the "ability to gain information about the meaning, pronunciation, and part of speech of new words from their prefixes, roots, and suffixes" (Nagy, Diakidoy & Anderson, 1991).

Students can learn to see the meaningful parts within words by using or creating lists of exemplary words. For example, Cunningham (2000) created a "Nifty Thrifty Fifty" list designed to show the most useful prefixes and suffixes in words that middle school students were relatively likely to know. It also contains words such as *happiness* and *forgotten,* which exemplify spelling problems that are related to adding affixes. A sample of Cunningham's list is shown in Figure 3.3.

Cunningham (2000) suggests that four or five of the words should be introduced each week and posted on a "word wall," a long-term display of words that students can reference when they are reading or writing. Notice that the list does not contain definitions for either the words or the affixes. Students arrive at the meanings through discussions about the words. The teacher might, for instance, ask them to explain what *antifreeze* is and then what the *anti* piece might mean. The teacher might then ask what *antiwar* would mean and what other similar words students know.

Blachowitz and Fisher (2002) suggest that students might also be involved in creating their own lists by compiling "affixionaries." As the name implies, these are collections

FIGURE 3.3 *Sample Prefixes and Suffixes*

Word	Prefix	Suffix
Antifreeze	anti	–
Beautiful	–	ful
Forgotten	–	en (double t)
Happiness	–	ness (y-i)
International	inter	al

The prefix "anti" means "opposed to" or "against"

Antifreeze	Antifreeze protects your car against freezing.
Antiwar	Five thousand people showed up to protest at an antiwar rally.
Antiseptic	Doctors use antiseptic to fight germs in operating rooms.
Antiglare	Without antiglare sunglasses, skiers can go snow blind.

FIGURE 3.4 *Sample Section from an Affixionary*

that are like a dictionary of prefixes and suffixes. The affixes are listed alphabetically, each on a separate page that includes a definition of the affix, several words that use that affix, and sentences that show how each word is used. A sample section is shown in Figure 3.4.

Students can collaborate to create affixionaries in small groups or even as a whole class project in which students are invited to add new pages or new examples to existing pages in the class collection. If students choose words from their reading to build a class list, the words they choose might not cover the most important affixes as systematically as Cunningham's (2000) list. On the other hand, they will feel more in control of their own learning, and they will be focusing on words that are in a meaningful context.

Blachowitz and Fisher (2002) argue that structural analysis activities are useful for English language learners. They point out, for example, that the Spanish word *excelente* can help a reader to identify *excellent,* and they suggest that English language learners might create bilingual lists that focus on affixes or root words that are common to both languages. They warn, however, that the process of using word pieces from the primary language to figure out words in English can lead to problems, giving the example of approaching the English word *excuse* from the Spanish word *excusado*—which means *toilet.*

Using Context to Identify Unfamiliar Words

Although the elements of word structure may be introduced and studied in isolation, structure cues are much more useful for identifying unfamiliar words when they are combined with meaning cues. Students in the middle grades need to be guided to use the context of sentences and passages in order to identify unfamiliar words. The modified cloze procedure described above is one way to do that. As students try to fill in the blanks, they need to consider what words would fit the syntax of the sentence and its meaning. They should also consider the overall meaning of the passage by looking at previous sentences as well as the sentences that follow the blank.

Contextual redefinition (Tierney & Readence, 2000) is another activity for developing the use of context. Unlike cloze passages, which provide context but few if any letter cues, contextual redefinition begins with showing the entire unfamiliar word without context. The steps for this activity are simple:

1. **Select a few unfamiliar words** that are important to understanding the material students will read.

2. **Write a sentence for each word,** using it in appropriate context and providing clues to its meaning.
3. **Present the words orally and in writing** but without a sentence context. You may want to pronounce each word repeatedly and ask students to repeat after you. Students then suggest possible meanings, discuss the possibilities, and choose the one that is most appropriate for each word.
4. **Present each word in the sentence you prepared** and ask students again to provide possible meanings and to discuss the reasons for their answers.
5. **Students verify definitions** from a dictionary or glossary. This can be done by selected volunteers or in small groups.

Contextual redefinition provides opportunities for modeling and practicing the use of many kinds of context clues. The activity is most productive if all the sentences presented fit the context of the whole text that students are reading. If the words that are chosen contain structural clues such as a recognizable prefix or word root, contextual redefinition allows students to practice cross-checking by considering whether meaning cues confirm structure cues.

Suppose a class of sixth graders is reading an article about protecting their health that contains the word *antiseptic.* When the word is presented in isolation, the teacher might ask if students recognize any parts within the word. Students with septic tanks at home might recognize that piece as well as the prefix *anti.* Students might use those pieces to predict that the word means "fighting or preventing dirt." The teacher might then present a sentence containing a contrast clue: *Doctors and nurses use an antiseptic rather than ordinary soap and water to clean out a cut.*

Students might discuss how the sentence confirms that an antiseptic fights dirt, but that it is different in some way from soap. A look in the dictionary might then verify the conclusion that antiseptics fight germs as well as visible dirt. The teacher should conclude this activity by encouraging students to use structure and content clues in a similar way as they are reading the article.

Learning Words through All the Language Arts

People have four types of vocabulary: listening, speaking, reading, and writing. The *listening* vocabulary is, of course, the earliest to develop and the largest. This vocabulary is composed of all the words people hear and understand and serves as the foundation for learning other vocabularies. The second vocabulary to develop, the *speaking* vocabulary, includes all the words a person uses appropriately in everyday speech. The *reading* vocabulary consists of the words a person recognizes or can figure out in print, and the *writing* vocabulary encompasses those words a person can use appropriately during written communication.

"Knowing" a word involves being able to understand it when it is heard, to use it when speaking, to recognize it when reading, and to use it and to spell it appropriately when writing. Experiences in all the language arts work together to develop the knowledge required for the "reading the words" component of proficiency. New words encountered during listening, for instance, can be added to speaking, writing, and reading vocabularies. Words that are learned during reading are reinforced by speaking, writing, and listening.

For very young readers, writing and reading are equally important ways to learn about the match between letters and sounds (Durkin, 1966; Fountas & Pinnell, 1999). In the middle grades, students can continue to learn and apply insights about letters, sounds, and words through both reading and writing. As students attempt to spell the words that are already in their meaning vocabularies, they must carefully consider the matches between letters and sounds (the graphophonemic system) and the meaningful "chunks" that make up longer words (the semantic system). Teachers can help all students learn the patterns of English words as they are writing by doing some or all of the following:

- When students are trying to spell an unfamiliar word, encourage them to "rubber band" the word by stretching it out so that they can hear its sounds.
- Create a classroom word wall or have students keep a personal spelling list that includes "sight" words that cannot be spelled phonetically.
- When a student is stuck on spelling a word that has a "regular spelling pattern," suggest writing a rhyming word that they know and then changing the beginning.
- Encourage students to make some attempt at spelling difficult words. Ask them to, at least, draw a line that roughly matches the length of the word and add a beginning letter. Encourage them to add other letters that match the sounds they hear.
- Use dialogue journals in which you write to students and they write back by "borrowing" spellings of words from your written message.

A Balanced Perspective on Word Reading

Many key applications from interactive models of reading have been drawn together by the concept of "balanced literacy instruction." A number of different interpretations of this concept exist (Fitzgerald, 1999; Rycik, 1997; Strickland, 1996), but we believe that the definition offered by Morrow (2001) best expresses the principles that are most relevant for teachers in the middle grades.

> Balanced literacy is grounded in a rich model of literacy learning that encompasses both the elegance and complexity of reading and language arts processes. Such a model acknowledges the importance of both form (phonics, mechanics) and function (comprehension, purpose, meaning) of the literacy processes and recognizes that literacy occurs most effectively in a whole-part-whole context. This type of instruction is characterized by meaningful literacy activities that provide children with both the skill and the desire to become proficient lifelong literacy learners. (p. 20)

As Morrow's definition suggests, balanced literacy instruction is reflected in a "whole-to-parts-to-whole" framework for planning instruction. This means beginning with a focus on the overall meaning of a text. Then, the teacher guides students to apply specific reading strategies or to focus on particular passages or words in the text. Finally, the teacher guides students back to considering the overall significance of the text, perhaps by encouraging them to apply text ideas to their own lives.

For example, as students read Gary Paulsen's historical novel *Mr. Tucket* (1994), initial discussions centered on the dangers of the westward migration in the 1840s and all the new things the main character, Francis Tucket, had to learn after he was separated from his family's wagon train.

As students continued to read the book, the teacher focused attention on some of the unfamiliar words in the book. Many of these words referred to objects and events from another time and place such as *war-bride, venison, haunch,* and *sorrel.* Discussions of these words included their pronunciations and spelling patterns as well as their meanings. For English language learners, the teacher modeled the correct pronunciation and then students repeated the word, reinforcing the pronunciation. Eventually, the discussion turned back to the whole text as students considered the plot and themes such as "coming of age."

Researchers have demonstrated that vocabulary is learned through a balance between extensive reading and more formal instructional activities (Armbruster & Osborn, 2002; National Reading Panel, 2000). Readers need multiple exposures to a new word before they truly learn it (Stahl, 1999). As they read a book or an article on a particular topic, readers are likely to encounter a new word related to that topic many times in slightly different sentence contexts. Gradually, they can arrive at a definition for the word inductively. Moreover, they will have a feel for the kind of situation in which the word is actually used that they could not obtain from a dictionary or thesaurus. On the other hand, this process can be helped by vocabulary activities that focus on specific strategies for figuring out words.

Our notion of balanced literacy also includes balancing reading with the other language arts. We agree with the principle that "language arts learning activities are seldom discrete—'just reading,' just writing,' or 'just viewing,' for example. Each medium relates directly or indirectly to every other" (National Council for the Teachers of English, 1996, p. 6). For example, the structure (syntax) of the sentences used in books is typically more complex and formal than the language that middle grades students hear from peers or family members. Students who read extensively are more likely to acquire these complex sentence structures and to use them in their own writing.

In this book we have placed reading in the foreground, but if you look closely, you will notice how the other language arts are connected to reading in the instructional activities we recommend. Speaking and writing play an important role in interpreting texts, and viewing and representing ideas visually are excellent ways to extend and elaborate the ideas of written language. This balanced approach especially benefits the English language learners who need a variety of experiences with the English language to improve their oral, written, and literacy skills.

Summary

In this chapter, we examined interactive models of reading that show how readers integrate various kinds of language cues in order to recognize words and construct meaning. We have also shown how students can use structural analysis and context to figure out the meaning of words they have not previously heard. Finally, we have suggested that the idea of balanced literacy instruction can place "reading the words" in the proper perspective as just one part of a comprehensive reading program in the middle grades.

Assessing Comprehension and Applying Ideas

- Suppose that three different readers read the sentence, *"He felt a tingle in his fingers that told him they were warming up."*
  - Reader A: He felt a tickle in his fingers that told him they were warming up.
  - Reader B: He felt a tackle in his fingers that told him they were warming up.
  - Reader C: He felt a tigel in his fingers that told him they were warming up.

  Based on this sample of oral reading, which reader would you judge to be the most effective? Why? What might you discuss with each reader in a Retrospective Miscue Analysis?

- If the parents of one of your students told you that she was struggling because she "needs more phonics," how would you respond? What assessments could you use to investigate the statement?

A Case to Consider

Ying is a sixth-grade student whose family recently arrived in the United States from China. She studied English in China, but quickly found out that the demands of reading, writing, speaking, and listening in an American middle school classroom far exceeded what her classes in English taken in China prepared her for. Ying feels intimidated to present the projects she completes as assignments and sometimes gets embarrassed when asked to answer questions in class. Although she can read long paragraphs fluently, she has little confidence in her spoken English. She has to concentrate when the teacher gives directions. Her teacher speaks rapidly, uses many colloquialisms, and has a southern dialect. Her English classes in China did not prepare her for the "kind" of English spoken by her teacher.

1. What are some ways that Ying's teacher could help her to learn English vocabulary?

2. What could her teacher do to assess her knowledge of letters and sounds?

3. What classroom practices might help Ying learn strategies for coping with the challenge of learning a new language?

Key Terms to Know and Use

interactive models	miscue analysis	informal reading inventory
syntactic system	RMA	morphology
modified cloze	affixionary	dialogue journal
structural analysis	balanced literacy	
semantic system	graphophonemic system	

Possible Sentences

Use two or three terms in the columns above and write a sentence stating one idea you now know about reading the words. Write four or five such sentences using different words until you have a nice summary paragraph.

Beyond the Book

- The role of word identification in reading has been a subject of intense controversy. Often this controversy has been expressed as a conflict between "phonics" and "whole language," which is characterized as a method for teaching reading that emphasizes literature instead of word identification. You can go to www.middleweb.com and investigate by typing in either phonics or whole language at the search page. Be sure to examine enough of the available links so that you are sure you understand both sides of the controversy. How does the concept of balanced literacy address this conflict?

- Administer a passage from an Informal Reading Inventory with a middle grades student, or listen to a student who is reading orally from a book that you suppose to be appropriate in difficulty. You may want to record the reading so you can listen to it more than once. List each of the reader's miscues next to the text word in a chart like the one in Figure 3.2. Interpret the results by answering the following questions:

  1. What does the reader's performance tell you about whether the difficulty level of the book is appropriate?

  2. What characteristics of a proficient reader does this reader show?

  3. What would be the first thing you would try to teach this reader about using cues more effectively?

References

Anderson, R. C., & Freebody, P. (1983). Reading comprehension and the assessment and acquisition of word knowledge. In B. Hutton (Ed.), *Reading/language research: A research annual* (pp. 231–256). Greenwich, CT: JAI Press.

Armbruster, B. B., & Osborn, J. H. (2002). *Reading instruction and assessment: Understanding the IRA standards.* Boston: Allyn and Bacon.

Blachowitz, C., & Fisher, P. J. (2002). *Teaching vocabulary in all classrooms* (2nd ed.). Upper Saddle River, NJ: Merrill.

Clay, M. M. (1993). *An observational survey for early literacy achievement.* Portsmouth, NH: Heinemann.

Cunningham, P. M. (2000). Big words for big kids: The morphology link to meaning and decoding. In K.D. Wood & T. S. Dickinson (Eds.), *Promoting literacy in grades 4–9: A handbook for teachers and administrators.* Boston: Allyn and Bacon.

Durkin, D. (1966). *Children who read early.* New York: Teacher's College Press.

Fitzgerald, J. (1999). What is this thing called "balance"? *The Reading Teacher, 53*(2), 100–107.

Fountas, I. C., & Pinnell, G. S. (Eds.). (1999). *Voices on word matters.* Portsmouth, NH: Heinemann.

Gaskins, I. W., Ehri, L. C., Cress, C., O'Hara, C., & Donnelly, K. (1997). Procedures for word learning: Making discoveries about words. *The Reading Teacher, 50*(4), 312–327.

Goodman, K. (1976). Reading: A psycholinguistic guessing game. In H. Singer & R. B. Ruddell (Eds.), *Theoretical models and processes of reading* (pp. 470–496). Newark, DE: International Reading Association.

Goodman, Y., & Marek, A. M, (1996). *Retrospective miscue analysis.* Katonah, NY: Richard C. Owen.

Harris, T. L., & Hodges, R. E. (Eds.). (1995). *The literacy dictionary.* Newark, DE: The International Reading Association.

Harris, A. J., & Sipay, E. R. (1990). *How to increase reading ability: A guide to developmental and remedial methods* (9th ed.) New York: Longman.

Johns, J. L. (2001). *Basic reading inventory* (8th ed.). Dubuque, IA: Kendall/Hunt.

LeBerge, D., & Samuels, S. J. (Eds.). (1977). *Basic processes in reading: Perception and comprehension.* Hillsdale, NJ: Erlbaum.

Moore, R. A., & Aspegren, C. M. (2001). Reflective conversations between two learners: Retrospective miscue analysis. *Journal of Adolescent and Adult Literacy, 44*(6), 492–503.

Morrow, L. M. (2001). *Literacy development in the early years.* Boston: Allyn and Bacon.

Nagy, W. E., Diakidoy, I. N., & Anderson, R. C. (1991). *The development of knowledge of derivational suffixes* (Technical Report No. 536). Champaign Urbana, IL: Center for the Study of Reading.

Nagy, W. E., & Herman, P. A. (1987). *Limitations of vocabulary instruction* (Technical Report No. 326). Champaign Urbana, IL: Center for the Study of Reading. (ED 248 498)

National Council for the Teachers of English and International Reading Association. (1996). *Standards for the English language arts.* Urbana, IL: Authors.

National Reading Panel (2000). *Report of the National Reading Panel: Teaching children to read: An evidence-based assessment of the scientific research literature on reading and its implications for reading instruction.* Washington, DC: National Institute of Child Health and Human Development.

Paulsen, G. (1994). *Mr. Tucket.* New York: Bantam Doubleday Dell.

Rasinski, T., & Padak, N. (2000). *Effective reading strategies: Teaching children who find reading difficult* (2nd ed.). Upper Saddle River, NJ: Merrill.

Ruddell, R. B., Ruddell, M. R., & Singer, H. (1994). *Theoretical models and processes of reading* (4th ed.). Newark, DE: International Reading Association.

Rumelhart , D. E., & McClelland, J. L. (1982). An interactive model of context effects in letter perception: Part 2: The contextual enhancement effect and some tests and extensions of the model. *Psychological Review, 89*(1), 60–94.

Rycik, J.A. (1997). Common sense and common ground: The appeal of balanced literacy programs. *Ohio Reading Teacher, 31*(1), 19–21.

Sachar, L. (1998). *Holes.* New York: Bantam Doubleday Dell.

Stahl, S. A. (1999). *Vocabulary development.* Cambridge, MA: Brookline Books.

Strickland, D. S. (1996). In search of balance: Restructuring our literacy programs. *Reading Today, 14*(2), 32–45.

Tierney, R. J., & Readence, J. E. (2000) *Reading strategies and practices: A compendium* (5th ed.). Boston: Allyn and Bacon.

Vacca, J. L., Vacca, R. T., Grove, M. K., Burkey, L. C., Lenhart, L. A., & McKeon, C. A. (2003). *Reading and learning to read* (6th ed.). Boston: Allyn and Bacon.

Weaver, C. (1988). *Reading process and practice: From sociolinguistics to whole language.* Portsmouth, NH: Heinemann.

White, T. G., Power, M. A., & White, S. (1989). Morphological analysis: Implications for teaching and understanding vocabulary growth. *Reading Research Quarterly, 24*(3), 283–304.

Woods, M. L., & Moe, A. J. (2003). *Analytical reading inventory* (6th ed.). Upper Saddle River, NJ: Merrill.

4

Mastering Messages: Learning the Purposes and Forms of Written Language

Activating Prior Knowledge and Making Connections

Cindy, Maria, and Robert were sitting nervously outside of the library classroom. The door opened and another group filed out looking slightly shaken. "Lots of luck," said one of the departing students. "Those guys are tough." The new group filed in and faced the panel of community members who were acting as judges. They were consulting the form that the group had submitted nominating Albert Einstein for the first annual "I Have a Dream Award" in memory of Dr. Martin Luther King.

For the past several weeks, these seventh-grade students and their classmates had been reading biographies from a list that featured prominent women, members of minority groups, and political activists. The librarian had provided materials ranging from picture books to adult biographies and reference books. Students were assigned to teams and instructed to choose one person to nominate for the fictitious award based on the criteria given on the nomination form. Each class then presented one group to represent them based on their nomination form and the persuasiveness of a presentation they made in support of their choice.

Now the judges listened attentively as Cindy, Maria, and Robert took turns speaking about the slides they had prepared. They highlighted Einstein's scientific contributions, his attempt to help European Jews during the Holocaust, and his later efforts supporting peace and opposing nuclear weapons. After the presentation, the students referred to their notes and cited particular books to answer the judges' probing questions about how Einstein exemplified the principles espoused by Dr. King. Eventually, they learned that their nominee had finished second to Mahatma Gandhi.

Before you continue reading, consider the following questions about this project:
1. What kinds of texts were students required to read and to write?
2. How did oral language and written language support each other?
3. What might they learn about the different forms and purposes of written language?

Mastering messages means becoming increasingly aware of the reasons why people send and receive messages and the forms those messages can take. In this chapter, we will examine literacy proficiency from the perspective of an individual's overall ability to use language to communicate. Then, we will consider some of the implications of this perspective for the kinds of language tasks English-speaking students and English language learners should be asked to do. Finally, we will suggest some specific practices for effective instruction and assessment in the middle grades.

Communicative Competence and Reading

Language users know a great deal about what language can do for them in a variety of situations. They learn about these various purposes for language from the people around them. They also learn—usually through trial and error—how to accomplish these purposes. By the time they get to the middle grades, young adolescents know how to wheedle privileges from their parents, what slang expressions will get them accepted by their peers, and what they cannot say in a classroom. They also know how to use reading and writing both for school tasks and for staying in touch with their friends. Mastering messages in reading is one aspect of *communicative competence,* "the ability to use any form of language appropriate to the demands of social situations" (Harris & Hodges, 1995, p. 37).

Communicative competence involves both the ability to produce a wide range of language forms (productive competence) and the knowledge that is needed to understand messages from a wide variety of individuals (receptive competence). Competence requires understanding how language is used in particular settings and situations and how it is used differently by various individuals and groups. Those with high levels of communicative competence can effectively exchange messages with males, females, and with individuals from many occupations, social classes, and age groups.

One of the Standards for the English Language Arts (National Council for the Teachers or English and International Reading Association, 1996) recommends that, "Students adjust their use of spoken, written, and visual language (e.g., conventions, style, vocabulary) to communicate effectively with a variety of audiences for a variety of purposes" (p. 3). To meet this standard, students in the middle grades need to widen their understanding of the purposes for communication, the forms that messages can take, and the relationship between those who send messages and the audiences who receive them.

The Purposes of Language

Smith (1977) identified ten uses for language and suggested that they should all be part of the experiences students have in school:

1. Instrumental: "I want." (Language as a means of getting things, satisfying material needs.)
2. Regulatory: "Do as I tell you." (Controlling the behavior, feelings, or attitudes of others.)
3. Interactional: "Me and you." (Getting along with others, establishing relative status.) Also, "Me against you" (Establishing separateness.)
4. Personal: "Here I come." (Expressing individuality, awareness of self, pride.)
5. Heuristic: "Tell me why." (Seeking and testing knowledge.)
6. Imaginative: "Let's pretend." (Creating new worlds, making up stories, poems.)
7. Representational: "I've got something to tell you." (Communicating information, descriptions, expressing propositions.)
8. Divertive: "Enjoy this." (Puns, jokes, riddles.)
9. Authoritative/Contractual: "How it must be." (Statutes, laws, regulations, agreements, contracts.)
10. Perpetuating: "How it was." (Records, histories, diaries, notes, scores.) (p. 640)

Notice that some of these purposes are personal, but most of them involve communicating with others. When language is used for purposes that involve social interaction, participants need to understand *pragmatics,* the cues that signal the social purpose behind the message. For example, if you are sitting alone at a table in a cafeteria and someone approaches and asks, "Is anyone sitting here?", you recognize that the person wants permission to sit down and not information about the proportion of occupied chairs in the cafeteria.

Individuals who are unable to interpret pragmatic cues have difficulty understanding sarcasm, slang expressions, or any other use of language where the words that are used do not really mean what they say. This is often difficult for English language learners, especially if they do not have many opportunities to engage in informal conversations.

The Genres of Language

Traditionally, the term *genre* has been applied only to literary writing such as short stories, poems, and plays. More recently, however, genres have been defined as "any type of discourse that possesses typified, distinguishable, conventions of form, style, or content in recurring contexts" (Harris & Hodges, 1995, p. 96). According to that definition, a grocery list is a genre because it has a typical form (single words and phrases that are arranged top to bottom rather than left to right), a typical content (food items that are needed), and a typical context (going shopping).

Notice that the "contexts" for various genres are situations that are common in a particular culture. That means that genres that exist in one culture may not exist in another. For instance, grocery lists do not exist in cultures where people have no choices about what they eat or in societies where people obtain food every day rather than buying it and storing it. Cultural differences in the kinds of texts that are used may be a source of difficulty for readers.

Proficient Reading from a Communication Perspective

Communicative competence is a concept that includes both oral and written language. With written language, however, competence may be more difficult to achieve. Understanding the sometimes subtle meaning behind the words becomes more difficult because readers do not have the cues provided by a speaker's tone of voice and body language. Proficiency from a communicative perspective involves drawing on knowledge acquired through face-to-face interaction and through experiences with texts. From this perspective, proficiency in reading might be described as follows:

- **Readers use their pragmatic knowledge to understand words and phrases.** In the previous chapter, we examined the cues that readers use in recognizing words. Pragmatic cues also play a role in word identification. If one character in a novel exclaims, "You bloody twit!" to another character, an American reader can recognize that this is an insult without knowing the meaning of the words. On the other hand, common words and phrases may be difficult to understand if the reader is unable to identify their intent. Consider for instance, a pun like this: "Are you working hard, or hardly working?" The sentence makes no sense unless you recognize both the play on words and its intent of teasing someone.
- **Readers recognize the form and function of different genres.** Luke and Freebody (1999) noted that treating different genres as "text types" tends to focus attention only on the form of written language rather than the connection between the forms that writers use and the purposes they are trying to achieve. Readers are most effective when they are able to see how each part of a text is related to its overall purpose. When reading the manual that comes with an appliance, for instance, a reader needs to be aware that part of it consists of cautions to the user (intended to protect the manufacturer from liability), part of it consists of warranty information (intended to show the limits of the manufacturer's responsibility for correcting problems), and part of it explains the basics of operation (intended to provide information the consumer needs).
- **Readers are aware of authors and their intent.** Message mastery involves *critical literacy,* an awareness that texts are created by authors who are shaped by their society and culture. In practical terms, this means that readers need to ask, "Who says so and why?" Critical literacy is not only concerned with looking for deception or manipulation. Readers simply need to keep in mind that authors are limited by the time and place in which they live and the values of the people around them. A writer for a computer magazine, for instance, may be unaware that all the articles in the magazine assume that everyone has access to the Internet or wants the latest technology. Criti-

cal literacy also includes considering the relationship between the senders of messages and the receivers. For example, if the students in a particular class draw up a list of rules for classroom behavior and post it on the wall, the list will have a different meaning than it would if the teacher posted the very same list.

- **Readers can use a wide range of texts for a variety of purposes.** Teachers are naturally concerned about students' proficiency with the kinds of texts and tasks that are done in school. Those tasks are certainly vital to their students' future, but it is important to remember that students may be proficient outside of school with many genres that teachers do not or cannot read. This is especially true of electronic texts and media. Adolescent readers may routinely navigate websites, online magazines as well as email, instant messaging, and text messaging to cell phones. Often they can also "read" media such as music videos, anime, comic book novels, and video games at a high level of proficiency. The notion of *multiple literacies* acknowledges that these new texts and tasks do count as part of an adolescent's overall communicative competence even if they have not traditionally counted in school.

Implications for the Classroom

The notion of communicative competence has several important implications for the classroom. It suggests that teachers must involve students in reading and writing a wider range of texts for a wider range of purposes than ever before. To do so, teachers need to create environments that provide opportunities for oral communication and genuine reasons for reading and writing.

Expanding the Range of Texts

Mastering messages requires opportunities to read more than textbooks and to write more than essays. In particular, teachers may need to devote more attention to nonprint texts such as movies, television, and multimedia. Luke and Freebody (1999) argue forcefully that the pervasive influence of popular media make it vital to include critical media literacy in the curriculum. When students are guided to consider who produced the media they are watching and what effects were intended, they are learning ways of thinking that will serve them in their lives as well as in using print texts.

Electronic literacies may be treated as either a gateway or an obstacle to understanding the forms and purposes of language. For example, Landrum (2001) points out that students who use instant messaging have developed a whole vocabulary of abbreviations such as *u* (you), *r* (are), and *b4* (before) that are used and understood by a select audience. She reports that some English teachers were upset when these forms showed up in school—even in students' informal writing—but that other teachers were glad to see students choosing to write. Hefferly, Rivas, and Wofford (2003) suggest that teachers conduct a lesson that will help students to explore the relationship between purpose, audience, and language by writing an email for a particular scenario such as a thank you to a grandparent who has sent a gift, and then evaluating the appropriateness of the language that is used.

Authentic Literacy Tasks

Students cannot develop communicative competence if the reading and writing they are doing does not genuinely communicate with anyone. When reading and writing activities are done for real purposes such as the ten listed by Smith (1977), they are said to be "authentic." On the other hand, tasks are said to be inauthentic if they are done just for practice. Workbook pages and essays written to formulas are examples of inauthentic literacy activities. Not every literacy experience will be authentic. Students may practice reading words or making meaning with excerpts from a text or from individual sentences, but mastering messages requires experiences with real tasks.

Exploring Genres

Teachers can be deliberate about having students explore a variety of genres. They can keep a list of the kinds of texts that students have read and the purposes they serve. They could bring in examples of brain teasers or riddles, for instance, and note their "divertive" function, or guide students to examine how school rules are structured to accomplish their "regulatory" purpose. Discussions about the ways in which the forms of text relate to their purpose can range from the use of red herrings in mystery stories to the use of inside addresses and return addresses on business letters.

Understanding genres is one of many instances in which writing plays an important role in supporting reading. As they write initial drafts, students may be focused entirely on getting their thoughts on paper, but later they can be guided to think about the audience for the piece and how they can most effectively structure the message to have the intended effect on that audience. Teachers can also direct student authors to examples of published works that exemplify the form that is usually used for a particular purpose. They might, for example, show an example of a eulogy to a student who is writing a piece about the death of a grandparent or a travel guide to a student who is writing about a summer vacation trip.

Implications for English Language Learners

Herrell and Jordan (2004) note that English language learners need opportunities for both basic interpersonal communication and more cognitively demanding academic tasks. They identify some characteristics of instruction that will meet the needs of students learning English that will also support the language learning of other students.

- **Comprehensible input.** English language learners cannot acquire new language if they do not understand the intent of the messages that surround them. Teachers can use media and other visuals as well as their own facial expressions and vocal intonations to carry this pragmatic information that is necessary for interpreting the words.
- **Verbal interaction.** Teachers need to be sure that the classroom environment provides sufficient opportunity for interaction. Recent immigrants may not be afforded the opportunities to use the English language necessary for improvement. One high

school Chinese immigrant stated, "How can we learn English if no one speak it with us? No Americans speak with us. A friend would be best, but it is a puzzle. If you don't speak English you can't have American friend. So how do we learn English?"

- **Contextualized language.** In many cases, the content of the message can actually help a student to understand its form. If the student is familiar with a topic from previous experiences, the words can follow. Teachers need to make sure that students can make a connection to their own background so that they can draw on their prior knowledge as a resource in interpreting the language. Media of all kinds can be important for this purpose.

- **Security.** English language learners need a safe environment in which to put together the forms and purposes of language during informal conversation and small group academic tasks. They cannot master the forms of messages unless they feel safe to try and communicate. Take for example this tenth-grade Filipino boy who immigrated to the United States at age 14. He says, "There is lots of teasing me when I don't pronounce words right when I speak or read. Whenever I open my mouth I wonder. I shake and worry, will they laugh?" Teachers need to pair English language learners with students who view working with them as an opportunity to learn about another language and culture rather than as a nuisance.

- **Active involvement.** In a class where students have diverse language abilities and cultures, teachers will need to find ways for all students to build on what they do know about language as they learn to create and interpret new kinds of messages. Students who are beginning language learners may tend to withdraw if they are not given ways to participate actively. "Hands-on" projects encourage interaction, but do not require a high level of language knowledge. As students work through tasks of building, drawing, or using technology, the English language learners have a chance to acquire language gradually as they learn content.

Applications for Instruction

Teachers need to create classroom environments in which everyone has a place and everyone uses written texts for a wide variety of personal, social, and academic purposes. This means viewing the class as a literate community characterized by positive social interactions among students and between students and teacher.

The opening scenario of this chapter illustrates many instructional applications that result from a focus on mastering messages. The three students have each read several different biographies for the authentic purpose of gaining information about a person who interests them. They have produced a wide range of texts including an application form and a multimedia presentation in which they combined spoken language with pictures and text. Their presentation to a panel of judges has required them to think about the most effective way to structure their message to meet the expectations of an audience of adults who are relative strangers.

As Table 4.1 illustrates, Cindy, Maria, and Robert's presentation to the judges was preceded by other experiences that required them to consider the ways in which audience,

TABLE 4.1 *Genres Used in the "Dreaming a World" Unit*

Texts	Audience	Purpose	Concepts
"I Have a Dream" speech	Whites and blacks at the March on Washington, television audience	Reassure, inspire, persuade	Appeal to audience
Documentary film about "I Have a Dream" speech	Americans of a later generation	Inform	Visual interpretation of events
"Dream" poems	Self, peers	Express a mood and thoughts about justice and dreams	Poetry as powerful words arranged in patterns
Biographies	Children, adults, English- and Spanish-speaking youth	Inform, inspire	Chronological vs. nonchronological order
Life maps	Self, peers	Reflect and summarize, inform, persuade	Categories of life events
Dream Award nomination form	Peers, judges	Inform, persuade	Interpreting forms
Dream Award presentation	Peers, judges	Inform, persuade	Combining oral, visual, and written language

purpose, and form come together in print and nonprint texts. The first of these was a reading of Reverend Martin Luther King's "I Have a Dream" speech. Many of the students were familiar with the speech, but most had not studied it as a message that was organized to achieve some very specific affects on various members of the audience.

Guided by the teacher, they considered which parts of the speech were directed at African Americans, which were directed at whites, and which were directed at everyone. As students watched a videotape of the speech, they could see how the camera focused on different individuals or groups in the audience to match each passage.

The teacher pointed out how speeches use many of the same devices as poetry and asked students to examine the language of Dr. King's speech and to select powerful words and phrases that conveyed feelings of "hope and determination," "righteous anger," or "sadness and suffering." These words and phrases were discussed and categorized. Then they became part of a "bank" that the class could use in their own writing. The teacher also read several "dream poems' by Langston Hughes aloud and students practiced reading them as a whole class and in pairs.

Students then used large sheets of paper and colorful markers to create their own "dream" poems by choosing an emotion (e.g., hope or anger) and drawing from the words in the "bank" they had created. They used words from the "bank" and a few simple devices such as alliteration and repetition. The focus was on conveying emotion through language. For example, one student wrote:

When You Have a Dream
When you have a dream
You are walking in a sunlit path,
With joy and freedom
You feel free at last
You have love in your heart,
And peace in your mind,
That will keep you confident
All of the time.
No slaves, no suffering
No dark lonely nights,
Just keep a dream to
Chase away all your frights.

To gather information for their "Dream Award" nominations, students selected biographies to read from a list that featured prominent women and members of minority groups. To accommodate various linguistic and literacy abilities, the list contained books that ranged from picture books to adult biographies. After they had finished reading, students represented what they had learned in the form of a "life map," a drawing that portrayed the person's life as a road marked by obstacles, "turning points" (major decisions), and "milestones" (i.e., achievements). To be sure that a viewer could interpret the map, the students created a map key with symbols to mark each significant event. They quickly developed a visual "language" that included using four-leaf clovers for strokes of good luck and rain clouds or black cats for misfortunes.

Projects such as the "Dream Award" allow students to learn about genres by seeing the many kinds of texts, audiences, and communicative purposes that can be connected to the same topic. They allow students to learn about language at the same time that they are using it for authentic purposes.

Accommodating Differences

As students read and created the various texts related to the "dream" project, the teacher needed to be aware of the range of abilities within the class. Some activities such as viewing the video and reading poems in unison allowed all students to participate. Once the class had created the word bank, beginning English language learners were able to choose words and to create drawings that illustrated them rather than writing poems. The librarian was able to supply some Spanish-language biographies to go along with English-language books, and the multicultural list allowed many students to read or hear about a well-known figure from their own culture. Students with knowledge of presentation software could help with typing in information and running the slides even if they did not have the language abilities necessary for speaking or composing.

Applications for Assessment

Assessing students' knowledge and ability in sending and receiving messages involves answering three questions:

1. What do students know about the forms and purposes of various genres?
2. What kinds of messages do students send and receive?
3. How well can they accomplish a communicative purpose for an intended audience?

Teachers can find answers to these questions through examining written products, but they can also gain valuable information through students' self-reports and by observing their performance during actual communication tasks.

Message mastery requires knowledge and abilities that are beyond traditional school tasks. We believe that it is important for teachers to have as clear a picture of their students' literacy practices as possible. One way to assess the multiple literacies of adolescents is simply to ask about them. Bean, Bean, and Bean (1999) collaborated to document all the different kinds of print and nonprint texts used by two adolescent girls. This informal study reveals that even students who are successful in school have a significant literacy life that includes many kinds of communication that are more technologocial and interactive than academic literacy.

Students whose greatest capabilities are with out-of-school nonacademic literacies should not, of course, be excused from learning to accomplish the reading and writing abilities that are necessary for academic success. Nevertheless, it is important to discover and acknowledge their abilities as well as their limitations. Figure 4.1 is adapted from the form Bean, Bean, and Bean (1999) used to keep a record of the girls' literacies. Teachers could use such a form to gather information about their students' use of various literacies. Students could also be asked to complete a questionnaire in which they try to remember just one day of text use.

If they are encouraged to share the results of such assessments, students can see the many ways in which they *are* competent, and teachers can use the information to build bridges between the literacies that students use outside of school and those that they need to succeed in school.

Teachers sometimes hesitate to ask students to engage in oral language or media tasks for real audiences because they are concerned about evaluating such "real-world" events. Any communication activity can be evaluated, however, through the use of performance assessment. Performance assessment has four basic steps:

1. Identify three or four key traits that you want to see students display.
2. Consider what excellent performance would look like for each of those traits and write a description.
3. Describe what you would want to see for each trait in order for you to consider a performance to be satisfactory.
4. Construct a rubric that shows minimal and excellent performance and also describes a level in between.

FIGURE 4.1 *Completed Log of Student's Multiple Literacies*

Name ___Katie D.___ Dates reported: ___March 20___ to ___March 26___

Directions: Use the key below to show how many minutes you spend doing each activity every day for the next week.

	Magazine reading	Reading books you chose	Assigned reading and writing	Email or websites	Video, TV, video games	Practical reading and writing
Monday	20 mins.	—	30	30	2 hours	15
Tuesday	—	—	1 hour	30	2 hours	10
Wednesday	30	—	1.5 hours	30	1 hour	20
Thursday		—	30	30	2 hours	20
Friday	20	—	—	—	—	30
Saturday		—	—	2 hours	2 hours	10
Sunday		—	—	30	3 hours	10

Summary by categories:

Magazines: Read new issue of *American Dressage* and some *People* while waiting at the dentist.

Novels: None, except assigned novel for English class.

Assigned: English novel, history book, math book, wrote science lab and English essay.

Computer: Instant messages, some regular email. Movie and music websites.

Video/tv: Rented 2 movies, watched 4 favorite reality shows, channel surfing.

Practical: Directions for digital camera, labels and stuff, notes to friends, assignments in PDA.

Adapted from Bean, T. W., Bean, S. K., & Bean, K. F. (1999). Intergenerational conversations and two adolescents' multiple literacies: Implications for redefining content area literacy. *Journal of Adolescent and Adult Literacy, 42*(6), 438–448.

Table 4.2 shows a rubric that the judges could use for the "I Have a Dream" award competition. Notice that the lowest level on the rubric is still satisfactory. In this case, that is sensible because only the best teams from each class were sent to the competition. Rubrics that focus only on levels of satisfactory performance have the advantage of communicating high expectations. If a performance does not meet that standard, students may try again.

TABLE 4.2   *Judge's Rubric for "I Have A Dream" Award Presentations*

Key Trait	Excellent (9–10)	Good (7–8)	Satisfactory (5–6)
Audience Awareness	Addressed audience directly, anticipated questions, used formal language effectively.	Looked at audience, responded to questions at length, used informal language when responding to questions.	Looked at audience occasionally, answered direct questions, sometimes used slang.
Command of Content	Detailed how nominee overcame obstacles, stood up for principles, and put others first. Chose excellent examples for each trait. Good knowledge of facts with few glances at notes.	Explained reasons for one or more traits without vivid examples. Needed notes to answer questions.	Explanations of some traits were weak. Few vivid examples. Answered most, but not all questions adequately.
Use of Visuals	Slides showed key points; clear, attractive format; used photos/ other illustrations.	Slides showed key points; clear, attractive format; used only clip art graphics.	Slides may have contained too much or too little information; format was clear, but not attractive.

Total = 30 points

Message mastery does not always turn up directly in standardized tests or other high stakes assessments because it is difficult to assess in short-answer formats. Nevertheless, teachers need to gather information about students' current performance to design activities that will enlarge their range of effective communication.

Summary

Proficiency in literacy includes both using and expanding knowledge of the forms, rules, and uses of language. Message mastery requires the ability to interpret and create a wide range of texts. It also involves awareness of the motivations of authors and the expectations of audiences. Message mastery with written texts is part of communicative competence. The ability to use oral or written language in classroom conversations allows all students, especially English language learners, to develop communicative competence by learning about the pragmatics of language, the intended message that is sometimes just the opposite of the stated message.

Applying Key Ideas

- Make a chart in which you list the ten purposes for language use identified by Smith (1977). Match each use with a particular form of text and a potential audience for that text. How many of the texts that you identified do middle grade students typically read or create in school?
- Choose a topic that might be a subject for learning in a middle grade classroom. Use the chart in Table 4.1 as a model for thinking about how you could involve students in reading and writing several different forms for different audiences and purposes. Include some oral language activities and media. How would the activities you chose include English language learners at the beginning, intermediate, and advanced levels of English proficiency? How would they have to be modified?

A Case to Consider

Katie D. is a 14-year-old middle school student who achieves good grades in all subjects, including English. Examine the chart in Figure 4.1 that details her use of various print and nonprint texts during one week. Then respond to the following questions either in writing or through discussion:

1. Would you rate Katie's overall level of literacy as high, medium, or low? Why?
2. What connections can you see between Katie's school-related and nonschool-related literacy?
3. What connections could you make if you were her teacher?

Key Terms to Know and Use

communicative competence	pragmatics	multiple literacies
performance assessment	critical literacy	authentic reading

Possible Sentences

Use two or three terms in the columns above and write a sentence stating one idea you now know about mastering messages. Write four or five such sentences using different words until you have a nice summary paragraph.

Beyond the Book

The National Council of Teachers of English and the International Reading Association have collaborated to create a collection of lessons called ReadWriteThink. These lessons are sorted into three categories: (a) *learning language* (activities in which students use language with others in their everyday lives), (b) *learning about language* (activities in which students try to figure out how language works and explore its impact), and (c) *learning through language* (in which students learn how to use language to learn about something or to do something). The "learning about language" lessons are most closely related to message mastery.

Visit www.readwritethink.org. and find the *ReadWriteThink* lessons related to "Learning about Language." Evaluate a lesson that is intended for middle grades to see how well it meets these criteria:

    a. Promotes audience/author awareness.

    b. Invites reflection about the purposes and typical forms of a genre.

    c. Involves reading or creating authentic texts.

References

Bean, T. W., Bean, S. K., & Bean, K. F. (1999). Intergenerational conversations and two adolescents' multiple literacies: Implications for redefining content area literacy. *Journal of Adolescent and Adult Literacy, 42*(6), 438–448.

Harris, T. L., & Hodges, R. E. (Eds.). (1995). *The literacy dictionary.* Newark, DE: The International Reading Association.

Herrell, A. L., & Jordan, M. (2004). *Fifty strategies for teaching English language learners.* Columbus, OH: Prentice Hall.

Hefferly, L., Rivas, S., & Wofford, L. (2003). *Audience, purpose, and language use in electronic messages.* Retrieved from www.readwritethink.org/lessons/lesson_view, March 26, 2004.

Landrum, C. (2001). *Do u rite gr8? Some English teachers say no.* Retrieved from www.GreenvilleOnline.com, March 26, 2004.

Luke, A., & Freebody, P. (1999). A map of possible practices; further notes on the four resources model. *Practically Primary, 4*(2), 5–8.

National Council for the Teachers of English and International Reading Association. (1996). *Standards for the English language arts.* Urbana, IL: Author.

Smith, F. (1997). The use of language. *Language Arts, 54*(6), 638–644

5

Engaging with Texts: Motivation and Personal Reasons to Read

Activating Prior Knowledge and Making Connections

Mr. Jones was dissatisfied. As he began his third year teaching seventh-grade language arts, he negotiated many of the hurdles faced by beginning teachers, but he felt that he could be doing better. Most of his students completed their assignments reasonably well, but there were too many days when they seemed to just be going through the motions. Some students either could not or would not complete the assignments at all. Some of the English language learners appeared to disengage from learning. Colleagues told him not to feel bad because those same students were failing in all their classes. They reminded him that he could not expect to reach everyone, but it still bothered him.

Mr. Jones thought back over the past few weeks. Some of the boys had been complaining that the assigned novel, Katherine Patterson's *Jacob Have I Loved* (1980), was a "girl's book" and used that as an excuse not to read it. Not all the girls were reading it either. When he gave them class time to read, some students rolled along through the entire assigned chapter, but others sat aimlessly turning pages or struggling their way through less than half the chapter. During class discussions, few students responded to his questions, and some of the minority students and English language learners never participated.

Now he sat looking through their first written assignment of the unit, an analysis of the main character. He was struck by the wide range of ability represented in his class and the lack of effort some of his students showed. In addition, the papers were incredibly dull. He wished there was something he could do to change things, but he could not imagine what that might be. With a sigh, he continued his grading.

Before you go on with this chapter, consider these questions. You might want to write about them or talk about them with others:
1. What, if anything, is the problem with Mr. Jones' classes?
2. What are some of the ways in which his students differ from each other?
3. If Mr. Jones wants to change things, what might be his first step?

Notions of proficient reading must include readers' feelings and attitudes as well as their skills. In this chapter, we will examine motivation as a component of proficient reading, beginning with a brief overview of the problem of aliteracy in the middle grades. Then, we will introduce the concept of reading engagement and suggest some applications of this concept for assessment and instruction. Finally, we will examine other perspectives on students' attitudes and feelings regarding reading and writing, including cultural factors and the role of reading in the identity development of young adolescents.

The Problem of Aliteracy

Beers (1998) identifies the characteristics of an avid reader and contrasts them with four other kinds of readers who show different degrees of aliteracy (students who can, but choose not to read):

1. *Dormant readers* identify themselves as readers and have positive feelings about others who read. They believe the purpose of reading is to entertain. They enjoy reading but do not make time to read.
2. *Uncommitted readers* do not identify themselves as readers, but they do have positive feelings about others who read. They see reading as functional, something that is done to accomplish a practical purpose. They do not enjoy reading, but they think it is possible that they might enjoy it in the future.
3. *Unmotivated readers* do not enjoy reading or identify themselves as readers. Moreover, they have negative feelings about other students who do like to read. They see reading as functional, something that is done to accomplish a practical purpose. These readers define reading as "saying words" and always read to get facts, never for enjoyment or appreciation. They are sure that they will not read in the future.
4. *Unskilled readers* do not read very well or very often, except to practice skills. They are aware of their lack of reading ability, so they do not identify themselves as readers. They define reading as a matter of sounding out words. They do not enjoy reading, and a continued lack of success with reading leads them to choose never to read.

Beers (1998) concludes that the uncommitted and unmotivated readers came to school without enough enjoyable experiences listening to books that were read to them. As a result, when they came to school and began to do typical instructional activities, they developed the impression that reading was all about schoolwork. They began to avoid reading and fell into a cycle in which they avoided reading, which caused them to fall behind their classmates, which in turn, made reading even less enjoyable as it became more difficult.

Reading Engagement: Developing Skill and Will

The description of uncommitted and unmotivated readers given by Beers (1998) suggests that reading instruction in the middle grades must address both the skills of reading and the will to read. These two factors are combined in the concept of reading engagement. Guthrie and Wigfield (1997) define engagement as "the joint functioning of motivation with knowledge, strategies, and social interactions in literacy" (p. 5). Activities that are designed to promote engagement go beyond supporting the comprehension of particular texts to address the development of literate individuals over the long term.

Teachers should not assume that students who can comprehend text will choose to do so. Developing students' basic skills does not assure that they will be inclined to select books, read at appropriate times, persist through difficult material, and gain satisfaction from reading (Guthrie, McCann, Hynd, & Stahl, 1997, p. 754). Research related to literacy engagement identifies specific attitudes and beliefs that are necessary for students to become effective lifelong readers. Wigfield (1997) suggests that these factors can be summarized in three questions:

1. **Can I succeed?** A sense of efficacy (the belief that they have the ability to accomplish a particular reading task) makes it more likely that students will choose to do that task. Efficacy also makes it more likely that students will persist in the task when they encounter difficulties. Reading strategically and using repair strategies requires effort. Before they make that effort, readers need to have good reason to believe that their effort will pay off.

2. **Do I want to succeed and why?** According to Wigfield, a student's desire to succeed on a particular reading task depends not only on how much the individual likes or is interested in the task, but also how important and useful it is. Consider, for example, a student doing a comprehension "exercise" from a workbook. The task is unlikely to be interesting in and of itself. Completing it successfully may also seem to be a small and unimportant accomplishment. Finally, the assignment may seem to have little use. In fact, it will probably seem entirely useless unless the student can see how it connects with an important achievement such as learning to read the books that older and more capable students are reading.

3. **What do I need to do to succeed?** Being a strategic reader plays a role in motivation as well as in achievement. Being in control of one's own work brings satisfaction. As we presented in Chapter 2, using strategies allows readers to function as active decision makers who choose how to approach tasks, what to do when they encounter problems, and when to seek assistance.

Besides these general motivational factors, engagement also involves some characteristics of a particular reading task such as the degree of interest and ownership the reader feels. To some extent, interest is produced by the reader and by the situation. For example, most people do not consider a telephone book to be very interesting reading material, but if you are really hungry and looking for the number of a pizza place that delivers, that same phone book may become intensely interesting.

Schallert and Reed (1997) point out, on the other hand, that some books are likely to be more interesting than others. They note that a reader who picks up a particular book because it is "interesting" will only continue to read if the book has some features that create involvement. "For a text to pull in a particular reader, it must have some element of novelty and ambiguity, and it must somehow intrigue the reader" (p. 72).

Ownership involves being invested in a literacy activity and feeling a sense of pride and responsibility. Readers are most likely to feel ownership when they experience a high degree of *agency,* the freedom to choose personally relevant reading material and to decide when, where, and how to read it (Greenleaf, Schoenbach, Cziko, & Mueller, 2001). In contrast, readers such as the uncommitted and unmotivated readers identified by Beers (1998) generally see reading as a task assigned and controlled by a teacher. Perhaps these readers do not choose to read because they have never perceived that they *have* a choice.

Reader identity is related to many aspects of engagement, but it also includes the ways in which literacy achievement, attitudes, and practices are strongly influenced by such aspects of a reader's identity as gender, culture, and social class. Moore and Hinchman (2003) noted that these factors act as labels or "markers" that position students to think of themselves and to act in certain ways. They warn that "Influential teachers, parents, and friends who treat adolescent readers as struggling and slow as a result of such markers often produce, or at least reinforce, readers who act accordingly" (p. 17).

Ogbu (1992) observes that students from minority cultures that are in opposition to mainstream culture, such as many African American students, may face peer pressure to avoid doing anything that is approved by the mainstream culture. Students who want to succeed academically may have to choose from among these strategies:

1. Emulating the mainstream culture even though members of their own group ostracize them.
2. Accommodating to the mainstream culture in school but sticking to their peer culture group after school.
3. Disguising their serious attitudes toward academics by strategies such as playing the class clown or excelling in sports.
4. Attending private schools.
5. Buying protection from peers by helping bullies with their homework.

Ogbu (1992) advises teachers to show that they understand the problem of peer pressure and to help students examine the behaviors that might lead to a loss of social identity in order to distinguish those that are necessary for academic success from those that are not.

As we noted in Chapter 1, it is impossible to separate the literacy development of young adolescents from the many personal issues they confront. During the middle grades, students can use their literacy to help them sort out issues regarding who they are and who they want to be, but they may not be given the opportunity. Broughton and Fairbanks (2003) examine the identity formation of four sixth-grade girls and how the school and classroom culture addressed their needs and interests. They found "a disturbing lack of connection across the girls' interests and desires, the school context, and the language arts curriculum" (p. 432).

A Description of Proficient Reading

The concept of reading engagement and related notions such as ownership and identity all point to the conclusion that *being* proficient and *feeling* proficient go hand in hand. From this perspective, reading may be described as proficient when:

- Readers believe that reading is important and that the reading task they are doing is worthwhile.
- Readers believe that they can succeed, and they are prepared to use appropriate fix-up strategies if necessary.
- Readers feel challenged or intrigued by the text they are reading.
- Readers see their performance as a result of their own choices.
- Readers identify themselves as literate, one of the members of a literate community.
- Readers connect their literacy learning to personal, academic, and career goals.
- Readers see no conflicts between their identities as literate individuals and their identities as members of a family, a peer group, and a particular culture.

Implications for the Classroom

The ideal reading task for creating engagement appears to be one that (1) involves a text that is complex enough to be intriguing, (2) allows students to make decisions, and (3) encourages students to use reading strategies. Encouraging strategy use requires that teachers carefully consider the difficulty of the reading task. Students are most likely to use strategies with tasks that are difficult enough to require conscious planning and problem solving but easy enough that effort leads to success (Brown, 1987).

The notion of engagement also raises some important issues about intrinsic and extrinsic motivations for reading (Gambrell & Marinak, 1997). Students may be motivated to complete a workbook page (or any other reading task) if they are offered a reward for finishing or if they are afraid of receiving a failing grade. They may also want to outperform other students or comply with what adults expect of them. None of these extrinsic motivations, however, will be available outside of a school context. By contrast, intrinsic motivations such as the satisfaction that comes from mastering a challenging task or the pleasure of becoming "lost" in a book do not require a teacher to administer rewards. They are the motivations that last a lifetime.

Finally, supporting engagement requires attention to the *social context* for reading. Reading, like other language activities, influences and is influenced by relationships with other people. In the classroom, the kinds of interactions that students have with their teachers and with each other have an effect on how well and how willingly they read. For example, a classroom discussion about a story might consist of the teacher asking questions, students answering, and the teacher saying whether the answers are correct. This interaction pattern of I-R-E (teacher *initiation,* student *response,* and teacher *evaluation*) (Cazden, 1988) may influence readers to pay more attention to the facts of the story than to their personal associations and feelings about it. That may, in turn, influence their enthusiasm for reading. If they experience reading as a "teacher-pleasing" activity, students' interest in reading will depend heavily on how much they want to please the teacher.

Applications for Assessment

The "Why Do You Read?" questionnaire shown in Figure 5.1 is adapted from Wigfield (1997). Each section explores one of the factors related to motivation for reading. Teachers can use the questionnaire to gather some general information about how their students perceive reading. Students are asked to rank the various factors, so they have to decide which is most and least important rather than marking them all the same.

Students could also be given one or two factors at a time and asked to talk or write about them. Like all forms of classroom assessment, the questionnaire is most useful when students are involved in the process of interpreting it.

Applications for Instruction

Roe (2001) identifies the components of instruction that support the engagement of middle school students who do not read well. Most, if not all, of these components are equally appropriate for typical or highly proficient students. They include:

- **Control of literacy activities.** Students gain a sense of control when they are allowed to choose the materials they read and their topics for writing.
- **Models of engagement.** Roe points out that just as teachers of writing need to be writers, reading teachers need to be able to model the role of reader. When teachers are able to share their own preferences, responses, and especially their strategies for dealing with difficulties, they allow students to see what it is like to be a member of the literacy club.
- **Appropriate materials.** Roe emphasizes the importance of a wide range of reading materials so that teachers can match each reader with something appropriate. She also argues forcefully that assigned material must not be too difficult by stating that, "While I have changed my beliefs over the years, one remains intact: Students need to read texts that fit their instructional reading level and their interest. While extreme interest in a text can sometimes make a difficult book readable, overall, students become frustrated when a book is too hard" (p. 13).
- **Authentic literacy tasks.** Authentic tasks resemble those that readers and writers do in "real life," that is, outside of school. Roe emphasizes that it is natural for readers to engage in conversations about the books they read, but she asks, "When was the last time you could not wait to finish a book so you could answer a series of questions provided by a publisher or a computer program? How often have you been inspired to make a diorama?" (p. 14).

FIGURE 5.1   *Why Do You Read?*

Directions: Look at the statements listed under the bold headings below. Put a 1 next to the heading with the statements you most agree with. Put a 7 next to the heading with the statements you least agree with. Then put the numbers 2-6 where you think they should be.

_____ **Confidence**
- I know that I will do well in reading next year.
- I am a good reader.
- I learn more from reading than most students in the class.
- Compared to other school subjects, I am best at reading.

_____ **Challenge**
- I like hard, challenging books.
- I like it when the questions in the books make me think.
- I usually learn difficult things by reading.
- If a book is interesting, I don't care how hard it is to read.

_____ **Curiosity**
- If the teacher discusses something interesting, I may read about it.
- I read to learn new information about topics that interest me.
- I like to read about new things.
- If I am reading about an interesting topic, I may lose track of time.

_____ **Involvement**
- I make pictures in my mind as I read.
- I like mysteries.
- I enjoy a long, involved story in a fiction book.
- I read lots of adventure stories.

_____ **Recognition**
- My friends sometimes tell me I'm a good reader.
- I like hearing the teacher say I read well.
- I am happy when someone recognizes my good reading.
- My parents often tell me what a good job I am doing in reading.

_____ **Grades**
- I look forward to finding out my reading grade.
- Grades tell you how well you are doing in reading.
- I read to improve my grades.
- My parents ask me about my reading grade.

_____ **Social**
- I visit the library often with my family.
- My friends and I like to trade things to read.
- I talk to my friends about what I am reading.
- I like to tell my family about what I am reading.

_____ **Competition**
- I like to be the only one who knows the answer.
- I like being the best at reading.
- I like to finish reading before other students.
- I am willing to work hard to read better than others.

Adapted from Wigfield, A. (1997). Children's motivations for reading and reading engagement. In J. T. Guthrie, J. T. & Wigfield, A. (Eds.), *Reading Engagement: Motivating Readers through Integrated Instruction* (pp. 14–33). Newark, DE: International Reading Association.

An Emphasis on Response

If teachers are to avoid the kinds of tasks that may make readers feel powerless or uninvolved, they need an alternative approach that allows readers to draw on their personal backgrounds and to express their feelings about their reading experiences. Reader response theory (Rosenblatt, 1978) begins with the understanding that each reader creates a unique interpretation of a particular text and that this interpretation can be enriched by sharing it with others.

The kinds of responses that readers make range from aesthetic (focused on enjoyment and personal meaning) to "efferent" (focused on getting the facts straight). One of Mr. Jones' students might make an aesthetic response to *Jacob Have I Loved* (Patterson, 1980) by writing:

> When I read this story, I kept thinking of how my sister and I get jealous of each other, sometimes for no good reason. I wished that Louise would stop blaming her sister for everything and start thinking of what she really wanted. I loved the descriptions of how people lived on an island in the middle of nowhere. I could see how it would be boring to live there, but it could also be interesting in a way.

By contrast, an efferent response might look like this:

> The story takes place on an island. It is about two twin sisters who don't like each other. Their names are Louise and Caroline. Their father is a fisherman, and Louise goes to work with him while Caroline goes off to study music.

Both of these writings show an understanding of the story, but the first one shows a reader who is making interest by finding personal connections. Beers (1998) notes that aliterate students tend to approach every reading task from an efferent stance, whereas more avid readers moved back and forth between efferent and aesthetic reading.

Teachers can encourage readers to become more involved by conducting open discussions that invite readers' feelings and reactions through prompts such as these:

- Tell about a moment in the story when you were surprised.
- Tell an experience from your own life that was like what happened in the story.
- Tell about another story (or movie or TV show) that is like this one.
- Tell about a moment in the story that you liked.
- Tell about a moment in the story that you thought was unbelievable.
- Tell what makes the book hard (or easy).

Notice that none of these prompts has a right answer, and that they are not in the form of questions. These characteristics alone contribute to breaking the pattern that aliterate students have gotten used to.

Acknowledging Gender Differences

Given the emergence of secondary sex characteristics during puberty and young adolescents' need to develop a self-concept, teachers cannot ignore gender differences when planning instruction. Students need opportunities to explore and discuss gender issues

(Research for Action Inc., 1996). Reading classes can either help or hurt the process of building a positive gender identity depending on the materials and methods that are used.

Sprague and Keeling (2001) warn that adolescent girls are in much greater danger of problems such as depression, academic failure, and suicide than most teachers and parents believe. They note that self-esteem declines for adolescent girls and that they tend to hide their strong feelings, particularly anger, in order to gain approval from adults and peers. As a result, "They become unable to articulate who they are and what they value" (p. 47).

To address this situation, Sprague and Keeling (2001) recommend involving girls in "discussions about what causes girls to lose their confidence and voice" (p. 47). They developed the following set of criteria that can be used to select books that are particularly helpful for generating the desired discussion (see Figure 5.2 for a list of books meeting these criteria):

1. The main character is an adolescent female struggling to articulate her true voice.
2. The book demonstrates real and typical restrictions on females.
3. The heroine has to negotiate society, including males.
4. The book's appeal is not just for those with a special interest (e.g., sports).
5. It does not reinforce stereotypes of the woman being "rescued" by a man.

Jacob Have I Loved fits these criteria well. The problem for Mr. Jones is to open a discussion regarding the two different images of girls that are portrayed by the sisters and to help the boys to articulate their reactions to a book that is focused more on relationships than on plot.

Adolescent males, of course, have their own set of issues. Brozo and Schmelzer (1997) point out that many current social problems, including violence, poverty, and teen pregnancy, have been attributed to the lack of positive male role models. They suggest that literature can be used to "help boys appreciate honored character traits of males while they learn how authentic adult men and adolescent boys deal with themselves, other males and females, and difficult ethical and physical situations" (p. 5).

Brozo and Schmelzer (1997) also note that boys consistently exhibit lower achievement in reading and writing than girls do. They speculate that boys may see reading as an activity that is inconsistent with being male—at least with the image of being male that is portrayed in popular culture. They suggest building instructional units around some or all of ten male "archetypes": Pilgrim, Patriarch, Warrior, Magician, King, Wildman, Healer, Prophet, Lover (who is a caring and giving character), and Trickster (or joker). Brozo and Schmelzer believe that such units could focus on cross-cultural comparisons of male role models and could appeal to both males and females.

Addressing Cultural Differences

Cultural issues are too important to minority youth for teachers to ignore them, but cultural awareness is important for students from the mainstream culture as well, particularly during the middle grades. Young adolescents' "expanding social world and their increasing ability to understand others' perspectives contribute to early adolescence being an ideal time during which to teach appreciation and acceptance of all people" (Manning, 1993, p. 16).

FIGURE 5.2 *Books That Encourage Gender Dialogue*

Avi. (1990). *The true confessions of Charlotte Doyle.* New York: Avon (232 pages, readability grade 7, historical fiction).

Baczewski, P. (1990). *Just for kicks.* New York: Lippincott (182 pages, readability grade 6, caution: out of print, realistic fiction).

Creech, S. (1997). *Chasing redbird.* New York: Harper Trophy (261 pages, readability grade 7, realistic fiction).

Cushman, K. (1994). *Catherine, called Birdy.* New York: Clarion Books (212 pages, readability grade 8, historical fiction).

Duder, T. (1987). *In lane three, Alex Archer.* Boston: Houghton Mifflin (259 pages, readability grade 7–8, realistic fiction).

L'Engle, M. (1980). *A ring of endless light.* New York: Farrar, Strauss, Giroux (332 pages, readability grade 7, fantasy).

Levine, G. C. (1997). *Ella enchanted.* New York: HarperCollins (232 pages, readability grade 6, fantasy).

Levy, M. (1996). *Run for your life.* Boston: Houghton Mifflin (217 pages, readability grade 5–6, caution: out of print, realistic fiction).

McCaffrey, A. (1977). *Dragonsinger.* New York: Atheneum (240 pages, readability grade 6, fantasy).

McCaffrey, A. (1976). *Dragonsong.* New York: Atheneum (176 pages, readability grade 7, fantasy).

Patterson, K. (1991). *Lyddie.* New York: Lodestar (182 pages, readability grade 6, historical fiction).

Patterson, K. (1980). *Jacob have I loved.* New York: Harper Trophy (244 pages, readability grade 7, realistic fiction).

Spinelli, J. (1991). *There's a girl in my hammerlock.* New York: Simon & Schuster (191 pages, readability grade 5.5, realistic fiction).

Staples, S. F. (1989). *Shabanu: Daughter of the wind.* New York: Random House (240 pages, readability grade 6, realistic fiction).

Tate, E. E. (1987). *The secret of Gumbo Grove.* New York: Bantam Books (199 pages, readability grade 4, realistic fiction).

Voigt, C. (1982). *Dicey's song.* New York: Atheneum (211 pages, readability grade 6, realistic fiction).

Voigt, C. (1982). *Come a stranger.* New York: Atheneum (248 pages, readability grade 7–8, realistic fiction).

Voigt, C. (1986). *Izzy, willy-nilly.* New York: Atheneum (280 pages, readability grade 7–8, realistic fiction).

Walter, M. P. (1985). *Trouble's child.* New York: Lothrop, Lee & Shepard (157 pages, readability grade 4, caution: out of print, realistic fiction).

Wrede, P. (1990). *Dealing with dragons.* San Diego: Harcourt Brace Jovanovich (212 pages, readability grade 8, fantasy).

List adapted from Sprague, M. M., & Keeling, K. K. (2001). A library for Ophelia. In J. A. Rycik & J. L. Irvin (Eds.), *What Adolescents Deserve: A Commitment to Students' Literacy Learning* (pp. 45–57). Newark, DE: International Reading Association.

Jackson (1993–1994) emphasizes that mainstream teachers need to focus on affective aspects of learning, such as making sure all students feel they belong, as well as on the cognitive aspects. She also points out that students from minority cultures have always been expected to make the effort to become bicultural, so it is reasonable for them to expect teachers to do the same. Jackson made the following suggestions as part of a repertoire of instructional strategies to address cultural differences:

• Provide time for students to share their cultural backgrounds in small groups by telling about when and how their families came to the United States and some of their cultural customs.

- Recognize the importance of pronouncing students' names correctly and consider having them research and share the origin and meaning of their names.
- Try to learn more about students by observing them in nonschool settings, particularly by visiting their communities. Acknowledge their achievements in community organizations and activities.
- Provide a variety of ways to interact while learning. Sitting still and listening to the teacher is difficult for many students, but cooperative learning groups may be especially appropriate for culturally diverse classrooms.
- Explicitly model thinking processes and metacognitive strategies that must be used to be a successful reader. Students' previous experience may be with very different ways of thinking and approaching problems.
- Ask open-ended questions. These types of questions not only promote higher order thinking but also provide an affirmation that students have the knowledge and ability to think about important questions.
- Provide feedback that focuses on the academic components of the work rather than on personality variables. Begin by accentuating positive features, and then communicate specific ways to correct errors and to improve the overall quality of the work.
- Establish positive home-school relations by contacting parents to learn more about their perceptions of their child's strengths, weaknesses, and interests. Students might interview parents or grandparents by asking open-ended questions about topics such as ethnic traditions or world events.
- Both students from mainstream culture and those from minority cultures need opportunities to see a diversity of adults in the school. Parents, grandparents, and community members can be invited to social occasions, as an audience for student performances, or as participants in open-ended panel discussions on topics such as current events.
- Carefully analyze instructional materials to be sure that they accurately portray the perspectives and feelings of the groups that are portrayed and avoid clichés and stereotypes.

Many of Jackson's (1993–1994) recommendations would also apply to English language learners. Alvermann and Phelps (2005) assert that teachers who are native English speakers should be careful about viewing English language learners as deficient in language skills. They contend that bilingualism might well be considered more normal and healthy than speaking only English, stating that,

> Language differences should be more than tolerated; they need to be celebrated and affirmed. As teachers, we need to help students appreciate that having two or more languages or dialects at their command gives them the prerogative to choose from among them as circumstances dictate. (p. 45)

It is also important for teachers of these students to attend to the problem of ensuring that they are involved in literacy tasks that allow them to experience success and to feel some aspects of independence and control. For instance, Mr. Jones, from the situation described at the beginning of this chapter, might provide fairly advanced English language learners with the option of listening to the assigned book on tape during classroom reading time. For less proficient students, he could offer a choice of a number of easier books on the theme of sibling rivalry. Teachers with a combination of English language learners and English-only students should note in their grade books or seating chart their language proficiency level (beginning, intermediate, advanced). With this on hand, the teacher can differentiate instruction when planning lessons.

Summary

According to the standards of the International Reading Association, creating a literate environment is one of the competencies expected of all reading professionals (International Reading Association, 2002). In discussing this standard, Armbruster and Osborn (2002) make recommendations similar to those of many other educators cited in this chapter:

*   Teachers and others who model interest and involvement in literacy.
*   A large number of appropriate books and time to read them.
*   A physical environment that features easy access to books and technology and areas where students can work in small groups and independently.
*   An atmosphere that conveys a strong message that reading and writing are valued, where students have opportunities to share their personal responses and what they have learned from their reading.

We believe that teachers can most effectively create literate environments by keeping in mind the two goals of encouraging engagement and expecting and respecting diversity. In Part II of this book, we will show a variety of approaches for putting these principles into action.

Applying and Organizing New Information _____

Reread the vignette at the beginning of this chapter and consider the following questions:

1. What does Mr. Jones need to know about his students in order to help them engage more fully with reading and writing tasks? What assessment procedures might he use to find that information?

2. How might Mr. Jones change his novel study unit to create more student engagement?

3. To what extent does he have the power to change things? What factors can he control? What factors are beyond his control?

A Case to Consider _____

Jamaal is an African American student in a suburban middle school where the majority of students are of European descent. Neither of his parents went to college, but they expect him to do so. They have informed the school that they expect to be called immediately if his grades start to slip, but they are not otherwise involved with the school program. Like his friends, Jamaal likes rap music and professional sports, particularly basketball. He gets along with his teachers and all the students in his classes, but he eats lunch at a table with other African Americans. He rarely shows up at school social activities, and then only if his friends come with him. He struggles with writing, especially with spelling. When allowed to choose his own reading material, he picks *Sports Illustrated* or "the shortest book I can find."

Respond to some or all of these issues related to this case:

1. What environmental factors in the classroom encourage Jamaal's reading development? What factors discourage it?

2. What factors *outside* the classroom encourage Jamaal's reading development? What factors discourage it?

3. If you were his teacher, what would you tell Jamaal about his own reading? What, if anything would you want to assess?

4. If you were Jamaal's teacher, what might you do to promote his reading engagement?

Key Terms to Know and Use

engagement	uncommitted readers	reader identify
motivation	unmotivated readers	gender differences
aliteracy	unskilled readers	cultural differences
dormant readers	ownership	

Possible Sentences

Use two or three terms in the columns above and write a sentence stating one idea you now know about engaging with texts. Write four or five such sentences using different words until you have a nice summary paragraph.

Beyond the Book

- The September 1998 edition of *Voices from the Middle,* published by the National Council of Teachers of English, focuses on English language learners in middle grades. Further information about the articles in this issue and about English language learners can be found at www.ncte.org.

- Use the "Why Do I Read?" questionnaire (Figure 5.1) to interview an individual or to survey a group. To use it for an interview, ask a reader questions about several of the factors listed in each section. For the section on "Curiosity" for example, you might ask, "If the teacher discusses something interesting, are you likely to read more about it? Can you tell me about a time when that happened?"

- Two recent books on the topic of adolescent boys and reading are:

  Smith, M. W., & Wilhelm, J. (2002). *Reading Don't Fix No Chevys: Literacy in the Lives of Young Men.* Portsmouth, NH: Heinemann:

  Brozo, William G. (2002). *To Be a Boy, To Be a Reader.* Newark, DE: International Reading Association.

References

Alvermann, D.E., & Phelps, S.F. (2005). *Content reading and literacy: Succeeding in today's classrooms* (4th ed.). Boston: Allyn and Bacon.

Armbruster, B. B., & Osborn, J. H. (2002). *Reading instruction and assessment: Understanding the IRA standards.* Boston: Allyn and Bacon.

Beers, K. (1998). Choosing not to read: Understanding why some middle schoolers just say no. In K. Beers & B. Samuels (Eds.), *Into focus: understanding and creating middle school readers* (pp. 37–63). Norwood, MA: Christopher-Gordon.

Brozo, W. G. (2000). *To be a boy, to be a reader.* Newark, DE: International Reading Association.

Brozo, W. G., & Schmelzer, R. V. (1997). Wildmen, warriors, and lovers: Reading boys through archetypal literature. *Journal of Adolescent and Adult Literacy, 41*(1), 4–11.

Broughton, M. A., & Fairbanks, C. M. (2003). In the middle of the middle: Seventh-grade girls' literacy and identity development. *Journal of Adolescent & Adult Literacy, 46*(5), 426–435.

Brown, A. (1987). Metacognition, executive control, self-regulation, and other more mysterious mechanisms. In E. Weinert & R. H. Kluwe (Eds.), *Metacognition, motivation, and understanding* (pp. 65–116). Hillsdale, NJ: Erlbaum.

Cazden, C. (1988). *Classroom discourse: The language of teaching and learning.* Portsmouth, NH: Heinemann.

Gambrell, L. B., & Marinak, B. (1997). *Incentive and intrinsic motivation to read.* In J. T. Guthrie & A. Wigfield (Eds.), Reading engagement: Motivating readers through integrated instruction (pp. 205–217). Newark, DE: International Reading Association.

Greenleaf, C. L., Schoenbach, R., Cziko, C., & Mueller, F. L. (2001). Apprenticing adolescent readers to academic literacy. *Harvard Educational Review, 71*(1), 79–129.

Gullingsrud, M. (1998). I am the immigrant in my classroom. *Voices from the Middle, 6*(1), 30–37.

Guthrie, J. T., & Wigfield, A. (Eds.). (1997). *Reading engagement: Motivating readers through integrated instruction.* Newark, DE: International Reading Association.

Guthrie, J. T., McCann, A., Hynd, C., & Stahl, S. (1997). Classroom contexts promoting literacy engagement. In J. Flood, S. B. Heath, & D. Lapp (Eds.), *Research on teaching literacy through the communicative and visual arts* (pp. 753–762). New York: Simon & Schuster Macmillan.

International Reading Association. (2002). *Standards for reading professionals.* Newark, DE: Author.

Jackson, F. R. (1993–1994). Seven strategies to support a culturally responsive pedagogy. *Journal of Reading, 37*(4), 298–303.

Manning, M. L. (1993). *Developmentally appropriate middle level schools.* Wheaton, MD: Association for Childhood Education International.

Moore, D. W., & Hinchman, K. A. (2003). *Starting out: A guide to teaching adolescents who struggle with reading and writing.* Boston: Allyn and Bacon.

Ogbu, J. U. (1992). Understanding cultural diversity and learning. *Educational Researcher, 21*(8), 5–14, 24.

Patterson, K. (1980). *Jacob have I loved.* New York: HarperCollins.

Research for Action, Inc. (1996). Girls in the middle: *Working to succeed in school.* Researched and written by J. Cohen and S. Blanc with J. Christman. Washington, DC: American Association of University Women Educational Foundation.

Roe, M. F. (2001). Combining enablement and engagement to assist students who do not read and write well. In J. A. Rycik & J. L. Irvin (Eds.), *What adolescents deserve: A commitment to students' literacy learning* (pp. 10–19). Newark, DE: International Reading Association.

Rosenblatt, L. (1978). *Reader, the text, the poem: The transactional theory of the literary work.* Carbondale, IL: Southern Illinois University Press.

Rycik, J. A. (2001). From information to interaction: Involving parents in the literacy development of their adolescent. In J. A. Rycik & J. L. Irvin (Eds.), *What adolescents deserve: A commitment to students' literacy learning* (pp. 160–164). Newark, DE: International Reading Association.

Schallert, D. L., & Reed, J. H. (1997). The pull of the text and the process of involvement in one's reading. In J. T. Guthrie & A. Wigfield (Eds.), *Reading engagement: Motivating readers through integrated instruction* (pp. 68–85). Newark, DE: International Reading Association.

Smith, M. W., & Wilhelm, J. (2002). *Reading don't fix no Chevys: Literacy in the lives of young men.* Portsmouth, NH: Heinemann.

Sprague, M. M., & Keeling, K. K. (2001). A library for Ophelia. In J. A. Rycik & J. L. Irvin (Eds.), *What adolescents deserve: A commitment to students' literacy learning* (pp. 45–57). Newark, DE: International Reading Association.

Wigfield, A. (1997). Children's motivations for reading and reading engagement. In J. T. Guthrie & A. Wigfield (Eds.), *Reading engagement: Motivating readers through integrated instruction* (pp. 14–33). Newark, DE: International Reading Association.

Supporting the Literacy Development of All Students

6

Environments for Diverse Learners: Scaffolds and Literacy Routines

Activating Prior Knowledge and Making Connections

Ramon was writing about his family's vacation trip to Disney World, but he was stuck. He wanted to describe how their bags were searched before they boarded the plane, but he did not know how to spell the word *luggage.* His teacher, Mrs. Jackson, noticed his frustration and asked if she could help. When Ramon explained, she asked how he might solve the problem. "Use the dictionary," he replied wearily. "But how can I look up the word if I can't spell it?"

Mrs. Jackson asked Ramon if he had ever used the *Spelling Dictionary* that was in the class bookcase. "Since it doesn't have all the definitions," she explained, "you don't need to turn as many pages to find a word. If I'm pretty sure about the first three letters of a word, I can usually find it in here fairly quickly," she said.

Mrs. Jackson handed Ramon the book. He still looked dubious, so she said, "Let's try it out." She directed him to pronounce the word *luggage* slowly, drawing it out so that he could hear each sound. "What letters are you pretty sure are in the word?" she asked. He told her that he knew it began with *l* and that the next letters were probably *u* and *g* and the next one might be an *i.*

Mrs. Jackson showed Ramon the guide words on the top of each page in the spelling dictionary and explained that he should look for a page that would include words that start with *l-u* and then skim down to where there were words starting with *l-u-g.* Seeing that Ramon still hesitated to try, she said, "Let me show you how I use it. Recently, I was trying to spell the word *terrible,* and I couldn't remember if it ended in *a-b-l-e,* or *i-b-l-e,* but I knew it started with *t-e-r.* I looked for the section with the *t* words, and found this page with *teacup* and *terse* on the top. I knew I was close, so I ran my finger down the page like this, and there it was."

Handing the book to Ramon, Mrs. Jackson reminded him to look for a page with *l-u-g* words. She said that she would check back with him and moved on to help another student. When she returned, Ramon had found the correct spelling. She reminded him that he could use the book whenever he was editing. Later, Mrs. Jackson called the students together for a brief sharing time. She called on Ramon to explain how to use the *Spelling Dictionary* and when he would use it. In the days that followed, Mrs. Jackson observed him using the dictionary on several occasions.

Before you go on with this chapter, take a few moments to consider this classroom scenario:
1. How does the teacher determine what kind of support she should give?
2. How does she encourage Ramon to become independent?
3. How does she encourage students to help each other?

As you read the rest of this chapter, think about how this scenario illustrates the concept of scaffolding and how various literacy routines provide opportunities for this kind of instruction.

In Part II of this book, we present different ways for teachers to apply their understanding of literacy in order to support the learning of students with a wide range of abilities, including students who are culturally and linguistically diverse. In this chapter, we provide an overview by examining some of the characteristics of effective classroom environments. We begin by examining how teachers can use the process of scaffolding to help all students become more independent. Then, we examine how effective environments combine meaningful instruction with respect for diversity. Finally, we introduce the concept of literacy routines and explain how a skillful blend of these routines can both challenge and support diverse literacy learners.

Scaffolding to Meet Students' Needs

Scaffolding is the process of temporarily providing assistance so that students can do things that they would not be able to do on their own. Just as the scaffolds that are provided for construction workers are taken down after the building is completed, instructional scaffolds are designed to be gradually discontinued as students become more and more able to engage with challenging texts independently (Harris & Hodges, 1995). Mrs. Jackson demonstrates scaffolding in the opening scenario of this chapter. She does not simply give Ramon the correct spelling he is seeking. Instead, she guides him to accomplish his goal by showing him how to use an appropriate resource. Notice that she offers the minimum amount of assistance necessary and quickly allows Ramon to use his new learning on his own.

The Zone of Proximal Development

The influential theorist Lev Vygotsky (1978) describes the process of scaffolding through the concept of a Zone of Proximal Development (ZPD). This concept is important to understanding the nature of instructional scaffolds. In Figure 6.1, the circle in the center of the diagram represents *current performance*—what a learner can already do independently. The outer ring represents *potential performance*—what the individual is attempting to learn. The ring that is in between depicts the ZPD—the tasks that the learner cannot perform independently but can accomplish when supported by an adult or by more capable peers.

The ZPD implies a particular view of the role of teachers. Rather than being authorities who provide right answers, they become coaches who continually challenge learners and then offer them the support they need. That support often comes in the form of instructional "conversations" that are one form of scaffolding. As Dixon-Krauss (1996) explained, "Social interaction provides the context for guiding the child's learning. During instruction, the teacher mediates or augments the child's ability to perform various learning tasks by providing guidance and support, primarily through social dialogue" (p. 15).

Kinds of Scaffolds

Scaffolding then, is often a process by which a more proficient individual talks with a less experienced or proficient individual in ways that help the learner to do new things. It is a little like the movie scene where a person in the control tower with a better vantage point

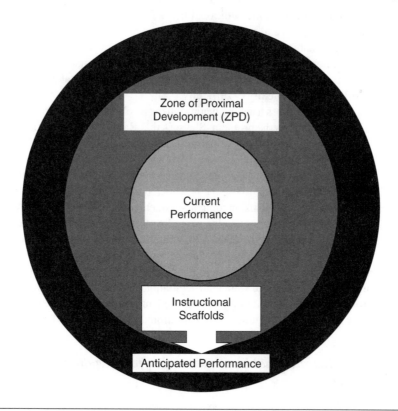

FIGURE 6.1 *Scaffolding and the Zone of Proximal Development*

and more experience tells an inexperienced pilot not to worry because, "I'll talk you all the way down to the ground." Teachers use their own language in a number of ways to help students to negotiate the unfamiliar territory of the ZPD. These ways include:

- Modeling or explaining the processes of using and thinking about texts.
- Posing questions that raise new possibilities and invite students to make new connections between ideas.
- Orchestrating conversations among students.
- Responding to students' attempts by inviting elaboration and clarification.
- Providing feedback that highlights students' successes and suggests appropriate next steps.
- Providing additional information that allows students to understand the purpose and significance of a passage or a text.
- Introducing, using, and reinforcing new words and language structures.

Assessment and Scaffolding

The notion of the ZPD underscores the importance of assessment. To create the necessary scaffolds, teachers need to identify what students can do on their own and what they might be able to do with some additional help. The assessment information that is provided by standardized tests and other school or district assessments may be of some help, but the information that is collected during day-to-day literacy activities is more important. By creating opportunities to listen to their students and to observe their reading and writing, teachers can identify the next steps learners are ready to take and guide them toward the next level of complexity or difficulty.

Mrs. Jackson's teaching begins when she observes that Ramon is having difficulty and asks him to explain the problem. She sees that Ramon has enough knowledge of sounds and symbols to get his thoughts down on paper and that he can spell many commonly used words. She decides that he is ready to learn some new ways to find and confirm spellings and that the spelling dictionary might be a good way to do that. Notice that she continues to observe Ramon's attempt to use the new technique so that she can continue to provide advice and encouragement. This ongoing assessment is crucial to the process of scaffolding.

In most states, English language learners take annual assessments on their ability to read, write, and speak English. Upon entering school they also receive an assessment on their primary language abilities. Teachers with a combination of English language learners and English-only students should note in their gradebooks or seating charts the language proficiency level of each student (beginning, intermediate, or advanced). That information provides a general guide for what the student can do—but the teacher will also want to use other assessments to guide their instruction, especially careful observation.

Using Instructional Strategies to Scaffold Reading Success

Scaffolds serve two basic purposes: providing enough guidance for students to read a particular text successfully and laying the groundwork for independent success in the future.

Teachers may create scaffolds spontaneously during their interactions with students as Mrs. Jackson did. They may also use their knowledge of their students' needs to plan scaffolds that will guide their students' engagements with texts. These planned scaffolds are often called *instructional strategies*. Sometimes this term causes confusion with the idea of *reader* strategies. The confusion is regrettable, but there is a good reason why the same word is used to describe both teaching and reading. A strategy can be defined as a "systematic plan consciously adapted and monitored to improve one's performance" (Harris & Hodges, 1995, p. 244). *Reader strategies* are plans that readers develop and implement to ensure their own success. *Instructional strategies* are plans that teachers develop for scaffolding a particular aspect of proficient reading.

An instructional strategy is a "how" that has been invented to help teachers get to a particular "what." For example, the Contextual Redefinition strategy that was introduced in Chapter 3 is a five-step procedure (the "how") that helps teachers to build students' relevant vocabulary knowledge (the "what") before they read. Like any tool, instructional strategies are only valuable if used at the right time and in the right way. Teachers can plan effective reading instruction by choosing the particular instructional strategies that are appropriate to the needs of their students and the characteristics of the text they are reading.

Expecting and Respecting Diversity

It is hard to imagine any group of human beings that does not show diversity. A group of friends gathered to eat dinner, for example, may "have a lot in common," but they would also show many differences. They may include both males and females and differ in physical characteristics such as eye color and height. More importantly, they may have different preferences about what they like to eat, different notions about when dinner should be served, and different standards regarding good table manners. It would be difficult, moreover, to introduce any topic of conversation that would be of equal interest to all of them. In spite of their diverse characteristics, however, it is possible for each of the dinner guests to feel welcome at the table.

Classrooms show much more diversity than a dinner party. Despite efforts to track or group them by ability or achievement, there are always important differences among students, including their cultural or religious background, their interests and preferences, and their past achievements. Nevertheless, teachers in the middle grades need to create classroom environments where each student feels welcome and experiences the proper balance of challenge and support.

In this section we consider some of the issues related to diversity by examining three ways in which students might differ. The variability shown by students in the middle grades goes far beyond these few factors, but the principle of expecting and respecting differences still applies.

English Language Learners

Throughout this book, we have referred to some of the needs of English language learners and some of the ways in which teachers can address those needs. We do so not only because the population of English language learners is growing steadily, but also because these students exemplify many of the issues related to diversity. First of all, English language learners exemplify the principle that differences in reading ability may not be related to either intelligence or effort. Second, they illustrate the enormity of the task of learning literacy and content at the same time. Consider, for instance, the following quotation from an eighth-grade student from Afghanistan.

> I get so tired, my head would hurt. All day, I sit in classes and hear English, English, English, and try so hard to understand, but I do not understand. I was afraid the teacher would call on me. I was trying to hear a word I knew. I was trying to figure out my science and my math. In the morning time it was better. I'd think, today I will understand. But by lunch my head was hurting, and I felt despair. By the last class in the day, I couldn't even listen any more—it was so hard. I just sat there and nothing made sense.

English language learners challenge teachers to consider differences as strengths worthy of respect. Alvermann and Phelps (2005) assert that teachers who are native English speakers should be careful about viewing English language learners as deficient in language skills. They contend that bilingualism might well be considered more normal and healthy than speaking only English, stating that,

> Language differences should be more than tolerated; they need to be celebrated and affirmed. As teachers, we need to help students appreciate that having two or more languages or dialects at their command gives them the prerogative to choose from among them as circumstances dictate. (p. 45)

Since school is such a highly verbal environment, students whose first language is other than English may face some formidable difficulties. Gullingsrud (1998) describes some of the ways in which he tried to give the proper respect to the language and culture of the Mexican American students in his classroom. He explains how he worked at learning and using Spanish (although he considered himself as only an English speaker) and how he tried to bring Spanish language texts into his room.

> I look for books I already have in English, or bilingual text within a single volume, so we can all enjoy the same works together. We read aloud side by side, one student doing a passage in English and another the same in Spanish. I take part as well, reading either language, and of course I encourage my English learners to try the new language. (p. 32)

For English language learners, teachers should modify instruction, not complexity. Teachers should focus on the key concepts within the standards and eliminate confusing activities or variables. The lessons should be even more organized and sequential and be focused on the most important concepts. Instruction is not thereby watered down. Instead, it is distilled to ensure that instructional time is used to help students understand the fundamental concepts or skills needed to master the standards.

Readers Who Struggle

Readers who struggle are sometimes difficult to identify. Allen (2000) notes that older readers have often developed elaborate strategies for camouflaging their reading difficulties such as studiously turning pages during silent reading time without reading at all. These students rarely ask questions or say they do not understand out of fear that their peers will make fun of them. They are usually not asked to read aloud as often as they were in the primary grades, so problems with decoding and fluency may not surface. Allen states that only a minority of struggling readers have problems with letter–sound relationships due to poor instruction or disabilities such as dyslexia. She cites lack of fluency, poor vocabulary, and limited background knowledge as factors that might limit readers' comprehension.

Hill (1998) notes that most middle level teachers do not know where to begin with struggling readers. They make accommodations such as reading content material aloud to students, having them listen to audiotapes, or arranging for them to read with a partner. They do these things to help their students through the curriculum, but "to reach that goal, they remove students from the very practice they need most: reading. Instead of practicing reading and writing, low-level students spend much of their time practicing listening" (p. 82).

Teachers should resist the temptation to look for deficiencies within their students or to blame parents or previous teachers. They may eventually decide to refer students to a specialist, but their first focus should be on adapting the classroom environment to provide appropriate learning experiences to fit students' needs (Ash, 2002). Teachers need to communicate that they are not shocked when students struggle with their assignments and that they believe they will eventually succeed.

Gifted and Talented Students

Baskin (1998) complains about the lack of attention to the reading needs of gifted students, noting that, "appallingly, instead of receiving reading instruction themselves, gifted pupils often acted as teacher surrogates" (p.6). She contends that a teacher's tendency toward "teaching to the middle" and heterogeneous grouping work against gifted students. Moreover, teachers often respond to their ability either by giving them more of the assignments they have already mastered or by creating special more rigorous assignments rather than by providing the specific differential planning gifted students need.

Planning instruction for gifted students during middle grades should begin with an understanding of their characteristics. Baskin (1998) argues against "one size fits all" instruction and insists that gifted students need appropriate materials and experiences.

> Since these students show exceptional comprehension, higher level books sometimes even at an adult level should be made available; since they have the capacity for sustained effort, longer books are reasonable options; since they can understand symbolic material, books including such components are possibilities. (p. 68)

Baskin also points out that, although highly capable readers should have opportunities to read advanced adult books, they might also profit from reading young adult books.

Academically talented students must deal with the same developmental issues that all adolescents face, and young adult books may provide valuable insight and moral support.

Characteristics of Effective Environments for Literacy Learning

The differences between the groups described above are striking. Nevertheless, these students have some common needs. They all need to feel that they are an integral part of a learning community rather than a problem to be dealt with or a junior teacher's aide. They also need opportunities to interact with the teacher in the way that Ramon did in the opening scenario. They also need to have opportunities to interact with others.

Student Collaboration

Providing opportunities for learners to help each other is an important way in which teachers scaffold learning. Some people might characterize students collaborating in pairs and groups as "the blind leading the blind," but it is more accurate to describe the process as partially sighted people learning by sharing what they see. Modeling, sharing information, and discussing among peers can have the same mediating effect as interacting with a teacher with the added benefit that the language students use to help each other may be more comprehensible than the language a teacher would use.

Access to Reading

Ivey and Broaddus (2001) report that sixth-grade students found activities such as "Drop Everything and Read" (DEAR) to be among the most valuable experiences in their language arts classes. The material they preferred included magazines, adventure books, mysteries, and scary stories. Most importantly, they wanted to choose the material they read.

Effective environments for literacy need to include time for reading in class rather than assigning all the reading for homework. They should include a good classroom library containing the things that students like to read, and they should include a balance between reading teacher-selected and student-selected materials.

Ongoing Informal Assessment

As we pointed out above, in effective environments, teachers can easily observe and respond to students' literacy processes. A teacher who finds out that students are struggling from their scores on a unit test is finding out too late. Teachers need to be able to move around the room and talk with students about their reading and writing on a regular basis. Students need to see assessment as the first step toward improvement rather than as a weapon to be used against them. Listening to a student read a passage aloud or asking for a summary of a story can allow a teacher to show students how much they *do* know as well as what they need to learn next.

Flexible Grouping

For teachers to be free to observe student talk, students need to be working independently and in small groups at least as often as they are listening to the teacher or engaged in whole class discussions. Students may form a group so that they can all read and discuss a book that they have chosen, or the teacher may temporarily call together a group to work with them on an aspect of their writing. Groups can be formed in many ways, but they should always serve to meet the students' needs, unlike an ability group where "low" students are always kept together as a way of managing the classroom.

Meaningful Instruction

Langer (2002) carried out a study that compared the instructional practices of effective and "typical" teachers. She was particularly interested in schools where students were "beating the odds" by achieving higher than might be predicted. She identified six factors that were common in effective instruction:

1. Effective teachers integrate the teaching of skills and knowledge with purposeful literacy activities.
2. Effective teachers did not focus on teaching to a test. They integrated instruction in skills, strategies, and knowledge into students' daily literacy activities.
3. Effective teachers made connections across lessons, classes, and grades and between in-school and out-of-school literacy.
4. Effective teachers directly taught strategies for thinking such as planning, organizing, completing, and reflecting.
5. Effective teachers focused on deeper understanding rather than on an immediate goal such as getting the "right" answers.
6. Effective teachers encouraged students to learn from each other through substantive discussions from multiple perspectives.

Creating an environment of respect that balances challenge and support, is comfortable with diversity, and consistently provides effective instructional practices would be an impossible task if teachers had to start from scratch each day. The key to managing the effort is to organize learning activities that are used repeatedly so that students can learn to function fairly independently, and the teacher can develop a clear connection between literacy goals and instructional procedures. This can be done by establishing a repertoire of literacy routines.

Classroom Literacy Routines

Rasinsky and Padak (2000) define routines as "regular blocks of time during which certain predictable types of activities occur" (p. 25). The words *routine* and *predictable* may imply activity that is done automatically or without enthusiasm, but literacy routines can create an environment that allows thoughtful teaching and powerful learning.

Mooney (1990) suggests three kinds of literacy routines that should be part of any balanced reading program: reading *to* students, reading *with* students, and reading *by* students. We have further divided this classification to identify eight literacy routines that we believe should be components of a comprehensive literacy program in the middle grades. As Table 6.1 illustrates, each of these routines comprises a pattern of teacher roles, student roles, and materials that work together to support particular literacy goals.

Note that all of the routines involve students in complex literacy tasks using real texts rather than in learning isolated skills from practice materials. They also combine reading with speaking, writing, and listening in a natural way. The remainder of this chapter provides a brief overview of each of the literacy routines.

Read-Alouds

Read-alouds continue to serve an important purpose throughout the middle grades, as Irvin and Strauss (2000) point out,

> Older children and young adolescents still benefit from hearing interesting stories or information from an informational text read to them. Read-aloud sessions give them access to text that they are not able to read themselves, expose them to an author or genre previously unknown or unappreciated, increase vocabulary development, aid in critical thinking, and encourage reading for sheer enjoyment. (p. 124)

In Chapter 7, we present a more detailed look at these reasons for read-alouds and some specific examples of ways in which students' vocabulary and comprehension can be developed during read-aloud experiences.

Student Oral Reading

Like teacher read-alouds, a picture of students reading aloud may be associated with beginning reading instruction. Oral reading can, however, still play an important role in the reading development of young adolescents. Many students in the middle grades are still developing reading fluency. Appropriate oral reading experiences can act as scaffolds for those students to develop ease and comfort with written language. Chapter 7 will also show some ways to guide and assess oral reading by students.

Guided Reading

Guided reading routines are often used in the primary grades (Cunningham & Allington, 1999; Fountas & Pinnell, 1999). The scope of instruction and the specific strategies differ in the middle grades, but the purpose of guided reading remains the same: to support students as they learn and apply effective reading strategies while reading challenging texts. Because guided reading involves modeling and support, it is an effective strategy for English language learners who have low reading ability. In Chapter 8, we discuss guided reading by showing frameworks teachers can use to combine instructional strategies into effective text experiences.

TABLE 6.1 *An Overview of Literacy Routines*

Literacy Routine	Purposes	Teacher Roles	Student Roles	Materials	Organization
Read-Aloud	• Promote fluency • Expose students to new genres, authors • Build comprehension • Elicit response • Build vocabulary • Build interest in reading	• Modeling fluent oral reading • Leading text discussions • Introducing vocabulary	• Active listening • Participating in text discussions • Writing responses Reading along with the teacher	• Adolescent literature (whole texts or excerpts) • Selections from anthologies or basals • Periodicals • Poems • Other	• Whole class • Small groups
Student Oral Reading	• Develop word identification • Develop fluency	• Introducing fluency criteria • Establishing pairs or groups • Assessing fluency	• Rehearsing oral reading • Applying fluency criteria to self and others • Assisting partner or group	• Instructional level text • Dramatic text • Content area passages	• Pairs • Individual • Small groups
Guided Reading	• Learn and apply reader strategies • Acquire new vocabulary • Comprehend challenging text	• Modeling reader strategies • Activating or building back-ground knowledge • Introducing vocabulary • Posing focus questions	• Silent reading from assigned texts • Whole-class and small-group text discussion • Using guide sheets • Writing to reconstruct, apply, or extend ideas	• Challenging text • Basal readers or textbooks • Fiction and nonfiction trade books	• Whole class • Small groups

(continues)

TABLE 6.1 *Continued*

Literacy Routine	Purposes	Teacher Roles	Student Roles	Materials	Organizatios
Guided Literature Study	• Read aesthetically from challenging literary texts • Learn tools and terms of literary analysis • Acquire new vocabulary and language structures • Experience some "classic" literature	• Guiding discussions about meaning within texts and between texts • Introducing concepts of literary analysis • Modeling attitudes and strategies • Introducing vocabulary, language structures, and background knowledge	• Silent reading from assigned texts • Whole class and small group text discussion • Formulating and applying literary criteria • Writing to explore themes, literary elements, connections	• "Classic" and contemporary young adult and adult novels • Selections from literature anthologies • Poetry and drama • Film and other media	• Whole class • Small groups
Literature Circles	• Gain experience and independence • Acquire new vocabulary and language structures • Develop favorable attitudes toward reading	• Establishing groups and group procedures • Monitoring and reinforcing techniques for reader response and text discussion • Monitoring and reinforcing use of reader strategies	• Choosing from selected books • Reading silently and independently. • Preparing for small group discussions • Doing journal entries or other informal writing	• Sets of young adult trade books appropriate for age and reading ability • Self-selections from basals or anthologies	• Small groups

Reading Workshop	• Gain experience and independence with a variety of material • Acquire vocabulary, language structures • Develop favorable attitudes toward reading	• Establishing procedures • Monitoring student progress through conferences and written responses • Assessing, reinforcing use of reader strategies	• Choosing from a wide range of genres • Reading independently • Writing responses, making creative products • Sharing, discussing, engaging in conferences • Keeping records, setting goals, and self-evaluating	• Young adult trade books appropriate for age and reading ability • Periodicals, "real world" materials • Internet and media	• Individual • Pairs • Small groups • Whole class
Writing Workshop	• Gain experience and independence writing a variety of products • Use new vocabulary, language structures • Develop favorable attitudes toward writing	• Establishing procedures • Monitoring student progress through conferences and reading students' written products • Assessing, reinforcing writing strategies	• Choosing topics • Drafting, revising, editing, and publishing • Engaging in conferences with teacher and peers • Keeping records, setting goals, and self-evaluating	• Computers and writing materials • Classroom library • Students' writing • Writers' reference tools	• Individual • Pairs • Small groups • Whole class
Unit-Centered Reading	• Use reading to explore a topic, theme, or genre • Learn new vocabulary • Learn to use text structures to guide comprehension	• Setting unit goals • Providing materials and/or guiding student inquiry • Monitoring progress and assessing learning	• Reading from a wide range of related fiction or nonfiction texts • Locating/ recognizing significant information • Creating informal and formal written products	• Textbooks • Fiction/nonfiction trade books • Newspapers and magazines • Internet and media	• Individual • Pairs • Small groups • Whole class

Guided Literature Study

During guided literature Study, teachers are concerned with helping students interpret, appreciate, and think critically about texts that have been created for an artistic purpose. Ensuring a smooth transition from middle school to high school is one reason to include some guided literature study in a comprehensive reading program (Wells, 1996). It opens the door for young adolescents to participate more fully in the cultural life of their society (Jago, 2000) by reading from both classic and linguistically and culturally diverse authors. In Chapter 9, we discuss the goals of guided literature study, present ways to analyze literature, bridge texts, and to accommodate student differences.

Literature Circles

A literature circle (Daniels, 1994) is a literacy routine in which students select trade books, read them independently, and discuss them in small groups. Students lead the groups using guidelines or procedures provided by the teacher. Literature circles are characterized by ample opportunity for small group discussion, the use of reading logs or journals, and an emphasis on readers' responses to the books they read. The term *book club* is often used as a synonym for literature circles. Literature circle and book club approaches to independent reading will be described in detail in Chapter 10, as will another common approach—the reading workshop.

Reading Workshops

Reading workshops, like literature circles, focus on students' reading high quality adolescent literature and include small group discussion. In Chapter 10, however, we will make a distinction between the two by describing a reading workshop that allows students to choose from a wide variety of materials including newspapers, magazines, and informational texts and is structured to allow students to read independently without belonging to a group.

Writing Workshops

Reading and writing workshops were developed as parallel routines (Atwell, 1987). Both workshops share procedures such as mini-lessons, the use of portfolios, whole-class sharing sessions, and conferences (both between students and between a student and the teacher). It is also important to note that reading workshops involve a great deal of writing about text, whereas writing workshops are structured to encourage students to use their reading as a source of ideas for their writing. Chapter 11 contains a description of a writer's workshop as well as guidelines for using writing assignments for connecting reading and writing.

Unit-Centered Reading

Units can be organized around an author, a genre, a topic, or a theme. They can also be focused on particular literacy processes such as integrating the language arts or information literacy. Alvermann and Phelps (2005) point out that many teachers are planning units rather than lessons because they have come to view their curriculum

> as comprising meaningfully interrelated concepts and themes, not simply as isolated bits of information to be learned by rote. All this implies that teachers will plan activities that enable students to make connections between content areas, between the real world and the world of the classroom, and between "knowing what" (facts and concepts) and "knowing how" (using facts and concepts in authentic ways). (p. 80)

In Chapter 12, we will explore a variety of units and examine some of the ways in which units help middle grades students to learn the vocabulary, concepts, strategies, and skills that proficient readers need.

The authors of the Adolescent Literacy Position Statement (Moore, Bean, Birdyshaw, & Rycik, 1999) assert that

> Adolescents deserve classrooms that respect individuals' differences. To promote respect, teachers encourage the exchange of ideas among individuals. They regularly set up paired, small group, and whole class arrangements so that everyone can have his or her voice heard. Believing that everyone has something to offer, they organize instruction so that students of diverse backgrounds share their insights into course topics. (p. 8)

Teachers can approach this goal by artfully combining literacy routines. Ash (2002), for instance, suggests a pragmatic framework for reading instruction that would attend to the needs of struggling learners aged 10 to 14. The framework includes five routines—daily oral or shared reading, guided reading in flexible groups, word study, self-selected extended reading and writing, and explicit comprehension strategy instruction.

Literacy routines combine to create a consistent environment that supports students as they develop positive habits of writing, talking, and thinking about texts. The amount of time devoted to various routines needs to vary according to a number of factors, only some of which a teacher controls. The particular emphases of state and local curricula, the limitations of the daily schedule, the preferences and expertise of the teacher, and, of course, the needs and interests of the students in a particular classroom will all influence how literacy routines are combined. We believe, however, that each of the routines adds a unique and crucial element to developing proficient readers in the middle grades.

Summary

Part II of this book focuses on the many ways in which teachers can support the reading growth of their students. Scaffolding is an important element of classroom environments where a variety of languages and reading levels exist. It may involve demonstrating, explaining, questioning, and responding to students' attempts. Instructional strategies and literacy routines both help teachers to plan and to carry out the process of scaffolding. An effective environment uses literacy routines to create a balance between oral and written language, between challenging text and easy reading, and between student independence and teacher guidance.

Responding to Reading

This chapter stresses that students need literacy activities that provide guidance and support, but they also need opportunities to use their literacy abilities independently. You might want to consider this point by placing each of the literacy routines described in this chapter (Read-Alouds, Oral Reading, Guided Reading, Guided Literature Study, Literature Circles, Reading Workshops, Writing Workshops, and Unit-Centered Reading) on this continuum:

| **High teacher guidance and control** | ←————————————→ | **High student independence and responsibility** |

A Case to Consider

Brittney is a seventh grader who thinks of herself as an "average" reader. She reads willingly from series books such as the "Alien" books of Bruce Coville (www.brucecoville.com), but she rarely attempts anything more challenging unless it is assigned. Brittney likes to talk with her friends, but she does not usually like to work in groups with the stories that are assigned in language arts. She feels that the other students in the group are likely to leave it up her to answer all the assigned questions.

Brittney thinks teachers can help with her reading by "teaching me the hard words" that turn up in the assigned stories. When asked to tell about a time when a teacher did something that helped the class understand what they were reading, she tells about a teacher who made up "think sheets" that helped students to recognize and write down what was important in the things they read. Brittney thinks that she would like reading more if she could choose her own books. On the other hand, she believes that what she most needs to learn about reading is "how to read harder books and stories."

Consider how to meet Brittney's needs as a reader by answering the following:

1. What are some of the strengths she needs opportunities to use?

2. What are some areas where she needs teacher guidance and support?

3. How would each of the instructional strategies and literacy routines that are described in this chapter support Brittney's reading development?

Key Terms to Know and Use

literature circles	instructional strategies	read-alouds
reading workshops	gifted and talented	guided reading
scaffolding	diversity	guided literature study
Zone of Proximal Development	effective environments	unit-centered reading
	writing workshops	

Possible Sentences

Use two or three terms in the columns above and write a sentence stating one idea you now know about literacy routines. Write four or five such sentences using different words until you have a nice summary paragraph.

Beyond the Book

- Try to recall some examples of learning to do new tasks from your own experience. For example, how did you learn to tie your shoes? Or, more recently, how did you learn to drive, or to register for college classes? Try to think of some experiences when you were successful and some where you struggled. Trade learning stories with some friends or classmates, and then discuss or write about the following:
  1. Which of these learning experiences were successfully scaffolded by someone with more knowledge and experience?
  2. Were there any experiences in which the learners "figured things out" on their own? If so, how were they able to do that?
  3. What "rules" can you give for when and how to scaffold learning? How would you apply those rules to literacy learning?
- If you have the opportunity, observe a reading or language arts class. Use the list from the beginning of this chapter to note the kinds of scaffolds the teacher uses. If you are currently teaching, you may apply the same list to analyze your own classroom. Also ask yourself which scaffolds were used for English language learners.
- Gwynne Ellen Ash (2002) suggests five literacy routines that should be included in teaching middle grades readers who struggle. To read her online article, go to the IRA website at www.reading.org and search the journal, *Reading Online.* Which of the routines that Ash recommends would you include in a program for all readers in the middle grades?

References

Allen, R. (2000, Summer). Before it's too late: Giving reading a last chance. *Curriculum Update.* Alexandria, VA: Association for Supervision and Curriculum Development.

Alvermann, D. E., & Phelps, S. F. (2005). *Content reading and literacy: Succeeding in today's diverse classrooms* (4th ed.). Boston: Allyn and Bacon.

Ash, G. E. (2002). Teaching readers who struggle: A pragmatic middle school framework. *Reading Online,* 5(7).

Atwell, N. (1987). *In the middle: Writing, reading, and learning with adolescents.* Portsmouth, NH: Heinemann.

Baskin, B. (1998). Call me Ishmael: A look at gifted middle school readers. In K. Beers, K. Samuels, & B. G. Samuels (Eds.), *Into focus: Understanding and creating middle school readers* (pp. 65–80). Norwood, MA: Christopher-Gordon.

Cunningham, P. M., & Allington, R. L. (1999). *Classrooms that work: They can all read and write* (2nd ed.). New York: Addison Wesley, Longman.

Daniels, H. (1994). *Literature circles: Voice and choice in the student-centered classroom.* York, ME: Stenhouse.

Dixon-Krauss, L. (1996). *Vygotsky in the classroom. Mediated literacy: Instruction and assessment.* White Plains, NY: Longman.

Fountas, I. C., & Pinnell, G.S. (1999). *Guided reading: Good first teaching for all children.* Portsmouth, NH: Heinemann.

Gullingsrud, M. (1998). I am the immigrant in my classroom. *Voices from the Middle,6*(1), 30–37.

Harris T. L., & Hodges, R. E. (1995). *The literacy dictionary: The vocabulary of reading and writing.* Newark, DE: International Reading Association.

Hill, M. (1998). Reaching struggling readers. In K. Beers, K. Samuels, & B. G. Samuels (Eds.), *Into focus: Understanding and creating middle school readers* (pp. 80–104). Norwood, MA: Christopher-Gordon.

Irvin, J., & Strauss, S. (2000). In K. D. Wood & T. S. Dickinson (Eds.), *Promoting literacy in grades 4–9: A handbook for teachers and administrators* (pp. 115–127). Boston: Allyn and Bacon.

Ivey, G., & Broaddus, K. (2001). "Just plain reading": A survey of what makes students want to read in middle school classrooms. *Reading Research Quarterly, 36*(4), 350–377.

Jago, C, (2000). *With rigor for all: Teaching classics to contemporary students.* Portland, ME: Calendar Islands.

Langer, J. A. (2002). *Effective literacy instruction: Building successful reading and writing programs.* Urbana, IL: National Council for the Teachers of English.

Mooney, M. (1990). *Reading to, with, and by children.* Katonah, NY: Richard C. Owen.

Moore, D. W., Bean, T. W., Birdyshaw, D., & Rycik, J. A. (1999). *Adolescent literacy: A position statement for the commission on adolescent literacy of the International Reading Association.* Newark, DE: International Reading Association.

Rasinsky, T., & Padak, N. (2000). *Effective reading strategies: Teaching children who find reading difficult* (2nd ed.). Upper Saddle River, NJ: Merrill.

Vygotsky, L. S. (1978). *Mind in society: The development of higher mental psychological powers.* Cambridge, MA: Harvard University Press.

Wells, M. C. (1996). *Literacies lost: When students move from a progressive middle school to a traditional high school.* New York: Teachers College Press.

7

Read-Alouds and Oral Reading Routines

Activating Prior Knowledge and Generating Questions

As the bell rings signaling the beginning of language arts class, the teacher picks up the book *Night Journeys* (Avi, 1979) for the day's read-aloud. The students have their notebooks open and the day's date written on the top of a fresh page. The teacher, Mr. Brodsky, begins by asking, "Who can summarize what happened in the chapter we read yesterday for Mark's benefit since he was absent?"

One student gives a brief recap, and the teacher calls on a few others to add other details. Then he says, "In the chapter we're reading today, it is important that you have a clear picture of the setting—where the action is happening—a particular part of the Delaware River. Otherwise you may get confused about what the characters are doing and why. Try to form a picture in your head as I read, and I'll stop a few times for you to draw a picture or diagram in your notebook." Then he begins to read.

> At that point the Delaware River is fairly wide, wider than anywhere else for some miles north or south. There in the river lies Morgan's Rock, set at unequal distances from the river's banks: fifty yards from the Pennsylvania side and perhaps three hundred or so from Jersey.
>
> A narrow island, Morgan's Rock is much in the shape of a teardrop, its pointed end to the south. At the northern end a mass of rock thrusts against the river's flow like the prow of a great ship, making the river split into two different paths. (p. 17)

The teacher pauses and says, "You may not have caught all of that, but draw a picture in your notebook of what you do know. Draw it fairly large so you have room to add some details as you learn more. Mark your diagram to show north, south, east, and west. On a map, usually north is at the top. As you'll see in the next section, the river runs from north to south." After a few minutes, he goes on reading.

On the eastern—Jersey—side of the island the water runs wide and fairly shallow, making it wild and fierce. On the western—Pennsylvania—side it's the reverse. There the narrow channel runs to a greater depth but is quiet as a church. But on that side a line of broken rock juts halfway into the river: the dangerous Finger Falls. (p. 17–18)

The teacher pauses and says, "Your drawing will be clearer if you put labels on it such as shallow and deep. Now listen for some details about the island in the river."

The land directly behind the rock itself is an island clear of water. The northern section, some sixty yards or more, is solid and fertile, being heavily overgrown with trees, bushes, and whatever else can grow there. Indeed, the foliage is so thick that it's hard to enter. Moreover, it holds masses of logs and branches, hurled up on the island by the rolling waters around the rock.

The island's southern end is but an ever narrowing strip of sand and silt, which lengthens and shortens depending on the river's height. . . . At one place near the middle the sand and trees commingle. Mostly open and easy to cross, it was there we meant to take our watch. (p. 18)

The teacher forms the class into small groups. The teacher then gives each group a large sheet of poster paper and a set of colored markers. He gives each student a copy of the passage he has just read. Group members use the passage and the drawings in their notebooks to create one complete and correct drawing of the setting (see Figure 7.1). These maps are hung on the walls of the classroom, and a brief discussion follows about any differences among them. As the remaining chapters of the story are read aloud over the next few weeks, the teacher often directs students' attention to these drawings to help them visualize the action.

Before reading the rest of this chapter, reflect for a moment on these questions:
1. What are the advantages of reading this passage aloud before giving it to students to read?
2. What did students learn in this lesson that they could apply to future independent reading?
3. What are some reasons why the teacher might have decided to read this entire book aloud to his students? Do you agree with his decision?
4. How does this teaching strategy help English language learners? What can the teacher do to make the lesson more comprehensible for students who are learning English?

Each of the classroom literacy routines introduced in the previous chapter plays a distinctive role in helping young adolescents move toward proficient reading. Routines that involve reading aloud by teachers and students are crucial for building fluency; for motivating readers; and as occasions for discussions about the content, forms, and purposes of texts. In this chapter, we will examine some of the specific purposes of teacher read-alouds in the middle grades and describe some of the many ways they can act as bridges to guided and independent reading. Then we will briefly discuss appropriate ways to use and assess oral reading by middle grade students.

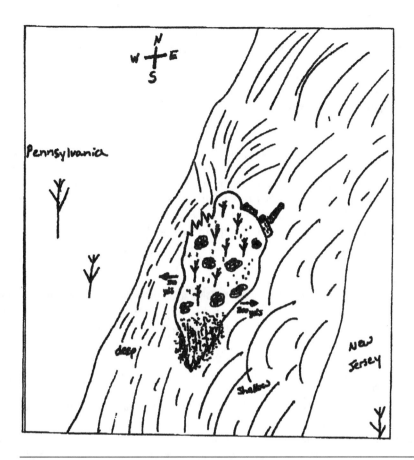

FIGURE 7.1 *Katie's Setting Drawing from* **Night Journeys** *Read-Aloud*

Reasons for Read-Alouds in the Middle Grades

The old adage says, "Give someone a fish and they eat for a day; teach them to fish and they eat for a lifetime." Nevertheless, we would not expect anyone to study angling without first tasting trout. Some middle grades teachers might be concerned that read alouds will make their students passive or dependent, but reading aloud to students actually whets their appetite for reading on their own. Reading aloud provides students with the unique opportunities for students to learn to feed themselves. Lesene (1998) reports that

> Twenty years ago, when I first started teaching middle school students, I read aloud as a way to entertain students and keep them quiet! I also read aloud to them to show them that I liked to read and that I knew good books for them to read. Now I read aloud to middle school students because I have discovered what primary grades teachers seem to have always known: being read to is an important part of reading development. (p. 246)

Many teachers who try reading aloud to young adolescents become devoted to the practice. Among the wide range of benefits that are cited, the following are mentioned most often.

Providing Opportunities to Experience "Unconscious Delight"

As Nilsen and Donnelson (2001) point out, children do not become enthusiastic and perceptive adult readers without first experiencing the "unconscious delight" of being lost in a story. Many children have this experience before they ever come to school, but others reach the middle grades without first-hand confirmation that reading proficiency is worth achieving. Strategy instruction is of little use unless students see literacy as both valuable and attainable. Reading aloud to students in the middle grades increases the likelihood that this will happen. In the best-selling book, *The Read Aloud Handbook* (Trelease, 2001), the author asks,

> Can we really believe that a child is going to develop a sense of "self" doing reading skills for forty minutes a day, five days a week, thirty weeks a year? Does an uninterrupted diet of skill and drill make a child want to escape into the world of books or away from it? (p. 10)

Creating a Classroom Community

Atwell (2000) contends that read-alouds "provide a communal reading experience in which we enter and love a book together" (p. 144). The read-aloud experience creates a sort of "level playing field" in which all students can participate regardless of their ability to decode the words of the text. English language learners benefit from a read-aloud in that it motivates and involves them in the reading process. During the discussions that often accompany read-alouds, struggling readers may find proof that they have the credentials to be members of a literate community. Just as importantly, their classmates have the opportunity to see them as capable participants in literacy events.

Listening to a common text can provide an occasion for young adolescents to explore their commonalities and differences. Richardson (2000), a strong advocate for reading aloud to students throughout adolescence, has given many examples of ways in which read-alouds provide a natural context for discussing issues of diversity and the developmental tasks of adolescence. For example, she points out that

> Simply telling students that cultures are diverse, and providing textbook reading or lecture examples, will not often achieve the impact that sharing personal events through literature can engender. A read-aloud is an effective, efficient means of introducing awareness that can lead to insightful discussion. (p·162)

During discussions about multicultural literature, English language learners and students from minority cultures can share their background experiences, affirm their identity and culture, and link new concepts to their daily lives.

Providing Opportunities to Expand Vocabulary and Concepts

Harvey (1998) shows how fifth-grade teacher Carol Quinby focused on vocabulary while reading aloud to a bilingual class that was studying explorers. She read aloud from the book *Encounter* (Yolen, 1992), which tells the story of Columbus's arrival in San Salvador from the point of view of the native Taino tribe. In one lesson, Quinby used an overhead transparency of a page from the author's note at the end of the book. Students sat on the floor around the projector with clipboards and copies of the author's note.

Quinby began by telling the class that the author's note explained the research that Jane Yolen did about Columbus and the Taino before writing the story. Then, prior to reading the first paragraph from the transparency, she instructed the students to raise a hand whenever she came to a word or concept they did not understand. Harvey (1998) describes the discussion:

> Fernando raised his hand. "Landfall," he said when Carol called on him. "I thought it meant that the land fell off, but that doesn't make any sense."
> "Does anyone know what landfall means?" Carol inquired. Bianca raised her hand and suggested that it might mean the place where sailors first saw land. "Why do you think that?" Carol asked. Bianca explained that it made sense when she read the sentence over. Carol asked if others agreed; they did and marked the meaning of landfall on their copy. Carol told the class that rereading the text as Bianca had done is an important strategy for clarifying meaning before heading to the dictionary. (p. 81)

After Quinby had continued the shared reading and group discussion of vocabulary for several more paragraphs, students finished the passage with a partner. They practiced figuring out the unknown words from context, only occasionally using a dictionary.

Harvey's (1998) emphasis is on the importance of nonfiction read-alouds, but all kinds of material can provide information that students can use in further reading and learning. Atwell (2000) describes how read-alouds can act as scaffolds for further reading by opening students' eyes to new possibilities. "The teacher's voice becomes a bridge for kids taking them into territories they might never have explored because they don't yet have schemas for a genre, subject, author, or period" (p. 144).

As students listen to a variety of materials, they acquire knowledge about both the world and the world of texts. A read-aloud at the beginning of a unit can establish a common starting point for class discussions and for future activities and projects (Muth & Glynn, 2000). It can also become a "touchstone" for comparisons and contrasts with other texts. The teacher might refer back to *Night Journeys* (Avi, 1979), for example, when introducing another book set in the colonial period, when leading a discussion about characters facing moral dilemmas, or in guiding students to identify the characteristics and challenges of the historical fiction genre.

Providing Opportunities for Developing Comprehension Processes

The lesson described by Harvey (1998) illustrates not only how a read-aloud can expand students' vocabularies, but also how it can become a scaffold for learning to use important reading strategies. Without the read-aloud, Yolen's text may have been too difficult for the students, and they probably could not have applied the strategies of rereading and using context as immediately or effectively.

Reading aloud provides a natural context for modeling and applying elements of strategic reading such as self-questioning, prediction, and rereading. During a read-aloud, a teacher can pause to ask questions such as "What do you think might happen next? What do you already know about the main character? What do you think the author is trying to get at here? Does this remind you of anything else you've read? Does it remind you of anything that's happened to you?" (Atwell, 2000).

Because read-alouds eliminate much of the risk of being wrong, students may be more willing to participate in discussions that match their perceptions and opinions against those of their classmates. As Cunningham and Allington (1999) observe,

> The best introduction to (and practice for) book conversations seems to occur when good books are read aloud in classrooms daily and teachers and students take time to mull over their reactions. Read-aloud time, then, is not finished with the last page of the day's chapter. That is when the second important phase of read-aloud begins: the talk-about. Whole-group discussion, besides providing an open forum for students, permits teachers to model the stance of the questioning, responsive learner. (p. 302)

Kinds of Read-Alouds

Teachers can employ many variations in read-aloud routines. Allen (2000) makes a distinction between a "read-aloud," in which the teacher reads short pieces and students listen, and "shared reading," in which students read the text silently as it is read aloud by a fluent reader. Based on her research with middle and high school students, Allen attributed significant gains in reading achievement to following along with the text during shared reading.

Some other variations in read-alouds include inviting the principal, a parent, or a community member to prepare and perform a "guest reading," or having one or more students prepare passages that they read in alternation with the teacher. In a classroom with a variety of cultures, there is an opportunity to invite literate adults from the represented cultures to read to the class.

As the opening vignette in this chapter illustrated, the teacher might choose to first read a passage aloud to provide an overall understanding and to then present students with photocopied passages so that they can engage in "close reading" activities with a limited portion of the text. Another option is to obtain or create books on tape. An unabridged recording (such as those available from Recorded Books Incorporated) allows a student to follow along with the text and to rewind and replay the tape at will. Teachers can also produce their own tapes or, better yet, involve students who are excellent readers in producing them.

Lesene (1998) identifies three approaches to reading aloud in the classroom. In "Read and Tease," the teacher reads a few sentences or a paragraph from a particularly appealing passage of a book in order to create interest for the students to read the book themselves.

This approach also allows teachers to learn about the reading interests of their students by noting their reactions to particular books, and especially by noting which ones they choose to read.

A read-aloud can also be used to introduce a new genre or topic. Hearing examples of a particular genre such as poetry or short stories, for example, allows students to arrive at some of the essential characteristics of that genre inductively before they take on the total responsibility for reading. A third approach is to read an entire book aloud one chapter at a time over the course of several days or weeks. Lesene (1998) notes that aliterate (students who can read, but choose not to read) or reluctant readers may need this experience to enjoy a book that they would not be likely to read on their own, but she also contends that more willing and capable readers also benefit from this approach.

Allen (2000) suggests using the shared reading approach when reading entire books. She believes that following along with the teacher's voice helps students to stay focused. Regardless of whether students have the text in front of them, however, the teacher will want to get the most out of the time invested in a whole-book read-aloud. The following section describes some instructional activities that are particularly appropriate when reading entire texts aloud.

Activities for Whole-Book Read-Alouds

Rycik (1986) studied eighth graders' use of prediction strategies during an extended Directed Listening–Thinking Activity (Stauffer, 1980) using Willo Davis Roberts' novel *Don't Hurt Laurie* (1977). After each day's reading, class discussions focused on what might happen in the story either immediately or in the end. Students then decided which events they deemed most probable and recorded them in "Prediction Logs." They also crossed off any previous predictions that no longer seemed to be supported by the text. A sample Prediction Log is shown in Figure 7.2.

Roberts's novel was particularly well suited to the DL–TA framework. It tells the story of Laurie, who is the victim of her mother's physical abuse. The action in the story centers on whether anyone will find out about Laurie's problem and put a stop to it. The au-

FIGURE 7.2 *Prediction Log*

Date	Stopping Point	Prediction	Reason

FIGURE 7.3   *Susan's Expectations Essay*

I thought Miss Mullen [one of Laurie's teachers] was gonna help Laurie. I was surprised when she was just taken out of the story. I guess it was better for her to be taken out because the story would have ended too soon. I also thought that Laurie's father was going to suddenly show up. I don't know why the author kept mentioning him in the story. It just made me think that he was going to come back.

I was thinking that Tim [Laurie's stepbrother] was going to tell his father without asking her first. If he did, I don't think that he would believe Tim. I'm glad that Laurie finally told someone herself even though she was forced into telling, because then she was able to get help and not have to be afraid of her mother any more.

---

thor introduces one character after another as candidates for this role, and it was natural for listeners to consider the likelihood of each one. Each time, however, some event deters Laurie from disclosing her situation. After students had heard the end of the story, they were asked to review their prediction logs and to write about three instances in which the story differed from their expectations. Susan's essay is shown in Figure 7.3.

During the read-aloud activities, students were equally able to participate in low-risk activities where no one had all the answers. Predicting seemed to make students more aware of the author's role as a choice maker. They could see how authors sometimes manipulate a reader's expectations in order to create conflict or suspense. Many students reported that combining listening with prediction helped them to think, understand, or remember more. Reexamining their predictions allowed them to become metacognitively aware of their own ongoing interpretations. Susan, for instance, concluded that, "I think it [predicting] did help because I could look back and see what I was thinking and if it turned out the way I predicted."

Prediction Logs take up a minimal amount of class time because the teacher does not have to explain the directions every day and the amount of actual writing is minimal. The emphasis is on participating in a discussion of possibilities and then choosing those that seem most plausible. A similar activity is a "Connections Log." The procedure is essentially the same, but the focus is on making connections between the text that is being read and the student's life or between the text and other stories, movies, or television shows.

Because students cannot always look back at the read-aloud text, summarizing can become a highly functional activity. The teacher might begin each session by asking students to recall the important events of the previous day's reading as Mr. Brodsky did in the opening vignette. As they attempt to refresh everyone's memory or bring an absent classmate up to date, students must engage in a process of distinguishing vital information from irrelevant detail. By writing down the summaries in bulleted form, English language learners can access the key ideas.

Occasionally, students can be asked to write a "So Far Summary." This assignment can be done as a five- or six-minute journal entry. It involves starting from the beginning and telling the story up to the latest stopping point. Writing summaries provides practice in the language of summarizing such as the use of sequence words (e.g., later, after a few weeks, after the king was crowned). The unique feature of So Far Summaries is that students can eventually look back over several of them to see how information that they in-

cluded in an early version was dropped from a later one. This helps them to see how dele-
tion of unnecessary information is an essential part of summarizing and to reflect on the criteria they use in deciding what is and is not essential.

Guidelines for Effective Read-Alouds

Given the pressures they face for their students to achieve and to demonstrate reading proficiency, teachers generally want to make the most of the time they spend in read-alouds.
To do so, they must walk a fine line between providing stress-free, inclusive experiences
and helping students to become independent with increasingly difficult and complex texts
(Knickerbocker & Rycik, 2002). The following guidelines are designed to ensure that read-
alouds will support both students' skill and will to read.

Read-Alouds Must Be Carefully Chosen and Planned

Several resources for locating potential read-alouds are provided at the end of this chapter,
but the key criterion for choosing a selection to read aloud is that the teacher is enthusiastic enough about the book to want to share it with students. Practical issues to be considered include whether it has illustrations, the overall length of the piece, and whether it has
reasonably short chapters or other convenient stopping points.

The match between text and students is crucial. This involves much more than considering the recommended reading level for a book. Teachers need to draw on their knowledge of their students in order to choose material that is interesting and thought-provoking
but also accessible. Sometimes this is a trial and error process.

Planning for reading aloud involves making choices about factors such as how long
a passage should be read in one sitting and where to pause for discussion. The most important choices, however, involve the overall focus for the read-aloud. Any of the purposes
listed above may be appropriate, but including all of them equally may not be possible. Students' enjoyment of the text may be lost if the read-aloud is weighted down with too many
other purposes.

Read-Alouds Must Present a Model of Fluency and Comprehension

In read-alouds, the teacher takes center stage to "show how it's done." The model that is
provided needs to be first rate. Atwell (2000) describes her own notion of what such an effective read aloud performance is like.

> When reading aloud, I go for it, changing my inflection for the different characters and
> moods of a text. I change my face too—smile, frown, show anger or surprise or the effects
> of suspense or enlightenment—and I modulate the volume, louder or softer, to match the
> mood. I read slower than I speak, and I pause before and after parts I want to stress, to let
> things sink in. I ask questions. . . . I show the illustrations. (p. 145)

The sort of performance Atwell (2000) describes does not just happen. The teachers' oral interpretations, the questions they ask, and the issues they raise grow out of their own careful reading of the text. There is no substitute for actually reading the text aloud before reading it to students. First, rehearsal greatly reduces the possibility of making a miscue on a word or misreading the sentence phrasing. Second, it allows the teacher to gauge how long it will take to read a given passage so that the stopping point comes at a natural break. Finally, rehearsing allows the teacher to determine the pace, volume, and expression that will best convey the meaning of the text. There is certainly room for sharing a spontaneous insight while delivering a read-aloud, but the best oral readers often "rehearse" those too!

Read-Alouds Should Be Intentionally Connected to Future Reading

Read-alouds can be an important bridge to independent and strategic reading, but teachers must pay careful attention to helping their students learn to apply independently the patterns of thinking and responding they develop during read alouds. One way to do so is to introduce activities such as Prediction Logs or So Far Summaries in the highly collaborative context of read-alouds and then continue them during guided and independent reading.

Another way to foster independence is to make frequent explicit statements about when, why, and how students might choose to apply a particular strategy. The teacher in the opening vignette, for instance, might advise, "When you come to a highly detailed description in your reading, you may have trouble creating a picture in your head. If the description seems important to your understanding, you could take a minute to make a sketch like the one we made to show the area around the river."

Read-Alouds and English Language Learners

Models of fluent reading from teachers and peers can be crucial for English language learners because they may have no other opportunities to hear English except at school. English language learners may not read in their primary language. Therefore, it is important to teach them how to interact with the text and to make sense of language in context. They need multiple opportunities to apply their knowledge.

English language learners need the experience of read-alouds and the instructional activities that go with them as support for moving from social interaction skills to academic language skills. With key concepts and vocabulary highlighted, English language learners can access the text. For example, teachers may want make a "word wall" with key vocabulary from the text.

Teachers must carefully consider the benefits for all students when they choose books for read-alouds. Historical novels such as *Night Journeys* (Avi, 1979) help native English language speakers to expand their historical knowledge and acquire uncommon vocabulary. Such books may, however, be harder for English language learners to understand than books with a contemporary setting and vocabulary. In classes with a variety of language groups, teachers will want to see if they can choose books that allow them to make cultural connections.

Teachers can also read aloud from books that help students consider issues related to moving to a new country and to learning a new language. *In the Year of the Boar and Jackie Robinson* by Bette Bao Lord (1986), for instance, tells the story of a 10-year-old Chinese girl who takes on the name Shirley Temple Wong when her parents move to the United States in 1948. After many struggles to adjust, Shirley learns English and becomes a fan of the Brooklyn Dodgers, but she also comes to an understanding about how she can maintain her identity and family heritage.

Students Reading Aloud

Teacher read-alouds put the language of books in students' ears and in their hearts. Student read-alouds can put that language in their mouths and in their memories. For this to happen, however, oral reading activities must be purposeful, carefully designed, and closely monitored. Many adults still carry the scars from experiences that required them to read "cold" from a text they had never seen before in front of an audience of impatient and critical peers.

Although proficient oral readers may enjoy the experience, "Round Robin" oral reading teaches little; it only exposes what a student already knows (or does not know) how to do. Instead of models of effective oral interpretation, students may find their ears filled with halting, emotionless, and laborious word calling. Teachers in the middle grades can choose from a variety of more effective oral reading activities.

For example, Wood and Nichols (2000) suggest paired reading as an alternative to calling on students to read individually. They describe an activity in which struggling readers in the middle grades were asked to "whisper read" the first two paragraphs of a selection with their partners and afterwards discuss what they recall from their reading. Carol Quinby used a similar technique in connection with the nonfiction read-aloud described earlier in this chapter. Wood and Nichols note that partners can assist each other with unknown words or concepts, relate what they have read to past experiences, and raise questions to be discussed with the class.

A Fluency Lesson Framework

The following Fluency Lesson Framework is designed to provide an alternative to Round Robin reading that is appropriate for developing reading fluency in the middle grades. It is adapted from similar frameworks intended for younger readers such as the Fluency Development Lesson (Rasinski, Padak, Linek, & Sturtevant, 1994) and the Oral Recitation Lesson (Hoffman & Crone, 1985). Specific elements of the framework may certainly be modified, but most of the principles of effective oral reading activities listed above are embodied in these five steps:

1. Students listen to a text read by the teacher or on tape. If possible, they should follow along with the text while listening. (This step may be repeated).

2. Students and teacher discuss the overall meaning of the text, any words that may be unfamiliar, and the appropriate expression to use in various parts.
3. The class reviews criteria for fluent reading: expression, pacing, and phrasing.
4. Students rehearse all or part of the text by doing repeated readings until they are sure they can read the piece fluently. They may read quietly to themselves, to a partner, or into a tape recorder.
5. Students do some sort of "finished" oral performance. One option for performing may include reading aloud in groups or choral reading. Choral reading can either be done with the group reading in unison or by assigning parts for individuals or small groups to read. The effect may be somewhat like a choir with some parts being done by a section of the class, some done in unison, and some done solo. In a choral reading of the poem "The Charge of the Light Brigade," for instance, the left side of the room might read "Cannons to the left of them," the right side might read "Cannons to the right of them," and the whole group would read, "Into the valley of death rode the six thousand."

Choral Reading   Choral reading allows all students to participate. This includes English language learners and students with low or high reading ability. Rasinski and Padak (2000) note, "In choral reading activities, less able readers benefit from the support they receive from the group, the camaraderie and joy of participating in a group activity with peers who have a variety of abilities, and the valuable practice of reading one text in a variety of ways" (p. 115).

Reader's Theater   Reader's theater is another way of involving students in a performance of oral reading. In reader's theater, students do not use costumes, scenery, or props. They simply read orally from a script using their voices in such a way that they convey the meaning of the text. Reader's theater scripts can be purchased, but the technique is particularly effective when students create their own scripts by adapting part or all of a piece they have been reading or hearing (Rasinski & Padak, 2000).

Assessing Oral Reading

Zutell and Rasinski (1991) created a rating scale for oral reading that identifies three elements of fluency: phrasing, smoothness, and pace. Teachers can use this multidimensional scale to identify students who need to work extensively on improving fluency. They can also use it later on to gauge a student's progress. As they engage in repeated readings to prepare for a performance, middle grades students need to have a clear conception of how a successful performance should sound. That understanding begins with the model provided by the teacher's reading aloud. It is further developed by discussions about what makes the teacher's reading successful or what qualities make reading unpleasant to hear. Finally, students can use a rating scale such as the Multidimensional Fluency Scale in Figure 7.4 to judge their own performance and that of the partners and groups with whom they read.

FIGURE 7.4 *Multidimensional Fluency Scale*

Use the following scales to rate reader fluency on the three dimensions of phrasing, smoothness, and pace:

A. Phrasing

1. Monotonic with little sense of phrase boundaries, frequent word-by-word reading.
2. Frequent two- and three-word phrases giving the impression of choppy reading; improper stress and intonation that fails to mark the ends of sentences and clauses.
3. Mixture of run-ons, mid-sentence pauses for breath, and possibly some choppiness; reasonable stress and intonation.
4. Generally well-phrased, mostly in clause and sentence units; with adequate attention to expression

B. Smoothness

1. Frequent extended pauses, hesitations, false starts, sound-outs, repetitions, and/or multiple attempts.
2. Several "rough spots" in text where extended pauses, hesitations, etc., are more frequent and disruptive.
3. Occasional breaks in smoothness caused by difficulties with specific words and/or structures.
4. Generally smooth reading with some breaks but word and structure difficulties are resolved quickly, usually through self-correction.

C. Pace (during sections of minimal disruption)

1. Slow and laborious
2. Moderately slow
3. Uneven mixture of fast and slow reading
4. Consistently conversational

From: Zutell, J. B. & Rasinski, T. V (1991). Training teachers to attend to their student's oral reading fluency. *Theory into Practice, 30*(3), 211–217.

Oral Reading for English Language Learners

According to Hadaway, Vardell, and Young (2001), oral reading activities can play a crucial role in scaffolding the oral language development of English language learners. They point out that students can pick up a great deal of vocabulary and syntax by reading along with teacher read alouds as long as they understand the general content of the text. They add that choral reading, reader's theater, and other rehearsed oral reading allows English language learners to work with the teacher or a small group on correct pronunciation, phrasing, and intonation. The Fluency Lesson Framework provides an appropriate scaffold for English language learners to move from listening to teacher read-alouds to fluent oral reading of poems or short passages from other books.

Poetry is an especially appropriate genre for English language learners and other students who are struggling with reading, according to Hadaway, Vardell, and Young (2001), because poems are generally short and are segmented into lines, which make them seem less intimidating. They may also have features such as repetition and rhyme that make them easier to understand. Hadaway, Vardell, and Young also point out that there are many collections of poetry that are in both English and Spanish, and they suggest that teachers set up listening centers where students can read along with recorded versions of poems and record their own readings.

Guidelines for Oral Reading Activities

Just as teachers in the middle grades may be reluctant to read aloud to their students, they may avoid having students read orally because they see silent reading as more "grown up" and challenging. Oral reading can, however, play an important part in the development of young adolescent readers. It allows students to engage fully with the vocabulary and syntax of a text as they work to produce accurate reading with proper phrasing. It promotes comprehension as students attempt to convey the appropriate nuances and emotions. It can also become an aesthetic experience as students create drama with their voices. These positive outcomes are much more likely, however, when oral reading activities follow these guidelines:

- Effective oral reading begins with an understanding of the meaning and purpose of the text.
- Students should be given time to engage in repeated readings of the text to ensure that they can read with fluency.
- Reading in unison with others or working with a supportive partner provides the security that is needed by students who struggle with reading, including English language learners.
- Students should always be aware of a functional purpose for their oral reading (e.g., to develop fluency, as a performance for others, or to share information).
- Students should be guided to identify criteria for effective oral interpretation and to apply those criteria to their own oral reading and that of others.

Summary

Read-alouds and oral reading routines are a motivating way to build fluency in reading. They also provide teachers with the opportunity to discuss content, purpose, and the structure of different texts. Read-alouds provide students with shared reading experiences, while expanding their vocabulary and conceptual knowledge. Comprehension is enhanced when students engage in predicting what will happen next in a story or passage. Students reading aloud can provide a vehicle for building fluency and meaningfully engaging with text. Repeated readings eliminate embarrassment and provide an effective alternative to "Round Robin" reading. Read-alouds and repeated readings are beneficial for English language learners as a strategy that bridges conceptual and academic learning.

Assessing and Extending Prior Knowledge _____

Review your responses to the questions accompanying the scenario at the beginning of this chapter. Have your answers changed? Consider the following:

1. What else might you ask students to do with the passage from *Night Journeys?*

2. Mr. Brodsky chose to read the entire book to his students over a period of weeks. How else might he have used read-alouds in connection with this book?

3. Which of the "Reasons for Read-Alouds" listed in this chapter do you think Mr. Brodsky is trying to accomplish? Which would *you* select as most important?

Cases to Consider _____

Franklin is a sixth-grade student who rarely reads for pleasure. When the class reads silently, Franklin is usually the last one finished. He resists reading orally, even when no one but the teacher can hear. When he does read orally, his reading is slow and laborious. He tends to read word-by-word with little expression. Consider the following:

1. What might explain Franklin's lack of reading fluency? Why is it important?

2. What role might teacher read-alouds play in improving Franklin's fluency?

3. What other oral and silent activities might help him?

Rosa is a seventh grader who moved from Mexico to the United States when she was in fourth grade. She has mastered social English and yet still struggles with academic English. She is able to read many of the words phonetically, yet she has no idea of their meaning. When she reads orally, students laugh at the way she pronounces words. Consider the following:

1. What prereading strategies will help Rosa to understand the text?

2. What role might teacher read-alouds play in improving Rosa's pronunciation and comprehension?

3. What other oral and silent activities might help her?

Key Terms to Know and Use _____

choral reading	readers' theater	Fluency Lesson Framework
Fluency Development Lesson	shared reading	multidimensional fluency
	Prediction Log	repeated readings scale

Possible Sentences

Use two or three terms in the columns above and write a sentence stating one idea you now know about read-alouds and oral reading routines. Write four or five such sentences using different words until you have a nice summary paragraph.

Beyond the Book

- The book *Read It Aloud! Using Literature in the Secondary Content Classroom* (Richardson, 2000) provides a comprehensive view of the kinds of texts that can be used for read-alouds and the ways in which read-alouds can be linked to a variety of learning objectives. The table of contents for the book and a sample chapter can be viewed at the Online Bookstore of the International Reading Association at www.reading.org.
- The ERIC Digest, "Children's Literature for Adult ESL Literacy" by Betty Smallwood, includes a list of recommended read-aloud books and guidelines for book selection.
- Jim Trelease's website (www.trelease-on-reading.com) provides excerpts from *The Read-Aloud Handbook* (Trelease, 2001). Those excerpts include an excellent list of "Read-aloud Do's and Don'ts." You will also find the "Treasury of Great Read-Alouds" that includes novels for young adolescents.
- You may want to try using the Multidimensional Fluency Scale to rate the oral reading of one or more middle grade readers. This can be done one-to-one or as a student reads orally in a whole-class setting. The student might also rehearse a passage and tape record a final version. In all these cases, you should briefly discuss fluency and explain that you are *not* assessing accuracy so that students will not be unduly concerned about any miscues they make. Note whether the student has had a chance to rehearse, since you would expect greater fluency if the reader has prepared.

References

Allen, J. (2000). *Yellow brick roads: Shared and guided paths to independent reading* 4–12. Portland, ME: Stenhouse.

Atwell, N. (2000). *In the middle: New understandings about writing, reading, and learning* (2nd ed.). Portsmouth, NH: Boynton Cook.

Avi. (1979). *Night journeys.* New York: Morrow Junior Books.

Cunningham, P., & Allington, R. (1999). *Classrooms that work: They can all read and write* (2nd ed). New York: Longman.

Hadaway, N. L., Vardell, S. M., & Young, T. A. (2001). Scaffolding oral language development through poetry for students learning English. *The Reading Teacher, 54*(8), 796–805.

Harvey, S. (1998). *Nonfiction matters: Reading, writing and research in grades 3–8.* Portland, ME: Stenhouse.

Hoffman, J. V., & Crone, S. (1985). The oral recitation lesson: A research-derived strategy for reading basal texts. In J. A. Niles & R. A. Lalik (Eds.), *Issues in literacy: A research perspective. Thirty-fourth yearbook of the National Reading Conference* (pp. 76–83). Rochester, NY: National Reading Conference.

Knickerbocker, J., & Rycik, J. (2002). Growing into literature: Adolescents' literary interpretation and appreciation. *Journal of Adolescent and Adult Literacy, 46*(3), 196–208.

Lesene, T. (1998). Reading aloud to build success in reading. In K. Beers, K., & B. G. Samuels (Eds.). *Into focus: Understanding and creating middle school readers* (pp. 65–80). Norwood, MA: Christopher-Gordon.

Lord, B. B. (1986). *In the year of the boar and Jackie Robinson.* New York: HarperTrophy.

Muth, K. D., & Glynn, S. M. (2000). The role of the literacy specialist. In K. D. Wood & T. S. Dickinson (Eds.), Promoting literacy in grades 4–9: *A handbook for teachers and administrators* (pp. 41–52). Boston: Allyn and Bacon.

Nilsen, A. P., & Donelson, K. I. (2001). *Literature for today's young adults* (6th ed.). Boston: Pearson/Allyn and Bacon.

Rasinski, T. V., & Padak, N. D. (2000). *Effective reading strategies: Teaching children who find reading difficult* (2nd ed.). Upper Saddle River, NJ: Merrill.

Rasinski, T. V., Padak, N. D., Linek, W., & Sturtevant E. (1994). Effects of fluency development on urban second-grade readers. *Journal of Educational Research, 87*(3), 158–165.

Richardson, J. S. (2000). *Read it aloud! Using literature in the secondary content classroom.* Newark, DE: International Reading Association.

Roberts, W. D. (1977). *Don't hurt Laurie.* New York: Atheneum.

Rycik, J. A. (1986). *Beyond story grammar: Students' predictions as a narrative map.* Unpublished manuscript.

Stauffer, R. (1980). *The language experience approach to the teaching of reading* (2nd ed.). New York: Harper and Row.

Trelease, J. (2001). *The read-aloud handbook* (5th ed.). New York: Penguin Books.

Wood, K. D., & Nichols, W. D. (2000). Helping struggling learners read and write. In K. D. Wood & T. S. Dickinson (Eds.), *Promoting literacy in grades 4–9: A handbook for teachers and administrators* (pp. 233–249). Boston: Allyn and Bacon.

Yolen, J. (1992). *Encounter.* San Diego, CA: Harcourt Brace Jovanovich.

Zutell, J. B., & Rasinski, T. V. (1991). Training teachers to attend to their students' oral reading fluency. *Theory into Practice, 30*(3), 211–217.

8

Guided Reading: Planning Students' Engagements with Texts

Activating Prior Knowledge and Making Connections

Ms. Taylor's seventh-grade reading textbook included the speech President Reagan gave after the space shuttle Challenger exploded in 1986 (EMC Corporation, 2001). Ms. Taylor liked the idea of studying a speech, but thought that her students would relate better to the more recent loss of the shuttle Columbia, so she looked on the Internet to find the speech President Bush gave on the day of that tragedy (see Box 8.1).

Ms. Taylor decided to take advantage of the prior knowledge of some students about space shuttles and the Columbia by engaging in a prereading version of semantic mapping (Readence, Bean, & Baldwin, 2000). She began by writing "Columbia Tragedy" on an overhead transparency and asked students to brainstorm words related to the subject. She recorded their responses to create this list:

astronauts	heat tiles	brave	accident	mistakes
exploring	fault	disaster	bright light	scientists
space	flames	scared	debris	insulation
blame	death	terrorism	dangerous	wings
Challenger	rocket	sadness	warning	explosion

As students contributed these words, Ms. Taylor made sure that all of the students, including the English language learners, understood what each word meant and how it was pronounced. She then asked for a brief explanation, such as, "Why do you think of terrorism when you think of the Columbia?" She then asked students which words seemed to belong together and arranged them in a web on a big sheet of chart paper. Finally, she asked them to label each of the groups. Figure 8.1 shows the map the class created.

Remarks by the President on the Loss of Space Shuttle Columbia

2:04 P.M. EST

THE PRESIDENT: My fellow Americans, this day has brought terrible news and great sadness to our country. At 9:00 A.M. this morning, Mission Control in Houston lost contact with our Space Shuttle Columbia. A short time later, debris was seen falling from the skies above Texas. The Columbia is lost; there are no survivors.

On board was a crew of seven: Colonel Rick Husband; Lt. Colonel Michael Anderson; Commander Laurel Clark; Captain David Brown; Commander William McCool; Dr. Kalpana Chawla; and Ilan Ramon, a Colonel in the Israeli Air Force. These men and women assumed great risk in the service to all humanity.

In an age when space flight has come to seem almost routine, it is easy to overlook the dangers of travel by rocket and the difficulties of navigating the fierce outer atmosphere of the Earth. These astronauts knew the dangers, and they faced them willingly, knowing they had a high and noble purpose in life. Because of their courage and daring and idealism, we will miss them all the more.

All Americans today are thinking, as well, of the families of these men and women who have been given this sudden shock and grief. You're not alone. Our entire nation grieves with you. And those you loved will always have the respect and gratitude of this country.

The cause in which they died will continue. Mankind is led into the darkness beyond our world by the inspiration of discovery and the longing to understand. Our journey into space will go on.

In the skies today we saw destruction and tragedy. Yet farther than we can see there is comfort and hope. In the words of the prophet Isaiah, "Lift your eyes and look to the heavens. Who created all these? He who brings out the starry hosts one by one and calls them each by name. Because of His great power and mighty strength, not one of them is missing."

The same Creator who names the stars also knows the names of the seven souls we mourn today. The crew of the shuttle Columbia did not return safely to Earth; yet we can pray that all are safely home.

May God bless the grieving families, and may God continue to bless America.

http://www.whitehouse.gov/news/releases/2003/02/20030201-2.html

---

Ms. Taylor decided to have students read with partners, making sure to pair beginning and advanced English language learners. She directed them to read the speech looking for the ideas that were included in the semantic web, and she allowed them to choose whether to read orally or silently.

After students finished reading the text, Ms. Taylor asked them to write in their notebooks what they thought the President was trying to say. She then conducted a whole class discussion about the speech using the semantic web. She asked about how each segment of the web related to the speech and which of the words students remembered reading. She invited students to suggest additional ideas to add to the web. She also asked them to note which words or ideas the President did *not* talk about in his speech and to speculate why. During the discussion, students concluded that mentioning the cause of the accident or try-

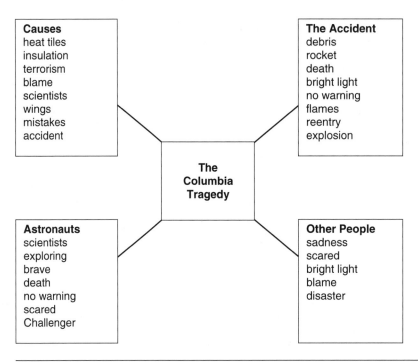

FIGURE 8.1   *Prereading Semantic Map*

ing to blame someone would be inappropriate for the occasion and that Presidents do talk about religious ideas in their speeches, especially on sad occasions.

Before reading the rest of this chapter, reflect for a moment on these questions:
1. Is Ms. Taylor right to substitute this speech for the one in the textbook? How does she know that her students will be able to understand it?
2. How well does her introductory vocabulary activity prepare students for reading? Why do you think she did not simply pick out vocabulary words herself?
3. What are some reasons why the teacher might have decided not to ask a series of comprehension questions to guide students' focus while they read? Do you agree with her decision?
4. What could Ms. Taylor have done to include English language learners in the discussion after reading? How well would they comprehend the key concepts that were being taught?

Whether students are reading from a basal reader, an assigned novel, or a traditional literature anthology, guided reading requires teachers to support students throughout their engagement with texts. In this chapter, we will examine options for preparing students to read, for helping them to use appropriate strategies while reading, and for encouraging them to review and extend text ideas.

Characteristics of Guided Reading Routines

Reading educators describe guided reading routines in slightly different ways (e.g., Allen, 2000; Cunningham & Allington, 1999; Fountas & Pinnell, 1996), but all the variations generally fit the characteristics that "the teacher provides the structure and purpose for reading and for responding to the material read" (Harris & Hodges, 1995, p. 102). While using guided reading activities, teachers carefully choose materials that are appropriate for student learning, and then provide just enough support to help students accomplish specific goals such as the following:

- Learning and applying strategies.
- Learning new words and language patterns.
- Learning about text structure and organization.
- Considering the processes and purposes of authors.
- Learning genre characteristics.

Notice that these goals encompass all aspects of proficient reading: reading words, making meaning, mastering messages, and engaging with texts. Teachers may highlight one or two of these aspects during a particular text engagement, but eventually they should all be included within guided reading routines.

Ms. Taylor drew students' attention to words during the semantic web activities. She focused their attention on meaning construction by the purpose she set for reading and through their writing and discussion. She engaged their interest by inviting them to share their knowledge and feelings about an event of national importance, and she extended their understanding of messages by raising issues about the role of the audience and the occasion in the ways speeches are written.

Scaffolding for Independence

Reading instruction in the middle grades should include scaffolding that helps students to experience success with the texts they want and need to read. Successful experiences are important for maintaining the willingness to read. Teachers in the middle grades must also pay close attention, however, to the way in which scaffolds lead to reading independence.

Joseph (2001) provides an example of the gradual release process by describing how she guided the reading of her eighth-grade students throughout the year.

> While we read a book in class, students have a comprehension packet of questions in front of them that they need to answer by the end of each section of the book. I try to use the questions as guides for their reading and to help keep their focus on the text. Even when students read independently or with partners, I want them to have packets to help guide their reading. During the year, I design fewer and fewer of the packets; the students design their own. (p. 105)

Materials for Guided Reading

The materials students read during guided reading need to be challenging, but not frustrating. Many factors go into determining the difficulty of a particular text. Readability formulas such as the Fry (1977) and the Raygor and Wark (1980) are based on the length and complexity of sentences and the number of long or difficult words in the text. Other factors to be considered include the overall length of the text, its structure and organization, and its format. Small print or large areas of "gray" text without headings, illustrations, or white space can make a book harder to read. Teachers in many middle grades classrooms have access to materials that are specifically produced to fit the developmental needs of students and the goals of guided reading instruction. These materials may include basal reader programs and sets of leveled young adult books.

Leveled Books.   Guided reading routines have recently become associated with using sets of "leveled books." In this approach, students are generally reading entire books by children's authors, and each book in the set is designated with a level of difficulty. Teachers then use classroom assessments to assign each student to an appropriate level of difficulty (Fountas & Pinnell, 1996). Sets of leveled books are often accompanied by suggestions about the kinds of assessment and instructional activities that are appropriate for guided reading.

As many as ten levels of difficulty may be distinguished within a particular school grade. Scholastic Publishing (2000), for instance, developed sets of leveled books that included dozens of fiction and nonfiction titles for grades five and six, each of which is designated with a letter from *Q* to *Z* to show its relative level of difficulty. Level *Q* contains titles such as *Exploring the Titanic* (Ballard, 1999) and *Help! I'm Trapped in the First Day of Summer Camp* (Strasser, 1999). Titles in level *Z* include, *City: A Story of Roman Planning and Construction* (Macaulay, 1981) and *The Adventures of Tom Sawyer* (Twain, 1876).

Basal Readers   Basal readers are textbooks that are designed for a particular grade level and intended especially for teacher-directed instruction in skills and strategies. These textbooks are usually part of a comprehensive language arts program that is designed by the publisher. Often a basal program includes a recommended approach to instruction and a "scope and sequence" indicating what should be taught and when. Basal publishers offer a wide variety of materials including teacher editions, pupil texts, assessment materials, and student practice materials such as workbooks and skill sheets. Newer basals may include supplementary materials such as CD-ROMs and websites.

Teachers often believe that using a basal reading program saves them time because they do not have to search out developmentally appropriate stories, and they do not have to invent all of the activities that students will do to accompany the selections. Some teachers, especially those with little experience teaching reading, find that the sequence and organization of lessons in a basal program makes them more confident that they are "covering" important objectives.

Schools use basal readers and leveled books for guided reading to ensure that students are reading in the Zone of Proximal Development (ZPD) where teacher guidance will have the most effect. Published materials also provide a consistent direction for instruction and the convenience of suggested instructional activities. However, teachers still have the responsibility for making choices about what material students read and how those materials are used. Note that Ms. Taylor chose to have her students read the Columbia speech rather than the selection in the basal textbook because it was more timely and because she was confident that she could provide the scaffolding necessary for her students to read it.

Grouping Students for Guided Reading Routines

In traditional basal reading instruction, individual differences were supposed to be accommodated through the use of fairly permanent reading groups, each of which might be using a reader at a different level. Many adults today can recall some of the drawbacks of this approach, especially the way that students became keenly aware of who was in the "bluebirds" group and who became identified as "crows." According to research by Allington (1994), students in low reading groups tended to spend less time actually reading and more time on skill lessons, workbook pages, and nonreading management problems than other students.

Traditional grouping practices are generally ineffective for accommodating differences, especially for English language learners and other students who are not "typical." Students in each group can never be identical; they will still show a range of knowledge and reading ability. Furthermore, comprehension depends on factors in the reader (such as background knowledge, interest, or experience with a particular genre), thus, predicting how easy or hard a selection will be for students in a particular group is harder than it might seem. The problem is to use grouping patterns that help students with the specific skills and strategies they need but are flexible enough to avoid permanently categorizing readers.

In the example at the beginning of this chapter, Ms. Taylor begins and ends with whole-class activities. In between, she has students reading and discussing with partners. This allows her to move about the room briefly checking in with various groups to see how well they are managing the task. She might also have formed a group of three or four students in order to observe them more closely or to give them additional help. Many teachers form this sort of temporary cooperative learning groups. These groups are organized around a specific learning task or an assigned text and are dissolved as soon as the task is complete.

If sets of leveled books are used with guided reading, the teacher may form groups of students who are reading books at the same level. By assigning a text that is matched to students' general reading level and by observing and responding to students' needs in a small group setting, the teacher can do much to ensure student success. When the teacher meets with each guided reading group, the agenda is to implement the planned instructional support activities. This may include discussion of the previous day's reading, prereading guidance for the next section of the text, or assessing and giving advice about strategy use (Fountas & Pinnell, 1996).

Leu and Kinzer (2003) suggest that students should be placed in a group based on assessment data such as anecdotal records about the materials they read the previous year, informal reading inventories, and observations made early in the year, as well as from standardized reading tests scores. They cautioned, however, that teachers must be careful to continue to evaluate students' placement in guided reading groups and that, "If you choose to use guided reading groups, it is essential that you also use alternative grouping patterns during the year" (p. 488). Guided reading groups may, for instance, meet only three days per week, so that students can engage in other literacy routines or read with other kinds of groups.

Assessing Guided Reading

When students are reading material that is too hard for them, they will often become so overloaded with identifying the words in the text that they can no longer construct meaning. They are said to be reading material that is at "frustration level"—a level at which they will read with poor fluency and often miscue on words that they have previously read accurately in other texts. On the other hand, books at a student's independent level are appropriate for building enjoyment, background knowledge, and fluency, but they provide few opportunities to teach the strategies that students need to use when they encounter problems. The ideal text is one that is at an *instructional level* where students can be challenged, but still be successful.

Grade levels provided by a readability formula or the designations given to leveled texts provide some information to help teachers avoid frustration level, but the usual method for confirming that a book is appropriate for guided reading is to take an oral reading sample, or running record (Clay, 1997). This is one of the few exceptions to the principle that students in the middle grades should read orally only when they have a chance to rehearse and perform their reading. A student is asked to read a passage of about 100 words, and the teacher counts and notes miscues. If the reading is 95 to 100 percent accurate, the text is considered to be independent level. If the student's accuracy ranges from 90–94 percent, the text is appropriate for instruction in a guided reading setting. If the reading is not at least 80–89 percent accurate, the text is considered to be at frustration level.

Planning Guided Reading Engagements

You can think of a text engagement as a "lesson" as long as your notion of lesson is fairly flexible. Vacca and Vacca (1999) emphasize that a lesson does not necessarily take place in a single class session. They suggest a framework for planning that helps teachers envision the amount and type of guidance needed in order to (1) prepare students for reading, (2) help them maintain their interactions with the text, and (3) reinforce and extend ideas from their reading. In the following section, we will explore issues and options relating to each of these stages.

Preparing Students to Read

Sometimes, the activities that prepare students to read may take nearly as long as the reading itself. At other times, a fairly minimal introduction may be enough to ensure that students will start out in the right direction. Preparing students to read involves building both their willingness and their ability to engage with a text. Teachers have a variety of options in both the amount and the kind of support they give. They must draw on their knowledge of their students to decide whether the key element in preparation is text content, text language, or text interest.

If the text deals with topics or situations that are outside students' experience, the teacher can consider activating and building background knowledge by:

- Building text-specific knowledge through pictures, videos, or read-alouds.
- Comparing a new concept(s) to something that is familiar to students.
- Discussing what students already know.
- Telling students information that will be in the text.

In our opening scenario, Ms. Taylor might have discussed the word "tragedy" and asked English language learners if a tragic event had ever happened in their countries. After that she might have shown a brief video of the Columbia incident or read aloud from a newspaper account of the tragedy. She also could have directly told students what they needed knew about the tragedy in order to understand the speech.

If the text is not inherently interesting to some students, the teacher can help them find a personal connection to the text through activities such as:

- Having students share experiences and feelings related to the topic.
- Inviting students to ask questions about the topic and predict answers.
- Having students debate controversial issues that will be raised in the text.
- Posing a problematical situation from the text and inviting solutions.

Sometimes when a text is not naturally relevant to students, they can create *imaginary* relevance through role taking. Ms. Taylor might, for example, assign each student the role of a family member, a fellow astronaut, or a citizen of another country. She could then encourage them to read critically through the eyes of their assumed role and imagine how they would feel hearing the speech.

If the form or language of the text poses problems, the teacher can direct students' attention by providing guiding questions, modeling or reinforcing the strategies they should use, or highlighting structure of the text. Ms. Taylor might have reminded students of a comprehension strategy they could employ while reading. For instance, she might ask them to use a strategy of visualizing by imagining the President standing before the television cameras and the millions of people around the world watching and listening to the speech.

Ms. Taylor also wanted to point out that speeches are carefully planned to address the needs and feelings of all the people in the audience and that they have to be well organized so that people will remember them. She could have created a "pattern guide" such as the one shown in Figure 8.2. A brief explanation of the guide would help her students see the underlying structure of the President's speech.

Maintaining Interaction between Student and Text

Appropriate prereading activities introduce students to a new text, but teachers also need to take steps to keep the "conversation" going. The match between students and text will determine how much guidance students will need while reading and how often they will need it. The guidance that is provided may take three basic forms:

FIGURE 8.2 *A Completed Pattern Guide for the President's Speech*

President Bush's speech can be divided into four parts. For each part: (a) Write one sentence that summarizes what the President was trying to say. (b) Write whether he was speaking to the nation, the families, or the world. (c) Write some key words he used, especially those that are in our web.

Part 1: The Facts (paragraph 1)

Sentence: The Shuttle Columbia exploded over Texas, and all the astronauts were killed.
The audience: The nation.
Five key words or phrases: 9:00 A.M., Mission Control, lost contact, over Texas, debris falling, no survivors.

Part 2: About the Astronauts (paragraphs 2 & 3)

Sentence: The astronauts knew space flight was dangerous, but they were brave, and they wanted to explore outer space.
The audience: The families.
Key words or phrases: Faced dangers, noble purpose, courage, daring, idealism.

Part 3: Feelings (paragraphs 4 & 5)

Sentence: We feel sad for the astronauts and their families, but we will keep exploring space.
The audience: The nation (?), the families.
Key words or phrases: Grief, respect, gratitude, inspiration, journey.

Part 4: Encouragement (paragraphs 6–8)

Sentence: God cares about all people, and the astronauts are now in heaven.
The audience: The nation, the families (?)
Key words or phrases: Cause will continue, inspiration, desire to understand, comfort and hope, safely home.

Talking about the text with the teacher or with peers.   This may take the form of a midway discussion in which students can summarize, give reactions to the text, and raise questions and problems. These discussions allow the teacher to see if there are any misconceptions about the text and to refocus students' attention on elements of the text they should watch for and strategies they should employ as they finish the reading.

Self-monitoring activities.   Since "knowing if you know" is a major part of reading comprehension, teachers should encourage the use metacognitive strategies as students engage with text. Activities such as knowledge rating and learning logs call on students to reflect about what they have or have not understood and to take responsibility for using appropriate "fix-up" strategies—including asking for help.

Writing about the text.   During reading, writing can serve two purposes: helping students organize their thoughts and helping them to remember. Completing a graphic organizer or a pattern guide can do both. Teachers can also model other strategies for independent note taking or have students write answers to a focus question. With longer texts, teachers may want to collect written products to use as formative assessments—information that will help them know who needs help or what might need to be retaught.

Reinforcing and Extending Comprehension

Perhaps the most common instructional activity after students read is to give some sort of quiz. Evaluation is certainly an important part of guided reading, but testing reading is not the same as teaching reading. As we explained in Chapter 2, comprehending requires using a schema to see the "big picture," the significance of the ideas in a text. The activities students do after they read should encourage them to decide which ideas are most important, and to make connections (1) between ideas in the text, (2) between the text and their prior experience, and (3) between the text and other texts they have read.

Many of the activities described above for preparing students for reading and for maintaining their interactions with a text as they read can also be adapted and used after reading. Some options include:

- Discussion/debates about text ideas.
- Creating artistic products such as poems, drawings, or music.
- Process discussions about difficulties encountered and successful strategies.
- Sharing related personal experiences or recollections of related texts.
- Application of ideas or strategies to future texts.
- Writing or drawing to reconstruct text ideas.

For beginning English language learners, drawing about what happened or making a graphic organizer with the key events will help the teacher to see if the student understood the concepts. They may miss some details due to a lack of vocabulary, but their drawings or graphic organizers will enable the teacher to determine if they have comprehended the most important elements.

One other option for reinforcing and extending text ideas is to have students engage in reading another related text. Ms. Taylor, for instance, could have asked students to listen to or read President Reagan's speech from their textbook. She could also have them visit one of the web pages that commemorate the crews of the two disasters and leave appropriate messages of condolence. Finally, she could have them read the poem "High Flight" (Magee, 1941) that was quoted briefly in both speeches and invite students to write about the meaning of "let slip the surly bonds of earth . . . and touched the face of God."

Guided Reading for English Language Learners

Herrell and Jordan (2004) state that guided reading routines are especially appropriate for English language learners because they allow for individual coaching in pronunciations and opportunities to correct misunderstandings and clarify word meanings. They suggest a routine, adapted from Fountas and Pinnell (1996), that includes:

- Groups of four to six students who have similar needs, based on their running records, meeting at the same table.

- The teacher beginning with a "book talk," pointing out important vocabulary and building background knowledge. The teacher should use pictures, gestures, and real objects as necessary.
- Students reading aloud at their own pace and the teacher listening to them, asking them to reread when necessary and posing questions such as, "Does that make sense?"
- Students practicing reading the text in pairs.
- The teacher presenting a short lesson for the group based on observations of their needs.

Teaching Vocabulary during Guided Reading Engagements

The National Reading Panel (NRP) (2000) points out that there is a clear link between vocabulary knowledge and comprehension, and it concludes that students need both extensive opportunities to learn words while reading on their own as well as direct instruction about words. The instruction that the NRP recommends seems to be well suited to guided reading routines: "There is a need for direct instruction of vocabulary items that are required for a specific text to be read as part of the lesson" (p. 4–24).

Teachers must carefully choose the vocabulary that will be studied during guided reading. Whole-class and small-group discussion should focus on those words that are (a) conceptually important to the text, (b) developmentally appropriate, and/or (c) used repeatedly.

Working toward Definitions, Not from Them

Learning new words is clearly an important goal of guided reading, but teachers need to consider carefully why, when, and how they will teach vocabulary. Few instructional practices are as entrenched as assigning lists of words for students to look up, define, and use in a sentence, but few instructional practices are more questionable.

As students are involved in a text engagement, they should be gradually closing in on the exact meaning of words through repeated exposures to those words and opportunities to use them in all the language arts. Notice that Ms. Taylor begins with words that some students already know by eliciting much of the vocabulary that will be used in the text before students read. Students should also should be learning strategies for dealing with unfamiliar words such as use of context, etymology, and morphology, as well as using dictionaries.

Associating Words   Learning new words can begin with *associating* the new words with one another. Include some familiar words in vocabulary activities so that students can see the relationship between new words and familiar ones. Ms. Taylor guides this process visually by constructing the semantic web. She then invites students to make additional connections to the web as they encounter new words.

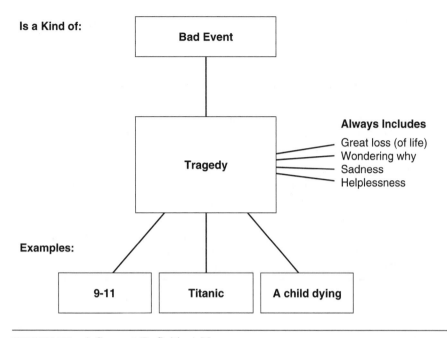

FIGURE 8.3 *A Concept (Definition) Map*

Analyzing concepts   Students' understanding is deepened by *analyzing* some concepts in depth. Ms. Taylor might reinforce and extend students' concept of "tragedy" by working with them to create a Concept of Definition Map (Schwartz & Raphael, 1985) such as the one in Figure 8.3. This graphic representation shows many of the elements that would go into a dictionary definition of a tragedy and could be constructed before or after consulting the dictionary.

Using New Words   Students learn new words by *using* them. Ms. Taylor asks students to talk about words and concepts in depth and provides opportunities for them to use those words in their informal writing. As she listens to them reading in pairs, she can assess their ability to pronounce the words and to explain their meaning.

Evaluating Guided Reading

The use of small groups, appropriate texts, and frequent informal assessment in guided reading routines makes it possible for teachers to ensure that all students are engaging successfully with texts. Teachers plan text engagements with an instructional framework that provides necessary scaffolding before, during, and after reading. A checklist that can help teachers evaluate their plans is shown in Figure 8.4.

FIGURE 8.4   *A Checklist for Evaluating Guided Reading Engagements*

1. Was the reading material at an instructional level and an appropriate match for my students' needs and abilities?
2. Were the assigned activities based on my knowledge of my students' match with the material?
3. Did I activate or build necessary background knowledge?
4. Did I allow/encourage students to share opinions and previous knowledge?
5. Could I monitor/support students' involvement with the text?
6. Did postreading activities reinforce and extend text ideas?
7. Did I provide multiple opportunities to analyze and use vocabulary that is important to the concepts in the text?
8. Did I model or promote sharing of ways to deal with obstacles in the text?
9. Did I provide feedback and encourage self-evaluation and reflection?
10. Did I plan activities that would involve beginning and advanced English language learners in pronouncing, understanding, reading, and writing new words?

Summary

Guided reading is a powerful and well-tested method for providing students with the support they need before, during, and after reading. Materials such as basal readers and leveled books can be used to ensure that students are reading instructional level texts during guided reading. Vocabulary development activities often enhance guided reading by helping students extend their understanding of important concepts presented in the text.

Reinforcing Text Ideas

Throughout this chapter, we have asked you to think about the opening scenario and to consider additional options the teacher might have used. Reread the scenario and evaluate the text engagement Ms. Taylor planned. What activities might you add or change to make the lesson better?

Key Terms to Know and Use

guided reading	role taking
pattern guide	concept of definition map
leveled books	semantic mapping
reinforcing and extending	scope and sequence
text engagement	visualizing
basal reader	

Possible Sentences

Use two or three terms in the columns above and write a sentence stating one idea you now know about guided reading. Write four or five such sentences using different words until you have a nice summary paragraph.

Beyond the Book

- One source for samples of effective guided literacy engagements is "ReadWriteThink," a joint project of the International Reading Association and the National Council of Teachers of English. Access the site through the IRA homepage at www.reading.org and explore the activities linked to "Learning about Language." Try to find an example that is similar to the scenario in this chapter and one that is different.
- Examine a basal reader and the accompanying manual or teacher's edition and check on the following (you might also consider what other items you might add to this list if you were evaluating the textbook for possible purchase by your school):
  1. Are the selections "real" and whole?
  2. Is there a variety of genres, including fiction, nonfiction, and poetry?
  3. Are many cultural groups represented in the selections?
  4. Do the activities that are recommended match well to the text? Or do they focus on learning words or strategies that are not necessary for understanding the text?
  5. Do postreading activities reinforce and extend ideas, or merely test comprehension?

References

Allen, J. (2000). *Yellow brick roads: Shared and guided paths to independent reading* 4–12. Portland, ME: Stenhouse.

Allington, R. (1994). What's so special about special programs for children who find learning to read difficult? *Journal of Reading Behavior, 26*(1), 95–115.

Ballard, R. (1988). *Exploring the Titantic.* New York: Scholastic.

Clay, M. M. (1997). *Running records for classroom teachers.* Portsmouth, NH: Heinemann.

Cunningham, P., & Allington, R. (1999). *Classrooms that work: They can all read and write* (2nd ed.). New York: Longman.

EMC Corporation. (2001). *Literature and the language arts: Exploring literature* (2nd ed.). Saint Paul, MN: EMC Paradigm.

Fountas, I. C., & Pinnell, G. S. (1996). *Guided reading: Good first teaching for all students.* Portsmouth, NH: Heinemann.

Fry, E. (1977). Fry's readability graph: Clarifications, validity, and extension to level 17. *Journal of Reading, 21*(3), 242–252.

Harris, T., & Hodges, R. (1995). *The literacy dictionary: The vocabulary of reading and writing.* Newark, DE: International Reading Association.

Herrell, A., & Jordan, M. (2004). Fifty strategies for teaching English language learners (2nd ed.). Upper Saddle River, NJ: Merrill Prentice Hall.

Joseph, J. J. (2001). "Is this really English?": Using Young Adult Literature in an Urban Middle School. In J. A. Rycik & J. L. Irvin (Eds.), *What adolescents deserve: A commitment to students' literacy learning* (pp. 103–110). Newark, DE: International Reading Association.

Leu, J. L., & Kinzer, C. K. (2003). *Effective literacy instruction: Implementing best practice* (5th ed.). Upper Saddle River, NJ: Merrill Prentice Hall.

Magee, J. G. (1941). High flight. In *The last high flight,* Washington, DC: Library of Congress.

Macauley, D. (1981). *City: A story of Roman planning and construction.* Boston: Hougton Mifflin.

National Reading Panel. (2000). *Teaching children to read: An evidence-based assessment of the scientific research literature on reading and its implications for reading instruction.* Washington, DC: National Institute of Child Health and Human Development.

Raygor, A. L., & Wark, D. M. (1980). *Systems for study.* New York: McGraw-Hill.

Readence, J. E., Bean, T. W., & Baldwin, R. S. (2000). Content area literacy: An integrated approach. Dubuque, IA: Kendall-Hunt.

Scholastic Publishing. (2000). *Non-fiction focused program.* Red edition. Accessed at http://www.scholastic.ca/education/guided reading/index.html

Schwartz, R. M., & Raphael, T. E. (1985). Concept of definition: A key to improving students' vocabulary. *The Reading Teacher, 39*(2), 198–205.

Strasser, T. (1999). *Help! I'm trapped in the first day of summer camp.* New York: Scholastic.

Twain, M. (1876). *The adventures of Tom Sawyer.* Hartford, CT: American Publishing Co.

Vacca, R. T., & Vacca, J. L. (1999). *Content area reading: Literacy and learning across the curriculum.* (6th ed.). New York: Addison Wesley Longman.

9

Guided Literature Study

Activating Prior Knowledge and Making Connections

Ms. Garcia was beginning a unit on short stories. One of the stories in the class literature anthology was "The Legend of Sleepy Hollow" by Washington Irving (1998). She knew that this story was probably somewhat familiar to most of her students, but she also knew that it was set in a time and place that was far from the experience of her eighth-grade suburban students. Furthermore, the story contained much unfamiliar vocabulary and required students to make some subtle inferences about the events of the plot and the motivations of the characters. Ms. Garcia knew that the story would be a particular challenge for the English language learners in her class. Despite these obstacles, however, she decided that her students should have the experience of reading the original version of this famous tale.

Ms. Garcia decided to prepare her students for reading by drawing their attention away from the Headless Horseman and toward the story's characters and their "love triangle." She did not want to embarrass her students by asking them to discuss their own romantic experiences, so she decided to use an example drawn from popular media. She created the situation found in Figure 9.1 for them to think about.

Ms. Garcia considered having students improvise possible outcomes for the situation, but she decided instead to have them use the discussion web found in Figure 9.2. The discussion web (Alvermann, 1991) was intended to focus students' attention on a plot device ("make someone jealous") that has been used in literature for centuries. Students completed the web in groups of three by filling in as many reasons as they could find on both sides of the argument. Then Ms. Garcia acted as a recorder until the groups had shared all the reasons they had generated on both sides of the issue.

Ms. Garcia also supported students' reading of this challenging text by having them do "sketch to stretch" activities in small groups. She was sure to group the beginning English language learners with the more advanced English language learners. Different groups drew a map of the setting or a depiction of one of the characters and labeled the drawings by using words from the text. After students had read the story, Ms. Garcia guided them to revisit the idea in the discussion web and to write about how their conclusion was related to the story.

FIGURE 9.1 *Saved by the Bell: The Unknown Episode*

You might have seen reruns of the TV comedy *Saved by the Bell*. Recently, part of a script was found for an episode that was never actually made. Read the summary below and think about how the story might come out.

> Kelly felt that her handsome boyfriend Zach was taking her for granted, so she decided to make him jealous. She began to flirt with Screech, the scrawny, slightly silly guy who hangs around with her friends. Screech feels that his dreams are coming true as a beautiful and popular girl seems to be falling for him. He begins to act like a "big shot" with his friends and to make fun of "nerds" who can't get a date. Zach notices what is going on and decides to put a stop to it by plotting with his friend Slater to humiliate Screech at the big Homecoming dance.

1. How do you think the episode would end?
2. Where would the humor come from?
3. What do you think each of the characters would learn at the end of the episode?

FIGURE 9.2 *Discussion Web**

Directions: List ideas that support or do not support this statement

> All is fair in love and war.
> Sometimes a person must do things that are not quite honest or fair to be able to get together with the person he or she is meant to be with.

Support	**Do Not Support**
_____	_____
_____	_____
_____	_____
_____	_____

Conclusion

_____

_____

_____

_____

*Adapted from Alvermann, D. E. (1991). The discussion web: A graphic aid for learning across the curriculum. *Reading Teacher, 45*(2), 92–99.

Before you continue reading the rest of this chapter, consider these questions about Ms. Garcia's plan:
1. Do you agree with her decision to use this story for guided literature study?
2. Given the characteristics of the story, what else might she do to prepare students for reading?
3. How can she accommodate the needs of English language learners or other students who might struggle with the difficult style and language of the story?

In the previous chapter, we examined the ways in which teachers could create scaffolds to support students' reading during guided reading routines. In this chapter, we will use "The Legend of Sleepy Hollow" to demonstrate classroom activities that support students' reading of literary texts. Although this story may not be appropriate for all students in the middle grades, it is familiar to most adults and is a useful vehicle for exploring issues related to reading and appreciating literature.

Goals of Guided Literature Study in the Middle Grades

Guided literature study is meant to develop both interpretation and appreciation—the *skill* and the *will*—to read literature. Students should be carefully guided to construct meaning from particular literary works, but they should also be allowed to experience the artistry of those works and be encouraged to use literature to enhance their understanding of themselves and the world. Guided literature study should address the following goals:

1. Acquainting students with some of the tools and terminology that are useful for constructing interpretations of literary works.
2. Helping students to engage with literary works in order to understand themselves and others. If there are a variety of cultures and languages in the classroom, the teacher can choose literature that promotes a better understanding of diversity.
3. Examining the language and structures used by authors of literary works.
4. Giving students first-hand experience with the powerful and subtle messages that can be conveyed by written language.
5. Sharing some of the works that have reflected and shaped the cultural understandings of the society in which students live.

Atwell highlights the differences between guided reading and guided literature study in the second edition of her book, *In the Middle* (Atwell, 1998):

For a long time, I had been reluctant to see myself as a teacher of literature; I preferred teacher of reading. But my seventh and eighth graders know how to read. While I certainly do teach lessons about comprehension, speed and strategies, I am primarily a teacher of literature. I can't forsake the power of literature and lore that changed me. (p. 46)

Atwell's increased emphasis on teaching literature surprised many readers who knew her to be a great champion of independent reading. Some teachers also questioned her statement that students "knew how to read," pointing out that most students still have much to learn about reading. Atwell was not, however, denying the importance of independent and guided reading experiences. She was rather arguing that students need experiences that emphasize the unique purposes and characteristics of literary works.

Materials for Guided Literature Study

Educators disagree over whether guided literature study should include only "classics" that have been read for generations or whether they can use works that were written for young adults (Bushman & Haas, 2001; Jago, 2000). Hipple (2000) asserted that

Those less familiar with young adult literature tend sometimes to believe that its thematic treatments are slight or superficial—"teenage," if you will. They are not. Like the best literature written for adults, good novels written for adolescents possess themes that merit and reward examination and commentary. (p. 2)

Whether "classic" or contemporary, the ideal text for guided literature study should have the qualities necessary to create significant literary experiences. One of these qualities is *literary significance,* which means that the work allows students to explore important authors, trends, and alternatives in the field of literature and to examine closely some of the forms and techniques of literary writing. The work should also have *developmental significance,* the potential to provide students with opportunities to explore their own identities, their feelings and values, and their relationships with others. Finally, literary works used for guided literature study should have *social significance,* potential for helping students to explore their place in society, critically examine society's values and conflicts, and consider other and better ways of life.

Guided Literature Study for English Language Learners

For English language learners, guided literature study presents both additional challenges and additional opportunities. Literary writing often depends on subtle shades of meaning, and it may include uncommon words or use familiar words in uncommon ways. Literary texts may also be so deeply rooted in a particular culture that they are difficult for "outsiders" to interpret.

On the other hand, literature can help English language learners to strengthen their cognitive skills by "working through" the difficulties posed by the text, and encouraging them to share their personal perspectives and to affirm their values. Because literature deals with universal themes and experiences, English language learners may be able to make personal connections that serve as anchors for language learning.

Guiding Interpretation: Literary Analysis

Guided literature study often uses tools and terms of analysis that have been developed over many generations. Literary analysis encourages readers to focus on specific elements within a text and to consider how each element is important to the whole. Verse structures such as meters and rhyme patterns, for instance, help to explain how the poet created a particular feeling or mood. Teachers must remember, however, that reading literature should always include both "head and heart." Analyzing literature is not an end in itself, and a literary work should not be "killed" so that students can practice "dissecting it." Teachers should draw on their own experience as readers (and lovers) of literary works to choose elements for analysis that will help students to construct a rich and satisfying interpretation. We will illustrate the process of analysis by using "The Legend of Sleepy Hollow" as an example.

Examining Plot

The plot of a story can be represented by a chart like the one shown in Figure 9.3. Such a chart is another kind of pattern guide that helps students to consider what is and is not crucial information in a work of fiction. As students use the same chart on a regular basis, they will probably find that the same elements appear in every story, but they will also come to realize that they are not always introduced in the same order or accorded the same degree of importance. English language learners will need modeling and scaffolding to complete a plot chart. This can be accomplished through whole-class instruction or in a teacher-directed small group.

Notice that the "conflict" of the story is identified as what is bothering the main character or what the character wants to accomplish. "Sleepy Hollow" contains both kinds of conflict: the *external problem* between Ichabod Crane and Brom Bones and the *internal problem* of Ichabod's desire to marry rich Katrina. Three other points need to be made about plot analysis. First, there is more than one "right answer." You might, for instance, have listed Katrina as a problem to Ichabod because you believed she was leading him on.

Second, although a plot chart can give a teacher some useful insights into a reader's understanding of the story, it is not primarily intended as a test. Its greatest value is as a starting point for discussion. If some students list Katrina as a "problem" and others do not, they can be guided to think about whether she is, in fact, the passive "trophy" that Ichabod and Brom fight over or the instigator of Ichabod's troubles.

Finally, the chart that students fill out on paper is less important than the chart they are building in their heads, the story schema that will help them recognize the importance of various "facts" in other stories they read. Teachers need to make this point explicitly so that students understand that the purpose of the instructional activity is not to "learn" a particular story, but rather to become a particular kind of reader—a thoughtful one who seeks to "make sense" of fictional events.

Analyzing Character

Ichabod Crane is one of the most famous characters in American fiction, but how much does a reader really know about him? In the opening scenario, Ms. Garcia chose to have

FIGURE 9.3 *Plot Analysis for "The Legend of Sleepy Hollow"*

Main Character(s)	Setting	"Trigger"	Conflict(s) or Problem(s)	Reactions/ Attempts	Climax	Resolution
Who has the problem or is the problem?	Where and when does this story occur?	What disturbs "business as usual" and starts the story?	What is the main character trying to accomplish? Who or what is bothering the main character?	What do the characters do about the problem? How do they feel about it?	What moment is the turning point when you know if and when the problem will be solved?	How has the problem changed at the end of the story? How are the characters different?
Ichabod Crane, a country schoolmaster. Abraham Van Brunt (Brom Bones), the strongest young man in town. Katrina Van Tassel, the daughter of wealthy Dutch land owner.	Greensburgh, also called Tarrytown, "one of the quietest places in the whole world." Colonial times.	Ichabod becomes interested in Katrina.	Ichabod is poor but wants to be rich. He wants to marry Katrina. Brom Bones plays jokes on him and wants to fight him. He is superstitious and lives in a a spooky town.	He tries to become a rich land owner by marrying Katrina. He sees Katrina quietly and refuses to fight Brom.	Ichabod attends a party at Katrina's house and decides to tell Katrina how he feels. Brom tells scary stories of the Headless Horseman.	Katrina turns him down. The Headless Horseman chases him out of town, and Katrina eventually marries Brom.

some students draw him because the story tells much more about his outside than his inside. Ichabod, like the other characters in "Sleepy Hollow" is a relatively "flat" character as opposed to a "rounded" character that shows complexity and potential to grow and change.

Analyzing the depth of characterization in fiction can be a vehicle for considering stereotypes in real life. In current slang, Ichabod is a "nerd." He is reasonably intelligent, but he is not exactly handsome or well dressed. He has better manners than most of the young men, but by comparison he is weak and rather cowardly. Discussions of characterization can help students to understand how labels such as "nerd," "flirt," and "jock" oversimplify people and reduce them to cartoon characters. This may also be a time to discuss stereotypes in relation to diverse cultures and languages.

The process of analyzing characters can be aided by a chart such as the one in Figure 9.4 that raises questions regarding what the reader knows about a character and the source of that information. Students who examined this chart would immediately notice that their knowledge of Ichabod is limited since there is no dialogue in the story and the author has not allowed them to hear Ichabod's thoughts.

Just as plot analysis charts help students discuss and clarify their interpretations of events, a character analysis chart is most useful when it is used to guide students' discussions about the process of characterization and the ways in which character interacts with plot. Some points for discussion in this story might include:

- How do Ichabod's looks affect what happens in the story?
- How do Ichabod's likes and personality traits affect what happens in the story?
- Why does the author come right out and tell you some information about Ichabod and the other characters, but not everything?

Narrative Strategy and Style

Whenever discussion focuses on the choices that the author made in telling the story, readers are considering narrative strategy. Point of view is one part of narrative strategy. The narrator in "Sleepy Hollow" is an outside observer who does not tell readers all the secrets of the characters' thoughts and feelings. This point of view can be labeled as "third person limited," but the terms used to describe point of view are less important than considering its effect on the reader. One way to explore point of view is to experiment with changing it. Consider, for instance, what would happen if Katrina told the story from a "first person" point of view. She might describe the events leading up to the story's climax like this:

> We all had a fine night of fun and entertainment, but Mr. Crane had to go and spoil it all. He asked me to marry him! What had I ever done to put that idea into his head? I'm sure I don't know. Brom was nowhere to be seen, but all I could think of was how he would laugh at me when he found out. Mr. Crane is nice enough, but he is certainly not the man of my dreams. I wasn't sure what to say, but I figured I'd better erase any doubts he might have. "I'm sorry," I said, "but my heart belongs to someone else." As I feared, he asked me who that might be. "Brom Bones," I said, and for the first time I knew it was true.

Notice how the change in point of view takes the focus away from Ichabod. How does it affect the mood of the story? Is it still funny? Students could be asked to work

FIGURE 9.4 *Character Analysis Chart*

Type of information	What character says about self	What other characters say	What the narrator says	What the character's actions show
Looks			Tall, lanky, narrow shoulders, long arms and legs, hands dangling out of sleeves, feet like shovels, baggy clothes, authoritative voice, green eyes, huge ears, spindle neck	
Likes (dislikes)		Easy life	Eating! Listening to and telling ghost stories	Money and land, Katrina van Tassel, parties, being better than others, dislikes fighting and embarrassment
Traits		Great learning	Poor, believed in witches, soft and foolish heart	Can be mean, superstitious, greedy, cowardly, unskillful rider, proud

alone or in pairs to rewrite various incidents of the story from Ichabod's point of view or Brom's or to become an all-knowing (omniscient) narrator who tells what all the characters are thinking, feeling, and doing. What, for instance, is Brom Bones doing while Ichabod is plodding along in the dark terrified that he might encounter the Headless Horseman? Activities such as inferring or rewriting can be challenging for English language learners. The teacher will want to provide scaffolding for this activity. Further, the beginning and intermediate level students may be paired with students with more language ability.

Style is the product of the author's choices about how to use language. Preferences for long words or short sentences are part of style, and so is the decision to whether to use formal or informal language or figures of speech. Allen (2000) suggests that students can learn about different language registers by "translating" slang into more formal language. Similarly, students can learn about the elements of an author's style by working with a partner to "translate" a short passage into their own language. Like the "behind the scenes" features on DVDs, viewing literature as the product of an author's choices provides an additional dimension to the experience of reading. Students can gain appreciation for these choices by considering questions such as these:

- Is the story told in order or by using flashbacks?
- Are all the major events told, or does the story "skip ahead" in time?
- Does the author use foreshadowing or other "hints" regarding what will come?
- Does the author deliberately mislead the reader to create a surprise?
- Does the author "tell" the ending or leave the reader to figure it out?
- How does the author use comparisons to create pictures in a reader's mind (such as, "big as a mountain" or "like a scarecrow")?
- Are the words the author uses like the ones we use, or are they "old-fashioned"?

Considering Themes

Theme is the aspect of literary writing that makes it more than entertainment. It is also, often, the most difficult aspect of literary analysis for students in the middle grades to grasp. Some students cannot move beyond looking for the "moral of the story" to conceive of theme as the "idea that holds the story together such as a comment about society, human nature, or the human condition" (Lukens, 2003).

One way to help students grasp theme is to raise the issue before they read. Ms. Garcia attempted to do this by using a discussion web to focus her students' attention on issues related to ethics in romance. She might also have guided her students toward the themes of the story through the use of a Three-Level Guide (Vacca & Vacca, 2002) as shown in Figure 9.5 on page 144. One advantage of such a reading guide is that it asks students to *recognize* themes rather than to formulate them. An Anticipation Guide or Reaction Guide (Readence, Bean, & Baldwin, 2000) can also be used to present possible themes either before or after students read so they can consider and discuss them.

Thematic discussions may be particularly important with classic works such as "The Legend of Sleepy Hollow." Such works may be chosen for their literary significance, but reading them will only become a meaningful experience if students are guided to consider the themes that give them personal and social significance.

Ms. Garcia's students could use the items in part three of the Three-Level Guide as well as their previous discussions about characters in order to compare the stereotypical roles of the story's characters to those in their school. They could then reflect on their experiences with being positioned in roles like "nerd," "jock," and "prep" and consider times when they stereotyped others. Finally, students could be guided to consider how their own society is (or is not) like the early American village in the story in terms of attitudes toward "social climbing," marrying for money, and the status of women.

Guiding Literature Study by Bridging Texts

An analytic approach to literature can help readers to make meaning by identifying the various elements within a single literary work and by considering how they work together. Guided literature study can also be approached by asking students to consider comparisons, contrasts, and connections among literary works or between literary and nonliterary texts.

FIGURE 9.5   *Three-Level Guide for "The Legend of Sleepy Hollow"*

I. Mark each item below that is directly in the story. (Be prepared to show where.) Leave the line blank if the item is false or unstated.

_____   **1.** Ichabod Crane is a poor schoolteacher.

_____   **2.** Ichabod is better educated than practically everyone else in the village.

_____   **3.** People in the village, including Ichabod, believe in ghosts and other superstitions.

_____   **4.** Ichabod decides to avoid Brom because he has challenged him to fight.

II. Mark each item below that you think is probably true, based on what happens in the story.

_____   **1.** Ichabod wants to marry Katrina for her money.

_____   **2.** Ichabod sees himself as superior to other people in the village.

_____   **3.** Brom is a bully who enjoys humiliating Ichabod.

_____   **4.** Katrina uses Ichabod to make Brom jealous.

III. Mark those statements below that you think the author might make, based on what happens in this story.

_____   **1.** People who are "social climbers," trying to be better than others, deserve to be punished.

_____   **2.** People should marry for love, not for money.

_____   **3.** It is easy to take advantage of the fears of superstitious people.

_____   **4.** Some people are just "born losers" who don't seem able to make others like or respect them.

This approach is sometimes called *bridging* (Brown & Stephens, 1995; Bushman & Haas, 2001). Bridging may involve using a work of young adult literature to prepare students for reading a classic work. For example, students might read a young adult novel about the European Holocaust of the 1940s such as *Number the Stars* (Lowry, 1990) as preparation for reading and performing the play, *The Diary of Anne Frank* (Goodrich & Hackett, 1956). Knickerbocker and Rycik (2002) point out that bridging might also work in the other direction. Students may be asked to reinterpret a classic text that they have read during guided literature study by making connections from the young adult literature they read later.

Brown and Stephens (1995) suggest a variety of other ways to create bridges between literary works, including the following:

- **Author study** allows students to note tendencies in one author's style, narrative strategy, and themes. Students can also enrich their reading by making inferences about the author's experiences, concerns, and beliefs and recording their speculations in a "reading the author" log. They might then do research to confirm their theories by exploring authors' websites, reference works, or autobiographical works. Gary Paulsen (2001), for example, has directly explained how the events in his "Brian" survival stories reflect his life experiences. Using the Internet for author studies provides equal access to technological experiences for many English language learners who may not have had the opportunity to use computers prior to entering school.

- **Genre study.** A genre is defined by similarities in structure, purpose, and content. Genre units can be organized by guiding students to read several works and to analyze similarities and differences. They might be guided, for example, to answer the question "What makes a poem?" by reading several poems and noting the kinds of language used, the way lines are arranged on the page, the subject matter, and the emotion being conveyed. Genre study can also be done with a much narrower category of literature such as "novels set during the Great Depression." Students could be asked to compare and contrast the conflicts, feelings, and changes experienced by the main characters in Christopher Paul Curtis's (1999) *Bud, Not Buddy* and Richard Peck's (2002) *A Year Down Yonder.*

- **Theme study.** The concept of theme can be easier to grasp when students see a particular theme explored in more than one work, especially works from different genres. In the previous chapter, for instance, the theme of "flying too high" was approached through a speech about the Columbia disaster and the poem "High Flight." The same theme could be further explored through the Greek myth of Icarus who perished by flying too close to the sun. Theme study should focus on some universal aspect of the human condition that is frequently explored in literature. This may be phrased as a statement or as a question such as, "Does having high hopes and big dreams lead to tragedy or to triumph?" Literary works then become the means to "answer" the question.

Bridging with Media

Adolescents live in a world that is saturated with media that comprise an important part of their nonschool lives (Luke & Elkins, 1998). Their interpretation and appreciation of literature can be strengthened by connecting the literary texts they read to the media "texts" they hear and view. The scenario that begins this chapter illustrates how a teacher may use popular media such as an old television series as a bridge to a challenging literary text. Other possibilities abound. Both the classic story "The Monkey's Paw" (Jacobs, 1902) and the poem "The Raven" (Poe, 1845), for instance, have been subjects for parody on *The Simpsons.* Students can be invited to bring in lyrics from popular songs to illustrate literary themes or the uses of poetic language.

Teachers can show all or part of feature films as bridges to literary works, either before or after students read. They may, however, need to reconsider the common practice of "rewarding" students with a film version of a book they have just read and asking them to find differences between the print and film versions—usually for the purpose of showing that the film is inferior. Teasley and Wilder (1997) point out that teachers need to respect both books and films as different means for conveying stories. They suggest pairing a book with a related film according to literary elements such as setting, genre, or theme.

Scenes from the classic films *Grapes of Wrath* or *Paper Moon* might, for example, be paired with the Depression era novel *Out of the Dust* (Hesse, 1997). A scene from the film *The Karate Kid* could be used along with the novel *A Single Shard* (Park, 2001) to explore how an old man can be a mentor to a young man who is trying to master a craft.

The visuals that films provide can be especially beneficial for English language learners. Although they should not be substituted for literature, films can provide a backdrop for understanding. English language learners may be more likely to understand the literary concepts if they are familiar with the story.

Learning New Words during Guided Literature Study

The principles and techniques for vocabulary learning that were discussed in Chapter 8 also apply to guided literature study. There, are, however, some special opportunities for learning words when students are reading literary texts. Yopp and Yopp (1992) recommend the use of *polar opposites* as a means to consider character traits. When using polar opposites, students consider where a particular character falls along a continuum between two antonyms. Doing so can simultaneously encourage a richer understanding of the characters and reinforce the meanings of the words that are used to describe them. Figure 9.6 shows how this technique can be applied to the characters from "Sleepy Hollow."

Polar opposites can also be used to draw comparisons between literary works. For instance, the settings of several literary works could be placed along a continuum from "isolated" to "cosmopolitan," and the mood could be rated from "melancholy" to "cheerful."

Accommodating Differences during Guided Literature Study

Guided literature study frequently involves reading works written for adults rather than young adolescents. Teachers may rightly be concerned about students who will struggle with such material, but avoiding difficult material may not be the answer. Jago (2000) argues that it is "antidemocratic" to deprive any students of the opportunity to engage with an important part of their society's heritage. She opposes limiting readers to contemporary or adolescent literature or substituting comic book adaptations or film versions of classic literature. She also cautions against substituting teacher read-alouds for students' direct experience with the text. If teachers agree with these arguments, they will need to consider how to accommodate differences in language and reading ability.

Although Jago (2000) opposes replacing student reading with teacher read-alouds, many literacy educators disagree. Graves and Liang (2002) identify reading aloud (or providing a recorded version of the text) as an appropriate choice for the "during reading" segment of their Scaffolded Reading Experience framework, and Combs (2003) discusses literature study almost entirely within the context of read-aloud routines. The shared reading approach we discussed in Chapter 7 may be particularly appropriate as an accommodation strategy because students are engaged with the original text rather than an adaptation,

FIGURE 9.6 *Polar Opposites for "The Legend of Sleepy Hollow"*

Directions: Think about the traits of your assigned character and mark an "X" in the right place on each line below. Jot down a brief explanation so you are prepared to discuss your decisions. **Example:** For Brom Bones, you might mark the line like this:

leader _____X_____ follower

Explanation: *He is the leader of a gang, but he acts the same as everyone else in town.*

Assigned character _____

CONTENT _____ DISSATISFIED

Explanation _____

_____

OPTIMISTIC _____ PESSIMISTIC

Explanation _____

_____

SELFISH _____ CONSIDERATE

Explanation _____

_____

BOLD _____ TIMID

Explanation _____

_____

ACTIVE _____ PASSIVE

Explanation _____

_____

and they are following along with the print rather than only listening (Allen, 2000). In many cases, a read-aloud may be the only way a beginning or intermediate English language learner can read through a text.

Wilhelm (1997) argues that drama should be a regular part of students' reading experience because it allows all students, including reluctant readers, to construct meaning actively by visualizing and imagining beyond the words on the page. In particular, he suggests that students construct a "tableau," a sort of dramatic snapshot in which they portray a particular moment from the story. Reader's theater asks students to portray a story with their voices but without movement. Wilhelm suggested that students can also work in groups to develop ways of acting out a part of the text that is read aloud by someone else. This kind of acting can help English language learners to develop and express their understandings of literature.

Readence, Bean, and Baldwin (2000) discuss accommodation as a middle course between undifferentiated whole class instruction and total individualization. The following suggestions are adapted from their recommendations:

- **Slice the reading into manageable segments.** Ms. Garcia was doing this kind of "slicing" when she had students focus first on the setting, then on the main character, and so on. Even if they do not read and do the activities for every segment of the story, all students have some opportunity to engage with the text. The teacher will determine the reading level of all of her students including English language learners and will plan lessons according to their capabilities.
- **Slice the scope of the assignment.** Most of Ms. Garcia's students gathered information about all three of the characters as a homework assignment before working with a small group to complete a character chart. Some students were required to gather information only about the character they would discuss in their small group. Similarly, some students could be assigned only to complete a Three-Level Guide and to prepare to discuss thematic statements while others were asked to use the statements in the guide to write an essay about themes.
- **Provide additional guidance.** One of the simplest ways to help readers is to give them page or paragraph numbers to show them where to find information. Another method is providing a "reading road map" (Wood, 1988), that tells students where to read quickly, when to slow down, and where to pay particular attention. Such road maps may also include focus questions or explanations of difficult terms keyed to particular pages in the reading.
- **Use small groups for a variety of purposes** such as debating, gathering information, or brainstorming. It is important that small-group tasks are structured so that every student is able to make a contribution. This may involve offering an opinion, contributing information, recording the group's ideas, or using the text to confirm answers. Students may be able to participate more fully in small groups when they are given the time and extra help they need to prepare for the group task. Students might, for example, be required to come to the group with notes or a "rough draft."

The teacher may need to assign appropriate tasks specifically for English language learners so that they can be a part of the group work. English language learners or students with limited writing ability may be talented at drawing, or they may be able to listen carefully and report the group's findings to the class.

Summary

Guided literature study, like all classroom literacy routines, offers particular strengths and limitations. Students are given little opportunity to choose the texts they will read or the activities they will carry out. On the other hand, teacher guidance can provide students, including English language learners, access to literary texts that can enrich their lives. Lukens (2003) summarizes the importance of guided literature study:

> Literature at its best gives both pleasure and understanding. It explores the nature of human beings, the condition of humankind. . . . What are people like? Why are they like that? What do they need? What makes them do what they do? . . . The answers, or mere glimpses of the answers to these questions, are found in the literary elements of plot, character, point of view, setting, tone, and style of an imaginative work; together, they constitute literature. (p.9)

In this chapter, we presented several ways to support students' understanding of literature. Through guided literature study, students can not only deepen their appreciation of story elements such as plot and setting, but increase their vocabulary as well. We explored the issue of using classic literature and suggested accommodations that can be made for students who find the text difficult.

Responding to Reading

Construct a discussion web using one of these statements:

- All students including English language learners should have the opportunity to read and discuss the classic literature of their culture.
- It is unfair to allow some students to do easier or shorter assignments than others.
- Literature is meant to be experienced, not studied.

If possible, use the web to discuss the statement with classmates. You might also use the web to explore the issue on your own by listing to as many arguments as you can on each side of the issue and then writing your conclusion.

Key Terms to Know and Use

discussion web	social significance	theme
plot	accommodation	three-level guides
characterization	bridging	polar opposites
literary significance	narrative strategy	
developmental significance	style	

Possible Sentences

Use two or three key terms in each of four sentences that describe your understanding of this chapter. Then, write two questions that you still have after completing the reading. Discuss these questions with your classmates.

Beyond the Book

- Examine a literature anthology that is intended for students in the middle grades. Identify the stories or poems that meet the criteria of having literary significance, developmental significance, and social significance. Try to find both classic and contemporary works. Share your findings in writing or discussion.

- Graves and Liang (2002) argue that teachers should not need to design totally original activities for every literature selection their students read. They describe a website that provides plans for Scaffolded Reading Experiences that are designed to support readers before, during, and after reading a literary text. Visit that site at www.onlinereadingresources.com and download one of the sample SRE plans. How does it support each of the goals for Guided Literature Study listed in this chapter?

References

Allen, J. (2000). *Yellow brick roads: Shared and guided paths to independent reading* 4–12. Portland, ME: Stenhouse.

Alvermann, D. E. (1991). The discussion web: A graphic aid for learning across the curriculum. *Reading Teacher, 45*(2), 92–99.

Atwell, N. (1998). *In the middle: New understandings about writing, reading, and learning.* Portsmouth, NH: Heinemann.

Brown, J. E., & Stephens, E. C. (1995). *Teaching young adult literature: Sharing the connection.* Belmont, CA: Wadsworth.

Bushman, J. H., & Haas, K. P. (2001). *Using young adult literature in the English classroom.* Upper Saddle River, NJ: Prentice Hall.

Combs, M. (2003). *Readers and writers in the middle grades.* Upper Saddle River, NJ: Prentice Hall.

Curtis, C. P. (1999). *Bud not Buddy.* New York: Delacorte Press.

Goodrich, F., & Hackett, A. (1956). *The diary of Anne Frank.* New York: Random House.

Graves, M. F., & Liang, L. A. (2002). On-line resources for fostering understanding and higher-level thinking. In D. L. Shallert, C. M. Fairbanks, J. Worthy, B. Moloch, & J. Hoffman (Eds.), *51st Yearbook of the National Reading Conference* (pp. 204–215). Oak Creek, WI: National Reading Conference.

Hesse, K. (1997). *Out of the dust.* New York: Scholastic.

Hipple, T. (2000). With themes for all: The universality of the young adult novel. In V. R. Monseau & G. M. Salvner (Eds.), *Reading their world: The young adult novel in the classroom* (pp. 1–14). Portsmouth, NH: Heinemann.

Irving, W. (1998). The legend of sleepy hollow. In C. Neider (Ed.), *The complete stories of Washington Irving.* New York: Da Capo Press.

Jacobs, W. W. (1902). The monkey's paw. In *The lady of the barge,* 6th ed. (1906), New York: Harper & Brothers.

Jago, C. (2000). *With rigor for all: Teaching classics to contemporary students.* Portland, ME: Calendar Islands.

Knickerbocker, J. L., & Rycik, J. A. (2002). Growing into literature: Adolescent literacy interpretation and appreciation. *Journal of Adolescent and Adult Literacy, 46*(3), 196–208.

Lowry, L. (1990). *Number the stars.* New York: Houghton Mifflin.

Luke, A., & Elkins, J. (1998). Reinventing literacy in new times. *Journal of Adolescent and Adult Literacy, 42*(1), 4–7.

Lukens, R. J. (2003). *A critical handbook of children's literature* (7th ed.). Boston: Allyn & Bacon.

Park, L. S. (2001). *A single shard.* New York: Clarion Books.

Paulson, G. (2001). *Guts: The true stories behind hatchet and the Brian books.* New York: Delacorte Press.

Peck, R. (2002). *A year down yonder.* New York: Penguin Putnam.

Poe, E. A. (1845). The raven. In *The American review: A whig journal of politics, literature, art, and science, Vol. I.* New York: Wiley & Putnam.

Readence, J. E., Bean, T.W., & Baldwin, R. S. (2000). *Content area literacy: An integrated approach.* Dubuque, IA: Kendall-Hunt.

Teasley, A. B., & Wilder, A. (1997). *Reel conversations: Reading films with young adults.* Portsmouth, NH: Heinemann.

Vacca, R. T., & Vacca, J. L. (2002). *Content area reading: Literacy and learning across the curriculum* (7th ed.). Boston: Allyn and Bacon.

Wilhelm, J. D. (1997). *You gotta BE the book: Teaching engaged and reflective reading with adolescents.* Urbana, IL: National Council of Teachers of English.

Wood, K. (1988). A guide to subject matter material. *Middle School Journal, 19*(1), 24–26.

Yopp, R. H., & Yopp, H. K. (1992). *Literature-based reading activities.* Boston: Allyn and Bacon.

10

Independent Reading: Literature Circles and Reading Workshops

Activating Prior Knowledge and Making Connections

Molly, Candace, Jose, and Blake were sitting with their desks pulled into a tight circle. They each held a copy of the novel *Wringer* (Spinelli, 1997). On each of their desks, they also had a spiral notebook and a printed list of "Suggestions for Book Discussions." During a brief whole-class meeting at the beginning of class, their teacher, Mr. Douglas, had reviewed some basic procedures such as setting a turn-taking plan so that everyone was invited to speak. He encouraged English language learners to share cultural experiences as they related to the reading, which provided enriching discussion for all students. He had also suggested that since this was the first day for discussion for these groups, they might consider why the first part of their book was or was not an effective beginning.

The students who were reading *Wringer* had previously agreed that they would read the first five chapters. Now they decided that they would each say the one thing they most wanted to say about those chapters, and then everyone would discuss whether those chapters were an effective beginning. Some of them opened their notebooks to pages where they had turned down corners. Others turned over their books at a certain page. Molly began by saying, "I knew from when we picked the book what a wringer was, but when he had the dream in the first chapter about holding a pigeon and everyone yelling 'Wring it,' it was still a surprise. "It seemed like just a nightmare, but I knew from the introduction that, in this book anyway, it was real."

The group members nodded, and José said, "I know. It was so weird, especially the part about the pigeon having orange eyes. I don't think that pigeons in Mexico have orange eyes. Is that true?" No one knew, so José went on. "I just couldn't believe that Palmer was thrilled with the kids giving him an old cigar butt and a sock with holes for his birthday. Or that he liked getting named Snots. That's disgusting."

Mr. Douglas had come to sit in with the group. He wondered if anyone would offer an explanation for Palmer's behavior. He was tempted to raise the question himself, but he decided to just sit and listen as Candace took her turn. "I really hated that kid Beans, and I

think he's going to be real trouble because even Palmer's Mom said so. I marked this part."
She opened the book to a part that she had marked with a sticky note, and read

> "He's a sneak and a trouble-maker," she had said. "He's got a mean streak." And she was
> right. But he was also the leader of all the kids on the street, at least the ones under 10 years
> old. It had always been that way. Beans was boss as surely and naturally as any king who
> ever sat upon a throne.

Blake said, "I wrote something about that." He turned to a page in his notebook with
the corner turned down and read, "Palmer is kind of pathetic. He wants Beans and the other
guys to like him so much that he lets them take away his new soccer ball and call him Snots.
I think all the boys are afraid of making Beans mad, but Beans is not really much of a
friend."

Mr. Douglas made a few notes on a sheet attached to his clipboard and moved on to
another group. After a while, he asked students to stop their conversations and spend some
time writing in their notebooks about how their discussion had added to or changed their
understanding of the book. Then he made lists on chart paper as the class discussed characteristics that make the beginnings of books effective or ineffective. He planned to raise
the question of whether students had identified a protagonist (a "good guy") and an antagonist ("bad guy") in their books during a mini-lesson at the beginning of the next class.

In this chapter, we will present some of the ways in which teachers can help students
in the middle grades to read independently through routines such as the Literature Circle
described above.

Before you continue to read the chapter, consider the following questions:
1. How can you tell that the students in this group understand the book?
2. How do you think Mr. Douglas has guided the class so that the groups know what to discuss
   and how to do so?
3. Why did Mr. Douglas decide not to ask his question about Palmer's behavior?
4. What do you think Mr. Douglas was writing on his clipboard?

Goals for Independent Literacy Routines

The previous chapters have illustrated how teachers can structure successful engagements
by carefully choosing texts and designing activities that are based on their knowledge about
reading, about texts, and about young adolescents. In this chapter, we will examine independent literacy routines such as literature circles and reading workshops. These independent reading routines are designed to complement the teacher-directed routines as part of an
overall program to support young adolescents' literacy development.

All independent reading routines share an emphasis on student choice, self-monitoring, independent use of strategies, and responsibility for learning. Although these routines
go by many names, we have grouped them together under the two headings of literature

circles and reading workshops. As we define them, the two differ in the amount of collaboration they entail, the range of materials that are used, and the mix of learning activities they include, but both are designed to address similar goals:

1. Reading from a range of authentic material to meet personal interests and purposes.
2. Becoming part of a community of young adult readers.
3. Developing independence in using strategies for comprehending and learning new words.
4. Becoming aware of reading preferences and ways of finding interesting reading material.
5. Becoming increasingly willing and able to engage in listening, talking, and writing about reading experiences.

Reader Response Activities for Independent Reading

Reader response activities play an important role in independent literacy routines. As we explained in Chapter 2, reader response theory begins with the assumption that each reader will create a unique interpretation of a particular text because each reader has a unique background of experiences—with reading and with life. This important insight about reading has led to many activities in which students reflect on their personal "transaction" with a text (Rosenblatt, 1978). Students are often asked, for instance, to keep some sort of journal of thoughts and feelings about their reading. Beginning to intermediate level English language learners may have difficulties with a lot of writing in English due to lack of English vocabulary. However during this time, they may find three of their favorite lines from the reading selection and copy those into the journal. They may also be encouraged to write responses in their primary language and then share their ideas in discussions with peers.

Responding to reading is not the same as *reacting* to reading. Reactions happen automatically, but response requires readers to step back from their initial feelings about their reading and take a "spectator's stance" (Galda, 1990). They do so by using language to reflect on the characteristics in themselves and in the text that produced a particular reaction. The ability to do this kind of reflection develops with experience and with the guidance of teachers. Through the thinking they model, the expectations they set, and the environment they create, teachers can help students in the middle grades become increasingly sophisticated in their understandings of literature and of themselves.

Researchers and theorists have built on Rosenblatt's (1938, 1978) original concepts about readers and their transactions with texts and have identified many categories of responses (Langer, 1995; Probst, 1998). Most recently, theorists have emphasized social and cultural aspects of reader response (Watt, 2002), especially the ways in which responses are entwined with the reader's relationships with other people. Readers' interpretations are influenced, for instance, by conversations they have with others (McMahon & Raphael, 1997; Peterson & Eeds, 1990). Responses are also influenced by the social situation in which the reading takes place. Reading a book that is suggested or assigned by a teacher, for instance, is a different experience than reading a book suggested by a peer or one that is actually forbidden by a parent. Finally, reader response is influenced by the reader's role or position in society. Gender, ethnic background, and age are all factors that influence a reader's interpretations and feelings about what a particular book means. In our opening scenario, for instance, the boys might have a much different reaction than the girls to Palmer's willingness to be mistreated by Beans.

Suggestions for responding to the text that incorporate some of these social and cultural insights are shown in Figure 10.1 on page 156. Students can keep such a list close at hand in case they are needed during discussions, and they can use the suggestions as possible topics when writing in literature logs. Teachers may occasionally choose an item from the list as a focus for modeling or discussion.

Reader response activities may certainly include elements of literary analysis or discussions of comprehension strategies, but their focus is on describing what happened when a particular reader got together with a particular text. By carefully drawing out student responses, teachers gain a greater understanding of how each reader constructs meaning and then gently assist that reader to see new possibilities. Teachers may want to provide sentence stems for the English language learners in order to help them with the discussion and with the writing activities.

Literature Circles: Characteristics and Organization

The terms *literature circle* and *book club* are often used interchangeably, and we will do so in this chapter. Most of their characteristics are illustrated by the scenario that opened this chapter. Notice that the students in the group all chose to read *Wringer* (Spinelli, 1997), while other groups were reading different titles. They were given class time for reading and preparing for their group discussion. They were given responsibility for deciding what they would talk about and how they would manage the discussion. The teacher functioned mainly as a facilitator, setting up basic procedures, monitoring the group's functioning, and watching for issues and ideas that should be addressed by the whole class. The teacher also made sure to provide instruction specifically for English language learners when needed.

Daniels (2001) insists that students' "voice and choice" are the key ingredients of literature circles. He cautions against "terminology drift" that might allow any sort of small group reading routine to be called a literature circle—even when the texts were assigned and the activities were entirely directed by the teacher. He acknowledges, however, that there are many ways for teachers to organize these necessary ingredients in order to support students' independent reading and discussion. McMahon and Raphael (1997), for instance, developed a popular book club routine that is organized around five components:

- **Opening Community Share** is a whole-class meeting focused on setting the stage for the day's events. The teacher may model a new reading strategy or present new information related to a theme that is common to the books the students are reading. Students may also be invited to recap the previous day's story events.
- **Reading** for at least 15 minutes should be part of every day, and students should read from texts that have genuine content that relates to their interests and helps to build their knowledge. Reading for middle grades students is generally silent, but it can include partner reading or reading along with an audio recording.

FIGURE 10.1 *Some Suggestions for Writing or Discussions*

What was the context for reading?
- If the book was assigned, how did that fact affect your reading?
- If you chose it, what made you pick this rather than something else?
- Did the time and place where you typically read the book make reading easier or harder?
- Did the time and place where you typically read the book make reading more enjoyable or less?

What were your feelings while reading?
- Did reading this work bring back memories of events and experiences in your own life?
- What particular aspects of the work did you most enjoy?
- What did you least enjoy?
- Did you ever feel confused or frustrated?

What is your interpretation of the work?
- How was this work like or unlike other things you have read?
- What will you remember most from this work?
- What particular parts of the work do you think are most important for understanding it?
- Did this work match your expectations, or did it surprise or confuse you?
- What do you think is the significance of this work? Is it more than entertainment?

How did you "read" the author?
- What do you know about the author's life and work?
- What can you guess about this author's knowledge, values, and experiences?
- How do you think the work was influenced by the author's ethnic background or by whether the author is male or female, rich or poor, young or old?
- What effect do you think the author intended to have on readers of this work?
- Do you think the author had someone like you in mind as the audience for this work, or someone with different knowledge, values, and experiences than yours?

How did you "read" yourself?
- What characteristics about you do you think influenced your reaction to this work?
- How much do you think your responses were influenced by your own ethnic background, age, gender, experiences, or values?
- Do you think the experience of reading this work has changed you in any way?

What were the effects of the discussion?
- Did your partners bring up ideas that were new to you?
- Did you bring up ideas that were new to them?
- Did you change your mind about the meaning of the work or parts of it?
- Did you go back and reread?

What are your plans for the future?
- Do you think you will read other works like this book?
- Do you think you will read other works by the same author?
- Do you think you might reread this work one day?

- **Writing** includes both daily writing in a reading log or more focused writing using "think sheets." Occasionally, students may write essays or content area reports by engaging in a guided process of planning, drafting, revising, and editing. This writing is published to reach an audience within—or sometimes beyond—the classroom.
- **Engaging in Book Club discussions** that are led by students and guided by their reading log entries is the heart of the book club experience as students introduce ideas from their reading logs and clarify their meanings in response to questions and comments from others.
- **Closing Community Share** focuses particularly on connecting across book club groups. Students may share ideas, responses, or confusions they have experienced so that the whole group can discuss appropriate fix-up strategies. By listening to the members of other groups, students are able to make connections between texts.

Guiding Discussions in Literature Circles

For literature circles to function successfully, teachers need to communicate clearly the purpose and the process of student-led discussions. English language learners at all levels should be included in these discussions. Roles can be assigned and taught, so that they feel valued and included in the class, no matter the language ability. In the book club routine described above, students learn about the kinds of responses they can make and the kinds of book talk that are valued during the Community Share times. McMahon and Raphael (1997) also suggest the use of "think sheets" that are similar to the literary analysis activities we presented in Chapter 9. These sheets guide and extend the kinds of responses that are included in student-led discussions.

Daniels (2001) suggests a way to guide book discussions by adapting the cooperative learning practice of assigning specific roles or tasks to each member of the group—including English language learners. Roles are meant to ensure that each student has a necessary, unique, and clearly defined responsibility to the group. Daniels identified four basic roles that students could take during literature circles and created "role sheets" to ensure that each student could contribute to their group's discussions.

Figure 10.2 shows the role sheet for the Literary Luminary, who may also be called the "Passage Master." The Connector role involves relating elements in the text to the reader's own ideas, feelings, and experiences with life and with other texts. The Questioner is responsible for noting points of confusion or points that aroused curiosity. The Illustrator is responsible for creating pictures or some other form of graphic that captures the meaning of the reading.

Many additional roles have been suggested including a Summarizer, a Word Wizard, and a Scene Setter (Daniels, 2001). Each of these roles focuses one reader's attention on a specific aspect of reading that is desirable for *all* readers. Daniels intended the role sheets to be a temporary scaffold for students to use until they learned how to talk about a text in ways that would add to their understanding and enjoyment. Too often, however, teachers have continued to use role sheets long after their purpose has been served, probably as a way to assess students. Daniels noted the common result:

> In some classrooms, the role sheets did become a hindrance, a drain—sometimes a virtual albatross around the neck of book club meetings. What had been designed as a temporary

support device to help peer-led discussion groups get started could actually undermine the activity it was meant to support. (p. 13)

Teachers must be careful that assignments do not jeopardize the goals of reading engagement and reflection. Some of the concerns Daniels raised can apply to literature logs, for instance (Cherniwchan, 2002). Writing about their reactions to reading can be a powerful vehicle for students to reflect about literature and their own reading. If, however, students are writing in order to "prove" that they have done their work, the literature log becomes no different from fill-in-the blank questions or book reports. Even online discus-

FIGURE 10.2 *Sample Role Sheet for Literature Circles*

Literary Luminary

Name _____

Group _____

Book _____

Assignment page _____ to page _____

Literary Luminary: Your job is to locate a few special sections or quotations in the text for your group to talk over. The idea is to help people go back to some especially interesting, powerful, funny, puzzling, or important sections of the reading and think about them more carefully. As you decide which passages or paragraphs are worth going back to, make a note about why you picked each one. Then jot down some plans for how they should be shared. You can read passages aloud yourself, ask someone else to read them, or have people read them silently and then discuss.

Page Number and Paragraph	Reason for Choosing	Plan for Discussion

Source: Daniels, H. (2002). *Literature Circles; Voice and Choice in Book Clubs and Reading Groups* (2nd ed.). Portland, ME: Stenhouse, p. 109.

sions and creative products can become obstacles if students perceive them as just another school task that is done to please a teacher and get a grade. As Peterson and Eeds (1990) point out, the essence of literature circles is the opportunity to participate enthusiastically in a "grand conversation" about literature.

> Meaning evolves in dialogue through heartfelt responding that seeks to cooperatively disclose meaning. People in dialogue need each other. They collaborate one with the other, striving to comprehend ideas, problems, events, and feelings. Working together, partners in dialogue call one another forth as they seek to comprehend the world. (p. 14)

Written assignments, guide sheets, and other forms of teacher guidance should be used as scaffolds to help students achieve this kind of dialogue. Teacher read-alouds are also an opportunity for teaching students to engage in "book talk." By inviting reactions, questions, and connections immediately after students have heard a passage, the teacher can affirm the value of students' responses in a low-risk situation and point out particularly valuable features of the class discussion. English language learners benefit from teacher read alouds. The teacher can facilitate questioning and response so that beginning level students can participate. For example the teacher may write the question on the board and then ask, "Was Cinderella the antagonist (bad person—frown face) or the protagonist (good person—happy face)?" The beginning English language learner would then point to the answer and the teacher would assist in pronouncing the word.

Whole class literature circles provide a similar opportunity. The teacher can target specific kinds of responses (such as associations and connections), and then give students an opportunity to prepare a few responses that they can share with the class. The teacher may either monitor the discussion to praise appropriate responses or take an occasional turn as a participant in the discussion to model the desired language.

Managing Literature Circles

Literature circles, like the other literacy routines, use a set of procedures that are designed to support particular kinds of literacy activities. In this case, the particular focus is on conversations about real books that help students clarify their thoughts and feelings and make them part of a community of readers. To support these conversations, teachers need to create an environment that is orderly yet flexible, student led but teacher monitored, and comfortable yet challenging. A tall order! The following suggestions point out some of the ways in which teachers can establish and maintain effective small-group discussions.

Selecting Materials. The reading material selected for literature circles may be either fiction or nonfiction, but it should be read as literature—with the heart as well as the head—rather than as information to be remembered. Books should be easy enough that most students can read them independently. It is certainly appropriate to provide a range of length and difficulty, but students should not, as a general rule, be assigned to read a particular book because it is at their level. For students who struggle to read any age-appropriate book, teachers can provide accommodations such as listening to a recorded version for some or all of the book. This may be especially necessary for English language learners.

The potential of a book to engage readers is perhaps the single most important characteristic of books used in literature circles. Book talk will not occur unless the book provides something to talk about. Spinelli's *Wringer* (1997), for instance, raises issues about peer pressure and the ethical treatment of animals that can intrigue, puzzle, and outrage young adolescent readers. As Roser, Strecker, and Martinez (2000) observe, "The better the book, the more gripping its plot, the more gray its choices, the more ethical dilemmas pull the reader in, the better the book talk" (p. 297).

Forming Groups. Groups of five or six students are typical for literature circles, but a major advantage of smaller groups is that each person has more opportunity to speak at length. Larger groups, on the other hand, allow a wider range of viewpoints and ideas. The total number of students and the amount of time available are important considerations in deciding group size because the teacher must be able to get around to each group on a regular basis. The size of the room is also a factor. If at all possible, groups should have clearly defined spaces with enough room between them so that students will not hear other groups. This may necessitate fewer and larger groups.

Assigning students to groups is often a worrisome issue for teachers. If students are allowed to choose groups, they may only interact with their friends, and some students may feel ostracized. On the other hand, if students are systematically separated from their friends, some of the potential enjoyment of literature discussions may be lost. The best solution may involve a careful balance between choice and assignment. For example, the teacher might allow students to choose which of three titles they will read and then carefully select subgroups for each title. Another approach is to assign the students to groups and then allow each group to choose which of the available titles they will read.

Group membership should rotate enough during the course of the year so that teachers can ensure that students are hearing the ideas of a wide range of their classmates. If there are several levels of English language learners, teachers may want to group an advanced learner with a beginner. Beginning level students will feel much less anxious and more willing to participate if there is a person who can provide primary language support.

Setting Guidelines for Participation. Modeling effective book talk and choosing engaging books will go a long way toward establishing student-directed literature circles, but you will still want to establish guidelines for appropriate participation. Clearly stated expectations can head off problems and help you to communicate the serious purpose of literature circles. The following guidelines may be appropriate not only for literature circles but for all small group discussions:

- Students should sit so that they do not have to speak loudly to be heard.
- Students' attention should be focused only on the members of their own group.
- Everyone in the group should be specifically invited to speak.
- The group should follow an agenda—either one set by the teacher or one that they create.
- Students may disagree with the statements of others, but they must do so respectfully.

- Comments such as "good point" and "I agree" should be a regular part of the group's talk.

As you and your students gain experience with the process of literature discussion you may collaborate to develop additional guidelines by considering the questions, "What kind of talk encourages people to share what they think and feel?" and "What discourages them?"

Monitoring Process and Progress.   Teachers are often uncomfortable with student-led discussion groups because they feel unsure about whether everyone is engaged in the assigned activities. Procedures for assessment both during and after literature circles need to be developed. By using the class guidelines, a teacher can move from group to group assessing whether group members are participating in appropriate ways. Many teachers award daily points for meeting these guidelines and use those points as one factor in giving grades for literature circles.

Students can be involved in a self-evaluation of the effectiveness of their group and the quality of their own participation. Figure 10.3 on page 162 shows a form that can be used for self-evaluation. Note that the form contains both checklist items and open-ended questions. Self-report items are especially useful for gauging the extent of each student's participation and pointing out groups that may need additional monitoring.

Although we have noted some cautions about using literature logs for evaluation, they can, nevertheless, provide crucial insights into the students' progress in interpreting and appreciating literature. Teachers can read these informal journal entries periodically and respond to them with comments, questions, and focused praise. They can also have assessment conferences in which students are asked to use their literature logs to document their performance in areas such as

- Making connections between books.
- Relating reading to personal experience.
- Identifying characteristics of form and content that make a book interesting.
- Identifying characteristics that make a book difficult or unenjoyable.
- Considering the significance of a book for understanding self and others.

Students can show their understanding and appreciation of the books they read through a variety of products including book reviews. Book reviews differ from book reports in two ways. First, reviews focus more on the reader's thoughts and feelings while reading than they do on displaying knowledge of the text. Second, they are written for an audience other than the teacher. They are meant to be read by other students so that they can make decisions about books they might like to read.

The principles of "voice and choice" suggest that students should be given a range of options for showing what they think about their book. Students may create visual projects such as book jackets, posters, and murals. Working collaboratively on a culminating project may be a logical extension of a group's collaborative book talk. This sort of activity is useful for beginning level English language learners as long as they are given a role. For example, they may be in charge of the title page or drawing the illustrations.

FIGURE 10.3 *Literature Circle Self-Evaluation*

How well did you follow guidelines for participating in literature circles? (Circle the appropriate answer.)

I kept up with my reading	sometimes	usually	always
I was prepared for the discussion	sometimes	usually	always
I brought my book and notes to the discussion	sometimes	usually	always
I participated by offering my ideas about the book	sometimes	usually	always
I reacted constructively to the ideas of others	sometimes	usually	always

Comments:

What kinds of responses did you make most often? (Circle the appropriate answer.)

Made connections with other books	rarely	sometimes	often
Made connections to my experiences	rarely	sometimes	often
Pointed out favorite parts	rarely	sometimes	often
Brought up questions for the group to discuss	rarely	sometimes	often
Noted parts that confused me	rarely	sometimes	often
Made judgments about the characters	rarely	sometimes	often
Discussed believability or usefulness	rarely	sometimes	often
Made judgments about the organization or style	rarely	sometimes	often
Discussed the author's purpose for writing	rarely	sometimes	often

Others:

Describe a time when your group brought up some ideas that were new to you.

Describe a time when you brought up an idea that was new to some of the group.

Other comments:

Reading Workshops

An excited buzz could be heard from the students in Mr. Ling's seventh-grade reading class as they moved about the classroom examining stacks of glossy magazines. Some of them were back issues from the school library such as *Model Railroader* and *The Smithsonian*. Others had been contributed by the students' families or by teachers in the building. These included *Vogue, Time, Newsweek, Sports Illustrated,* and *Popular Science*.

"You have five more minutes to browse," Mr. Ling announced loudly. "Remember that you may take as many as five different magazines back to your seat in addition to any you brought from home. Choose carefully, because you will not be allowed to come back to exchange them once we start reading."

When time for browsing was over, students gradually made their way back to their seats, and Mr. Ling reminded them that the next 25 minutes would be quiet reading and writing time. Students began to leaf through the magazines until they found a particular article that they wanted to read. From time to time, they stopped to fill out a Magazine Survey Form (see Figure 10.4). They continued this process until Mr. Ling instructed them to

FIGURE 10.4 *Magazine Survey Form*

Magazine title: _____ Date(s) of the issue(s) you examined: _____

According to the masthead information at the front, how often is the magazine published? _____

What is the price for a subscription? _____ For a single issue? _____

According to the Table of Contents, what are some of the "Departments" or "Regular Features" of the magazine? _____

_____

_____

What are some of the major articles in this issue? _____

_____

_____

_____

Browse through the magazine and find out what products are advertised: _____

_____

_____

_____

Read the article(s) you find most interesting and put a * next to the title(s) in the list above.

Based on your survey, who do you think is the audience for this magazine? (age group? men? women? both?)

What do the editors seem to believe will interest these readers? How do you know?

How likely would you be to browse through this magazine in a waiting room? Explain briefly.

How likely would you be to buy or subscribe to this magazine? Explain briefly.

complete their records of the day's reading and return the magazines they had been using to the class box.

Mr. Ling called the class together for the last 15 minutes and used the overhead projector to show them an article about the growing popularity of snowboarding. It began with a brief story that described how teenage snowboarders were "taking over" a ski resort in Colorado. Mr. Ling introduced the term "vignette" and invited them to tell about any articles they read that day that contained such vignettes. He led the class in a brief discussion of why so many informational articles in magazines begin in this way and told them to watch for more examples during the next day's workshop.

Characteristics and Goals of a Reading Workshop Approach

As the example from Mr. Ling's class illustrates, reading workshops are like literature circles in many ways. Students in a reading workshop have made choices about the material they will read, and they are given time to read in class. They do short writings to record their reading and their responses, and they are expected to share their reading with others. This workshop also differs from literature circles in several respects:

- Students can choose material that is of interest only to them.
- They can read and reread without having to keep pace with other group members.
- They are reading material that is not "literary."
- They can sample a variety of texts without an obligation to finish them.
- The emphasis is on individual reading more than group discussion.

Literature circles and guided literature study both encourage what Peterson and Eeds (1990) call *intensive* reading, the "conscious contemplation of a work of literature" (p. 12). In contrast, a reading workshop provides more opportunities for *extensive* reading during which interpretations are made "without conscious deliberation," and are "guided by the particular interests, background, and experiences [readers] bring to the text" (Peterson & Eeds, 1990, p. 11).

A reading workshop is designed to help students discover a wider world of texts and to learn their own preferences by giving them time to read and access a wide range of texts. Given the opportunity, some students in the middle grades will choose to reread old favorites from earlier years, including picture books. Others will indulge a taste for a particular genre such as science fiction, fantasy, or sports biographies. A supply of nonfiction, including magazines, is especially important. Many adults who think of themselves as nonreaders developed that opinion because of the consistent emphasis that was placed on fiction, at the expense of nonfiction, while they were in school.

As the example at the beginning of this section illustrates, teachers may organize a workshop that focuses students' attention on a particular kind of reading material. For example, students could engage in a poetry workshop, a short story workshop, or a nonfiction workshop. As readers gain extensive experience with a particular kind of text, they have opportunities to inductively "discover" the key characteristics of a genre and the most useful strategies for reading that genre successfully. Even these focused workshops, however, should allow students the widest possible range of choice in the topics, lengths, and difficulty levels of what they read.

Managing a Reading Workshop

A successful reading workshop requires teachers to decide how they are going to organize the use of time and materials and to communicate that information to students. A schedule and a set of procedures that is fairly typical is shown in Figure 10.5 on page 166. Note that the procedures allow students to begin without waiting for the teacher to give directions. The amount of time devoted to mini-lessons, sharing, and writing can be modified to fit the time available, but students should be given 15 to 20 minutes a day of Sustained Silent Reading time so that they have every opportunity to become involved in their reading without interruption.

Using Mini-Lessons to Provide Guidance.   Because teachers want to give students as much reading time as possible, they confine their guidance to conferences and to brief (10–15 minute) "mini-lessons." Atwell (1998) suggests that these brief lessons address four areas:

1. *Workshop procedures* include keeping records or finding certain kinds of books in the classroom library.
2. *Literary craft* includes characteristics of different genres such as the information about the use of "vignettes" in magazine articles that Mr. Ling points out.
3. *Conventions of writing* include pointing out words that exemplify different spelling patterns or the ways in which long sentences are punctuated.
4. *Strategies for reading* include how to choose the appropriate speed for reading or the characteristics of effective oral reading performances.

Materials for Reading Workshops.   Reading workshops in the middle grades require a huge range of materials. A good school library can be a vital resource for meeting students' needs. For the magazine workshop, for example, Mr. Ling borrowed a variety of magazines from the school library as well as collecting back issues that have been "cancelled." A well-stocked library is equally important for other genre units, and a knowledgeable librarian can be invaluable in helping students find books that match their reading abilities and interests.

Materials in a variety of languages are beneficial for English language learners. For instance, Mr. Ling collected back issues of *El Sol,* a magazine designed for teenagers learning Spanish at school. The Spanish-speaking English language learners in his class enjoyed an opportunity to read in their primary language, and they were able to help some of their friends who were learning Spanish.

Workshop teachers also need to build a classroom library. Mr. Ling's classroom is crammed with boxes, crates, and shelves holding periodicals, fiction and nonfiction books, reference works, and student-made texts. He also has a small collection of computer programs such as the *Science Fiction Encyclopedia* (Grolier, 1995) and *Encarta* (Microsoft,

FIGURE 10.5   *Reading Workshop Schedule and Procedures*

Typical Workshop Schedule

Opening journal writing about the previous day's reading or plans for the current day	5–7 minutes
Brief status reports from 5–6 students or whole-class instruction	5–7 minutes
Silent Sustained Reading	15–20 minutes
Reading, Writing, and Sharing	10–15 minutes
Recording and cleanup	3 minutes

When you come into the workshop:

- Have your workshop folder, a pen, and necessary paper on your desk.
- Pick up your book from the class box. If you are starting something new, have several possible choices on hand.
- Check the board for the suggested journal topic, or you may choose a topic from the suggestions in your folder. Begin writing immediately and continue until time is up.

During "status report" time:

- Be prepared to tell titles you have been reading, how much you have read, and your plans for today's reading.
- Listen to what others report so that you can decide if you might like to read the same things. You can add titles that sound good to the *Possible Titles* list in your folder.

During Silent Sustained Reading:

- Do not talk—even to the teacher. You will have the chance in a very short while.
- Stay with the book you have until the end of SSR. You can change for tomorrow.
- You should mark pages you especially like or those with unfamiliar words. You might also want to jot a brief note or two, but SSR is not a time for extensive writing.

After SSR:

- You may want to continue reading.
- You may have a brief conference with the teacher.
- You may want to make notes or meet with other students.
- Be sure to record your reading for the day on the *Reading Log* in your folder.
- If necessary, look for a new book for tomorrow.
- Be sure to put your book for tomorrow in the box for your class on the way out.

1994). These materials have been collected through school-provided funds, donations, and careful purchases from secondhand bookstores and garage sales. For the magazine workshop, Mr. Ling added to his collection by asking students, parents, and his fellow teachers to make donations. He also went to the newsstand and made some very selective purchases using the book *Magazines for Kids and Teens* (Stoll, 1997) as a guide.

Guiding Choice.   Surrounding students with reading material will not help unless they learn how to find the material that matches their abilities and interests. Some materials may be marked to show a difficulty level, but students can learn to make a quick judgment for themselves. One quick way of judging difficulty is the "Five Finger" procedure (Veatch, 1968). Students are directed to read a page and fold down the fingers of one hand every time they come to an unfamiliar word. If they form a fist before the end of the page, they know that the book they are holding may be difficult. Another approach is to adapt the "Goldilocks Strategy" (Ohlhausen & Jepsen, 1992) by creating a rubric that describes what a book is like when it is "too hard," when it is "too easy," or when it is "just right."

Allen (2000) describes a "book pass" activity that she developed to help students sample a range of texts and then to select material that matched their interests and independent reading levels. The basic procedure was to have students sit in a circle and give each student a different book. Students were allowed about 2 minutes to examine their first book by looking at the jacket "blurb," reading the first page and sampling a passage or two from the middle and end. They were then asked to fill in the first line of a form with columns for recording the title, the author, and a comment/rating showing how likely they were to read the book.

After students had examined the first book they were given, the teacher called out "book pass," and they handed their books to the right. The procedures were repeated until all the students had examined all the books. Allen uses a whole-class circle, but the process could easily be adapted to be used with several groups. Students would then have a little more time with each book, although they would also see fewer titles. Allen emphasizes that students should be given a chance to tell about any books they had seen that they were sure they would want to read. They then put the completed Book Pass forms in their workshop folder so they would have a list of possible books to read close at hand throughout the workshop.

A teacher can use the Book Pass form to assess students' ability to find appropriate and interesting reading material. You may want to add a space for indicating the number of pages in each book and one for rating the difficulty and interest level of the book. By examining students' ratings of various material, a teacher can begin to see whether:

- They are able to find at least a few interesting books.
- Length is a significant factor in their choices.
- They are able to assess difficulty and are willing to try a challenge.
- They have developed some criteria for judging potential interest.
- They are, literally, trying to judge a book by its cover.

Assessing Student Performance.   Students may be asked to keep a simple Reading Log on which they record the date, the title of the book, the pages they read that day (e.g., pp. 12–19), and a brief comment, question, or prediction. Dialogue journals are another way to assess understanding. In a dialogue journal, students write about the material they read with the expectation that the teacher or a peer is going to write back to them. They can use a list of suggestions such as those found in Figure 10.1 on page 156, if necessary. In the process of writing back to students or examining exchanges between students, teachers can see

FIGURE 10.6   *A Collaborative Book Review*

Ann says that *Matilda Bone* by Karen Cushman is a book she would recommend to people who like historical novels, especially to girls. She liked it very much because it showed what it was like to live in the Middle Ages.

The book is about Matilda, who is an orphan and has to go to work for a woman named Peg who is a "bone setter," a kind of doctor who helps poor people with broken bones. Matilda hates everything about her new job, and she can't do anything right because she has never learned to do anything useful.

Ann said that the book got a little bit confusing at times because there were so many words and things that they had in the Middle Ages that we don't have any more. One of her favorite parts was when Matilda was sent to the market to buy lunch, and she comes back with a disgusting old eel. She thought that Matilda was really spoiled and stuck-up at first because she thought that she was better than Peg when she really didn't know anything that was useful. After a while, though, Ann felt sorry for her because she was all alone in a strange place trying to learn some very hard things.

Matilda Bone reminded Ann of *The Midwife's Apprentice,* which was also about a girl learning how to do medical kinds of things in the Middle Ages. She said the big difference was that the character in *The Midwife's Apprentice* really wanted to be a midwife, but Matilda hated it at first.

whether readers are encountering problems. They can also take note of which books students find challenging, interesting, or thought provoking.

Book reviews may be used as part of the evaluation of a student's performance in the reading workshop. They provide a teacher with insights about students' interpretations of a text and about their preferences and attitudes as readers. It is important, however, to treat book reviews as more than a "test." They can be published within the classroom and, perhaps, beyond. Teachers can arrange exchanges of reviews with other classes; and many websites that feature books, such as Amazon.com, provide opportunities for publishing reviews. Although reading workshop routines can be more individual than literature circles, opportunities for book talk remain important. Teachers can give students a chance to talk about their reading by having them interview each other and create collaborative book reviews such as the one for *Matilda Bone* (Cushman, 2000) shown in Figure 10.6.

Learning New Words during Independent Reading Routines

Opportunity, choice, and responsibility are the key notions in every aspect of independent reading routines, and those principles can be applied to vocabulary learning as well. When students read extensively from books they have chosen, they have opportunities to encounter developmentally appropriate words and to see those words in a meaningful context in which they are most likely to "stick." Moreover, independent literacy routines allow students, including English language learners, to choose the words they will learn and the

FIGURE 10.7 *A Vocabulary Self-Collection Sheet*

Date	Word	Phrase or Sentence	Hypothesis	Definition

method they will use for learning them. They become responsible for their own vocabulary development rather than being dependent on their teachers.

Both literature circles and reading workshops lend themselves to variations of the Vocabulary Self-Selection Strategy (Haggard, 1986). The collecting of words can be done in a literature log, or by using a "Self-Collection Sheet" such as the one in Figure 10.7. Notice that this sheet puts a premium on noting meaningful sentence context and making hypotheses about meaning. Students can use the dictionary to determine the definition or synonym for the word. They may also ask a peer or parent. A similar collection sheet is one of the "think sheets" McMahon and Raphael (1997) suggest for students in book clubs.

The Self-Collection Sheet or literature log may be useful as a device for assessing (a) whether students can self-monitor well enough to notice unfamiliar or troublesome words, (b) whether they can generate sensible hypotheses, and (c) whether they know and use strategies to confirm word meanings.

When invited to identify the words they do not know in the book they are reading, many students will report that there are none. They may do this because they resist admitting that they ever have difficulty, or perhaps they suspect that they will have to look up every word they identify and learn its definition. Here are several suggestions for encouraging students in the middle grades to identify and collect new words:

- Ask them to identify words that *someone else* may not know. This not only preserves their ego, but also draws their attention to words that they may "kind of" know without being able to use them easily or to define them. Students may also be encouraged to consider *how well* they know words by putting them on a list and then doing a knowledge rating from one (totally unfamiliar) to five (I can read it, use it in writing, and define it).

• Set aside occasional "Just Ask" times. This may be as little as 5 minutes a day when students can ask about any word on their list, providing they have recorded the sentence in which it originally appeared. They can spell out the word if they cannot pronounce it. You can then simply explain what the word means—or what you think it means. You might ask the class for hypotheses, but avoid doing so when most students probably know the word. That way, the student who chose the word will not be embarrassed. Try to elicit more than one possible meaning and to acknowledge sensible guesses.

• Have students pool their words to create lists of "Words Worth Learning." This activity allows students to consciously apply the criteria of asking whether a given word is crucial to understanding the text, whether it appears repeatedly, and whether it is likely to appear in other texts. Students often find a great deal of satisfaction when their words make the list, and the discussions about the merits of each word reinforce both the words' meanings and the strategy of considering a word's importance in context.

Summary

Liner and Butler (2000) point out that teachers are often concerned by the reduced amount of control they feel in independent literacy routines:

> Trust is the real issue in giving students choices in their reading, writing, and talking. The plain fact of the matter is that it is hard for us to let go. What if they mess up? What if they don't read the right books? What if they write silly things? What if they don't learn enough vocabulary words? What if they don't learn? The answer is that they will mess up. They will read the wrong books, but many of the right ones as well. . . . Vocabulary will take care of itself, and they will learn more than lists of words can teach them. They will learn. (p. 151)

In this chapter we have only been able to introduce the basics of literature circles and reading workshops. Teachers continue to create new variations in independent literacy routines as they adapt to the requirements of academic standards, try to create a balance among literacy routines, and, most importantly, meet the needs and abilities of individual students including English language learners.

Responding to Reading _____

• Look back at the opening scenario in this chapter. Have your answers to the accompanying questions changed after reading this chapter?

• Some literacy educators believe that literature circles can meet all the objectives of the literacy curriculum. Others think that student-led groups should be part of a balanced literacy program that includes the other routines you have been reading about in this book. What do you think?

Key Terms to Know and Use

reader response	extensive reading	Vocabulary Self-Selection (VSS)
role sheets	status report	literature logs
intensive reading	Book Pass	reading workshop
mini-lesson	book clubs	SSR
Goldilocks Strategy	book talk	
literature circles	dialogue journals	
think sheets	Five Finger Procedure	

Possible Sentences

Choose two or three terms in the columns above and write a sentence summarizing what you now know about literature circles and reading workshop. Write four or five sentences using different words until you have a nice summary paragraph.

Beyond the Book

You can find out more about using literature circles by visiting www.literaturecircles.com. As you examine this site, consider the following;

- What are some of the variations that teachers use in forming groups for literature circles?
- What are some ways of finding appropriate books for literature circles?
- What are some of the benefits for students that are claimed by researchers and teachers who have used literature circles?
- How can English language learners be included in and benefit from literature circles?

To learn more about books that you can choose to add to your classroom library, consult "Young Adult Choices" published every year in the International Reading Association's *Journal of Adolescent and Adult Literacy.*

References

Atwell, N. (1998). *In the middle: New understandings about writing, reading, and learning.* Portsmouth, NH: Heinemann.

Allen, J. (2000). *Yellow brick roads: Shared and guided paths to independent reading* 4–12. Portland, ME: Stenhouse.

Cherniwchan, N. (2002). Revealing warmer shadows; Tensions in reader response. In M. Hunsberger & G. Labercane (Eds.), *Making meaning in the response-based classroom* (pp. 116–130). Boston: Allyn and Bacon.

Cushman, K. (2000). *Matilda Bone.* New York: Clarion Books.

Daniels, H. (2001). *Literature circles: Voice and choice in book clubs and reading groups* (2nd ed.). Portland ME: Stenhouse.

Galda, L. (1990). A longitudinal study of the spectator stance as a function of age and genre. *Research in the Teaching of English, 24*(3), 261–278.

Haggard, M. R. (1986). The vocabulary self-collection strategy: Using student interest and world knowledge to enhance vocabulary growth. *Journal of Reading, 29*(4), 634–642.

Langer, J. A. (1995). *Envisioning literature: Literary understanding and literature instruction.* New York: Teachers College Press.

Liner, T., & Butler, D. (2000). "You want to read what?": Giving students a voice in their own literacy and in the literacy program. In K. D. Wood & T. S. Dickinson (Eds.), *Promoting literacy in grades 4–9* (pp. 139–154). Boston: Allyn and Bacon.

McMahon, S. I., & Raphael, T. E. (1997). *The book club connection: Literacy learning and classroom talk.* Newark, DE: International Reading Association.

Microsoft. (1994). *Encarta [electronic resource] : The complete multimedia encyclopedia.* Redmond, WA.: Microsoft.

Ohlhausen, M. M., & Jepsen, M. (1992). Lessons from Goldilocks: "Somebody's been choosing my books, but I can make my own choices now!" *The New Advocate, 5*(1), 31–46.

Peterson, R., & Eeds, M. (1990). *Grand conversations: Literature groups in action.* New York: Scholastic.

Probst, R. (1998). Reader response theory in middle school. In K. Beers & B. G. Samuels (Eds.), *Into focus: Understanding and creating middle school readers* (pp. 125–138). Norwood, MA: Christopher-Gordon.

Rosenblatt, L. (1978). *The reader, the text, the poem.* Carbondale, IL: Southern Illinois University Press.

Rosenblatt, L. M. (1938). *Literature as exploration, for the Commission on Human Relations. A publication of the Progressive Education Association.* New York: D. Appleton-Century.

Roser, N. L., Strecker, S., & Martinez, M. G. (2000). Literature circles, book clubs, and literature discussion groups: Some talk about book talk. In K. D. Wood & T. S. Dickinson (Eds.), *Promoting literacy in grades 4–9* (p. 295–304). Boston: Allyn and Bacon.

Spinelli, J. (1997). *Wringer.* New York: Harper Collins.

Stoll, D. (ed.). (1997). *Magazines for kids and teens.* Newark, DE: International Reading Association.

The multimedia encyclopedia of science fiction. (1995). Toronto: Grolier.

Veatch, J. (1968). *How to teach reading with childrens books.* New York: Citation Press.

Watt, D. L. (2002). Writing in response: Reflections on learning how. In M. Hunsberger, M. & G. Labercane (Eds.), *Making meaning in the response-based classroom* (pp. 154–174). Boston: Allyn and Bacon.

11

Integrating the Language Arts: Writing Workshops and Writing Assignments

Activating Prior Knowledge and Making Connections

Maleeka asked for a writing conference with her teacher, Mrs. Murray, because she was afraid the piece she was writing about ice skating was "not interesting enough." As they sat down together, Mrs. Murray asked, "Why did you choose to write about this topic? Why was it interesting to you?"

Maleeka explained, "Because I've been skating since I was 7, and I like it a lot, and I know a lot about it so I thought I could write about it." Mrs. Murray nodded and asked Maleeka to read the piece aloud. As she read, she paused several times to make small changes in the text where something "didn't sound right" or she had left out a word.

When Maleeka had finished reading, Mrs. Murray said, "Wow! It's obvious that you do know a lot about skating! I never knew that skaters had to practice at 5 o'clock in the morning. What do you do in the practice sessions?" Maleeka explained about practicing "school figures" and about developing and rehearsing routines for competitions, and Mrs. Murray asked her several clarifying questions such as the meaning of an "inside edge." Finally she asked, "How did you get interested in skating?" Maleeka explained that when she was 7 her best friend started skating and told her about it. It sounded like fun, so Maleeka started taking lessons too.

Mrs. Murray replied, "Many people take up a hobby because someone else tells them about it. Maybe this piece should focus less on your own skating and more on why other people would want to be skaters. Most articles and books are not interesting to everyone. They are written for a specific audience. Maybe the audience for this piece is people who are not skaters but might want to be if they knew more about it. Why don't you go over to the Magazine Center and find several articles that are written to explain a sport or activity in a way that would get people interested? Then we'll talk about them."

Maleeka found an article in *Young Miss* about scrapbooking and one in *Junior Sports Illustrated* about snowboarding. Mrs. Murray helped her to see some of the similarities in content in the two articles such as a list of reasons why the hobby was worth doing and a warning that the hobby required time and money. Mrs. Murray also pointed out how the articles combined short "vignettes" about people who participate in the hobby with advice and explanations.

Maleeka decided that the audience for her piece would be girls between 8 and 10 years old who were not skaters. She read revised versions to her writing group several times, and one of the group members helped her to come up with her eventual title, "Landing a Triple: Three Reasons Why Figure Skating Might Be Right for You." The piece was published in an online magazine sponsored by the school district and made available to all the elementary school students.

Before reading the rest of this chapter, consider the following questions:
1. What connections did Mrs. Murray make between reading and writing?
2. How might the experience of writing this piece affect Maleeka's reading habits?
3. How is the writing conference described here like or unlike the literacy routines you have read about in the previous chapters?
4. What modifications, if any, would you make when working with English language learners?

Multiple Reading–Writing Connections

Educators sometimes talk about "*the* reading–writing connection," but there are actually many ways in which reading and writing are connected. All language activities are connected because they all have similar purposes, use some sort of symbols, and follow "rules." Teachers in the middle grades can make use of the connections between reading and writing to help students learn about the structure of written language, the process of constructing meaning, and the relationship between authors and readers. Figure 11.1 shows a list of reading–writing connections, some of which are discussed in more detail.

Language Connections

One obvious language connection between reading and writing is that they both rely on words to convey meaning, thus providing occasions for developing new vocabulary. Students will truly come to own new words they have encountered in their reading when they can use those words in their writing. Both reading and writing also provide opportunities for learning about patterns of letters and sounds. In the middle grades, awareness of morphology, the meaningful "chunks" within longer words, can be reinforced in mini-lessons connected to either reading or writing. Such mini-lessons are particularly useful for English language learners who may need differentiated instruction in these areas.

Reading and writing both require an understanding of genres. The scenario at the beginning of this chapter provides an illustration. Maleeka reads magazine articles and uses

FIGURE 11.1 *Connections between Reading and Writing*

- Both use the same language systems (semantic, syntactic, graphophonemic)
- Both draw on knowledge of text structures
- Both are used for social purposes (to exchange messages)
- Both involve planning and goal setting
- Both require monitoring ("How am I doing?")
- Both require strategies for problem solving
- Both involve refining or revising an emerging interpretation
- Both affect how we understand the world and how we express our knowledge

that experience to find an audience and form for her writing. Her experience with selecting and organizing information according to the "rules" for magazine articles will prepare her to read articles in the future with greater understanding of their structure and purpose.

Process Connections

Researchers in the 1970s carefully observed writers and identified particular stages they went through in producing a text (Elbow, 1973; Emig, 1971; Graves, 1975; Murray, 1968). These stages are more or less sequential, but that they are also *recursive.* That means that writers often go back to an earlier stage as they are working. Those stages generally include these elements:

- **Rehearsal** involves planning a piece of writing, by gathering initial ideas—either mentally or on paper—and imagining what the finished piece will be like.
- **Drafting** is a matter of getting ideas down on paper with an attitude that they may change and without being overly concerned about correctness.
- **Revision** literally requires the writer to "re-vision" the piece to see additional possibilities and to identify places for making additions, deletions, and clarifications of content.
- **Editing** includes all those things that writers do to make a piece more "publishable" and more attractive to an audience. Editing includes proofreading to correct errors in capitalization, punctuation, and other mechanics, but it also includes decisions about the appropriate style and format for the piece.

Tierney and Pearson (1983) describe reading and writing as "two sides of the same coin" because both readers and writers "compose" messages by patiently putting pieces together to construct meaning. Writers need to call upon many of the same metacognitive strategies of planning, monitoring, and problem solving that are used when reading (Olson, 2003). For that reason, it may be more useful to think of the writing process in terms of *strategies* rather than stages.

Teachers can help young writers by making them more aware of the process that authors use on the way from a good idea to a good result. Students in the middle grades can be guided to think and talk about the strategies that are most effective for them. The questionnaire in Figure 11.2 can be used to assess students' knowledge and application of strate-

FIGURE 11.2 *Twenty Questions about Your Writing Process*

Complete each of the statements below to show what is usually true about your writing.

1. My favorite place to write is . . .
2. My favorite writing materials are . . .
3. If I can choose between being alone and being with other people when writing, I will . . .
4. I will ask other people to read my writing when . . .
5. I know that I can always write about the topic of . . .
6. Some people write a draft straight through without stopping, and some people stop often to make changes as they write. I usually . . .
7. When I'm writing and I get "stuck," I can try these three things: . . .
8. The best way for me to organize my writing is . . .
9. Another person who reads or hears my writing can help by . . .
10. I will make changes in the content of my writing when . . .
11. When I do make major changes in the content of my writing, the changes are usually . . .
12. I avoid errors in final drafts of my writing by . . .
13. I know that I had better check for these kinds of errors: . . .
14. The final version of my writing is usually different from earlier drafts in these ways: . . .
15. I can make sure that I have done a writing assignment well by . . .
16. I sometimes use writing to help me think about . . .
17. One kind of writing I do well is . . .
18. One kind of writing I often find hard is . . .
19. One thing I do better now than I used to is . . .
20. One thing I know I need to improve is . . .

gies for writing. Students can complete it individually or use it to interview each other. A class discussion about the items in the questionnaire can raise awareness about the many ways that writers approach their craft.

"Authoring" Connections

All language involves connections between two people for some sort of social purpose. Reading and writing are, however, different from oral language because the two people who are communicating may never have met and may be separated not only by vast distances but also by centuries. Just as readers must read the author behind the text, writers must be able to envision imaginary readers. Composition requires a constant internal monologue in which the writer considers questions, such as, "Would they understand that?" "What would they want to know next?" and "Will they accept this idea, or do I need to convince them?"

When readers consider the purposes of authors and the "craft" they use to achieve those purposes, they are adding to the possibilities for their own writing. When students struggle to make their meaning clear and find themselves reaching out to unknown readers, they are gaining new respect for books and the people who write them.

Making Connections in a Writing Workshop

A writing workshop is designed to help students explore different possibilities for every aspect of the writing process. Figure 11.3 on page 178 shows a typical workshop schedule and a list of useful procedures. Notice the similarity between the routines for this workshop and the reading workshop in the previous chapter. This similarity helps students to learn procedures more quickly. It also helps to maintain a classroom environment in which students have consistent roles: working collaboratively, engaging and reflecting, listening and sharing, and communicating.

Writing grows out of a fertile soil of talking, listening, reading, and using media. The workshop includes opportunities for students to talk about their own writing and that of others; to listen to finished and unfinished writing; to read published pieces that are similar to their own; and to use ideas, techniques, and forms drawn from popular media.

Guiding Topic Selection

As Atwell (1998) points out, students who are always given topics for writing will never learn to find their own. Topics for writing come from two sources: the students' life experiences and the example of other writers. Writing response groups, whole-class sharing, and classroom publishing allow students to gather possibilities from the writing topics of their peers. They can find topics that they know about and care about by considering such questions as these:

- What do I know about that most people do not know?
- How do I most like to spend my time?
- What are some of my strongest memories?
- What are my plans and hopes for the future?
- If I could visit any place, where would I go?
- Who do I care about?

A Possible Topics List is shown in Figure 11.4 on page 179. Such a list ensures that writers will always have possibilities that they can write about on days when they do not have a "hot topic."

One of the most important reading–writing connections occurs when teachers suggest that students consider writing the kinds of things they like to read. Browsing through the classroom library can be an effective way to find topics and forms to try. Teacher read alouds can also suggest possibilities.

FIGURE 11.3 *Writing Workshop Schedule and Procedures*

Mini-Lesson/Daily Oral Language	7–10 minutes
Status of the Class	5–7 minutes
Silent Writing	15–20 minutes
Write and Conference	15–20 minutes
Group Share/Author's Circle	10 minutes
Recording and Clean-Up	3 minutes

Workshop Procedures

Your two-pocket writing folder should be used for nothing else. It should contain:

- A Possible Topics list.
- A Personal Spelling list.
- Guide sheets from the teacher.
- A Record Sheet that shows what you do in and out of class each day.
- All the drafts of writing you have begun or finished.
- Plenty of blank paper.

When you come into the workshop:

- Have your Writing Folder and a pen/pencil on your desk.
- Record writing you did at home last night.
- Decide what you will do today.

During Status Report time be prepared to tell which of the following you plan to do:

- Starting a new piece.
- Continuing a previous draft.
- Revising a previous draft.
- Editing.
- Having a conference with _____ to discuss _____.

Listen to what others report and add ideas that sound good to your Possible Topics list.

During Silent Writing time:

- Do not talk—even to the teacher. You will have the chance in a very short while.
- Make sure that every piece you work on is dated and has a working title.
- Be sure to skip lines or leave extra wide margins for later changes.
- Do not throw away anything you write.

When the teacher begins to circulate for Writing and Conference time:

- You may want to continue writing.
- You may have a brief conference with the teacher.
- You may have a 5–10 minute meeting with 1–2 students at the conference table.

During Group Share time we may:

- Meet with your designated writing group.
- Do an Author's Circle.
- Do a second "status" update.

Be sure to record your work for the day on the "Record Sheet" in your folder.

FIGURE 11.4 *Possible Topics for Writing*

During the writing workshop, I can draw from this "bank" of topics that I know about and care about enough to write about.

Date	Topic or title	Possible form
	My Worst Birthday	Nonfiction story

Guiding Rehearsal and Drafting

Readers are more effective if they take a few moments to draw on their prior knowledge and develop a plan for how to approach a text. Writers, too, need to pause early in the process of drafting a new piece to think about its content and form and its potential audience. Teachers sometimes insist on writers doing "prewriting" activities such as making a semantic web or jotting notes, but there are many ways to gather thoughts before putting them down on paper. Teachers may suggest

- Reading over previous pieces.
- Skimming through a similar piece written by someone else.
- Talking to a teacher or friend.
- Making a rough drawing that captures what you want to convey.

Some writers prefer to "just start in." These writers may occasionally want to try a "freewrite" (Elbow, 1973), a few minutes of writing whatever comes to mind without stopping to plan. Writers may also rehearse by talking about their intentions. When the teacher stops by a student's desk and asks, "How's the writing going?" the writer's answer may serve as a rehearsal for the next section.

Understanding the writing process means realizing that writers often shift back and forth between rehearsing ideas and writing them down. Teachers can point out that writers often make a web or outline when they are in the middle of a piece and can see where it seems to be heading. When students get stuck while drafting, the teacher may suggest the helpful strategy of skipping ahead to a part that they *can* do. This is a strategy that most experienced writers use, but writers in the middle grades often have the mistaken notion that a piece must be written in order from beginning to end.

Guiding Revision

Although most proficient adult writers think that revision is the key to effective writing, students in the middle grades often resist it for several reasons. First, they may see revision as an admission that something was "wrong" with their first drafts. Second, if they have come to see composition in terms of "getting done and handing it in," they may see revision as a waste of time. Finally, they may not have the skills that are needed to consider possible improvements and to make changes in content without starting all over. This is often the case for English language learners.

The first step toward addressing this resistance is to emphasize that a revision of a previous draft "counts" just as much as a new piece (if not more). If students know that the evaluation of the workshop depends on their demonstrating progress in all aspects of the *process* of writing rather than on the number of *products* they finish, they will have less reason to resist. The second step is to emphasize the distinction between revision and editing by continually reminding students that any piece of writing can always be revised in the following ways:

- **By narrowing the topic.** For instance, Maleeka could narrow her topic from skating to the reasons why she skates.
- **By broadening the topic.** Skating could be broadened into a piece on individual sports or Olympic sports.
- **By changing audience.** Mrs. Murray suggested that Maleeka consider an audience of nonskaters who were curious about how and why people take up the sport competitively.
- **By changing genre.** Maleeka was considering whether her piece should be a personal narrative (a first-person true story) or an informational article with a few personal anecdotes.
- **By adding or subtracting.** Adding is the easiest kind of revision. Writers resist subtracting text they have taken the trouble to create, but they may need to take out irrelevant details in order to make their point more clearly. The length of a piece may be limited by its potential interest to readers, limitations set by publishers, or even the author's own interest and energy.

If these suggestions become part of the day to day routine of a writing workshop, students will come to see that revision is about seeing new possibilities for their writing rather than finding flaws in it.

Guiding Editing and Proofreading

Students often need help with preparing a piece of writing for publication. More importantly, though, they need to learn how to edit and proofread for themselves. One way to assist students is through mini-lessons that model specific techniques for improving the style of the piece and for reducing errors. For example, the following strategies can be used:

- Read each sentence aloud starting with the last and working backward to the first. Ask yourself if any of the sentences are really fragments.

- Read the piece aloud and put a wavy line under any sentence that "sounds funny." Then ask a peer for an opinion about those sentences you underlined. Teachers can "set the stage" and use discretion when pairing an English language learner and an English-only student to keep the experience positive for both students.
- Use a handbook such as *Write Source 2000: A Guide to Writing, Thinking, and Learning* (Sebranek, Kemper, & Meyer, 1999) to check on usage errors you often make (such as "him and me" versus "he and I").
- Read through the piece and circle any word that you think might be misspelled. Then ask a good speller if those words are correct.
- Try writing the word several different ways and see if one looks right. If necessary, confirm the spelling in a spelling dictionary.
- Use the spell and grammar check in a word processing program.
- Keep a list of words that you know you are likely to misspell and check your piece against that list.

As this list suggests, peer editing conferences, handbooks, and checklists can all reinforce the editing strategies taught in mini-lessons.

Conferences in the Writing Workshop

Writing conferences are the teacher's main tool for guiding student writing. By the responses they make to early drafts, teachers can help students not only to improve their own writing but also to provide helpful feedback to their peers. Conferences are also very useful later in the process as a means to provide additional "screening" that can reduce errors. Conferences differ according to the needs of the student and the particular piece of writing that a student is trying to complete, but most conferences could follow this general outline:

- **Mirror content.** A teacher's first response to student writing should be as a person and as an interested reader rather than as an advice giver. Mrs. Murray's remark, "Wow! I never knew that skaters had to practice at 5 o'clock in the morning" shows that she understands the piece and tells Maleeka what information "stuck" with a perceptive reader.
- **Give focused praise.** To be helpful, praise must be honest and specific. Vague positive comments such as "good job" might make the writer feel good (if the compliment seems sincere), but writers need responses that help them to see what features of the text are effective. Mrs. Murray's remark to Maleeka that "It's obvious that you know a lot about skating!" helps her to recognize that one of her piece's strengths is the quantity and quality of the information it provides.
- **Ask clarifying questions.** In an effective writing conference, the teacher speaks less than the writer (Graves, 1983). Asking questions is a way to get the writer talking about the topic of the piece, the process of writing it, and some additional possibilities for completing it. When Mrs. Murray expresses curiosity about Maleeka's subject, she begins to tell about information that is not yet in the paper.
- **Suggest possibilities.** Writing is very much a process of considering options and making decisions. Teachers need to help students see the options but they should

avoid "taking over" the paper and telling students what to do—even when they ask. For students who struggle, including English language learners, the teacher may want to offer three possible suggestions and allow the student to choose which direction to write.

- **Discuss next steps.** Although most of the conference should be about seeing multiple possibilities, students should walk away with a plan for continuing the piece—or for abandoning it. As the workshop procedures state, students need not finish every piece they start. Sometimes a conference reveals that the student does not yet have the information, the focus, or the confidence to complete a particular piece. More often, the teacher and students can agree on some ways to move the writing forward. Maleeka left her conference with Mrs. Murray with the idea of checking through magazine articles to find a proper form and focus for her piece about skating.

The Importance of Publishing

Writing is meant to be read. Discussions of audience, genre, or writing mechanics and conventions are all "academic" unless the ideas an author is trying to express eventually reach a reader. Teachers who want to invite students into a world of literacy need to think about how to connect their student writers with real readers. Rubenstein (2000) notes that publishing is also crucial for helping young adolescents find a voice and the reassurance that they matter.

> Every time my students pick up a pen I remind them, "You are not writing for me. You are writing for the world." They balk at first, seeing my grade book as the ultimate destination for their work, but slowly with encouragement from me, from response groups, from outside readers whom they trust, they start to see that what they have to say matters more in the world than it matters to me. I am only one reader in a world filled with interested readers, and once a student's words touch another corner of that world, something miraculous happens. (p.10)

The possibilities for student publishing are nearly infinite. They include personal publishing such as letters to friends and family members. Classroom publishing can include class collections of poems or stories, or a simple anthology in which every student is invited to submit his or her favorite or best piece. Schoolwide publishing can include school newspapers and literary magazines as well as newsletters for parents or visitors.

Beyond the school, students can write fan letters or letters of complaint. Inquiries about favorite products can bring interesting information and may even result in free samples. Whenever a letter is answered, even with a form letter, students become more connected with the wider world that they are in the process of joining. Online publishing opens up a huge new world for student writers. Lee (2000) notes that there are thousands of "e-zines," online magazines, on the Internet and that there are a number of established sites that publish student work.

Some of these sites provide templates for the particular kinds of articles they feature, which can assist students in composing their articles. Others accept submissions in a wide variety of forms. Another option is to establish a "keypals" relationship with another teacher's class. Finally, many schools or districts establish their own web pages so that they can showcase quality student work. The potentially wide audience for Internet publication is a powerful incentive for working to improve written products. As Lee (2000) points out, "No one wanted to look 'dumb' in front of the whole world. Grammar and spelling suddenly mattered" (p. 24).

Writing Workshops for English Language Learners

A writing workshop empowers English language learners because it allows them to take risks, to engage deeply with written language, and to become involved with other readers and writers in their own classroom and outside of school. English language learners who are shy about speaking to their classmates can use writing as a way of experiencing the satisfaction of making themselves understood in their new language, and that may build confidence for face-to-face communication. The workshop emphasis on choosing the topics that writers know best allows English language learners to communicate about their culture and to share some of their feelings about the difficulties they face. English language learners especially benefit from seeing their writing published. They have worked hard to learn a second language. Seeing their writing in the school newspaper or newsletter affirms that their hard work is paying off.

The crucial element in a writing workshop is the freedom students have to use what they know rather than feeling anxious about what they do not know. Fu (1998) describes how Chinese English language learners who were encouraged to write every day gradually moved from writing in Chinese characters, to writing in English with Chinese syntax, to writing English. This sort of progress is only possible when students feel secure in knowing that their best will be good enough.

Drawing can play an important role in the writing of English language learners and other students who struggle with language production. Hubbard (1998) reports how English language learners who were new to America began their writing by drawing a picture that represented a place they remembered well. For beginners in the language, drawings work much the way they do for very young children. They use their drawings to remember their ideas while they struggle to find the words and symbols they need to put those ideas into written language.

Making Writing Assignments

The goals and procedures of the workshop can be extended beyond the workshop through the use of well-designed and well-guided writing assignments. The writing workshop routine encourages students to "read like a writer" by paying attention to the ways in which texts are structured to meet the needs and interests of an audience. Teachers also use writing as a vehicle to guide students' thinking about particular texts. Reading and writing can be connected through a variety of formal and informal composition activities that students do before, during, and after reading. Figure 11.5 on page 184 provides an overview of some of the ways in which writing can interact with reading to deepen students' understanding.

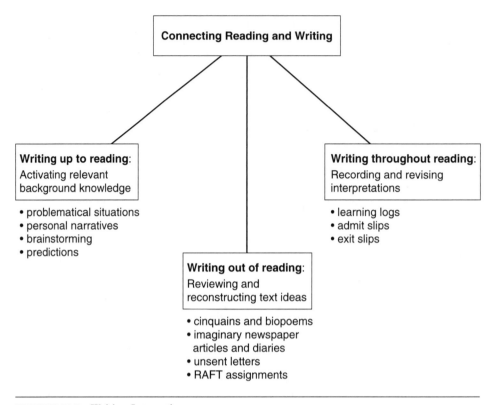

FIGURE 11.5 *Writing Interactions*

Informal Writing Activities

Informal writing activities generally result in "first draft" products that are intended to help students get ideas down on paper so they can remember them, discuss them, or reconsider them. Applebee (1984) suggests that when teachers read such products, they do so in the role of "the teacher as coach." In dialogue journals, for instance, students write their initial reactions to reading; and teachers respond by affirming ideas, posing questions, or supplying additional ideas or information. The role of coach contrasts with the more traditional role of "teacher as examiner" in which the teacher reads student writing primarily for the purpose of assigning grades.

Admit slips and exit slips provide another way for the teacher to "coach" students' reading. When students read outside of class, they can prepare an admit slip that states ideas they have learned, raises questions they would like to have answered, or even expresses a complaint about the text or the reading task. Students hand these slips to the teacher on the way into class as if they were a ticket for admission. The teacher begins class by reading through the slips aloud and responding appropriately. Schmidt (1985) noted that admit slips gave students in his math class immediate feedback to their questions and also provided them a chance to hear what other students were thinking and feeling.

When students read or discuss a text in class, they can complete exit slips to write any questions they have, to tell what they have learned, or to express how they feel about the reading. The teacher circulates to collect the slips as students finish their work, and she then takes the last few minutes to read and respond to some or all of them. Since students are accountable both for their reading and for completing admit or exit slips, they should put their names on the slips, although the teacher does not read the names aloud. English language learners might feel intimidated asking a question in class. The admit and exit slips give them a chance to ask a question in a nonthreatening way.

The literature logs that were discussed in the last chapter are one example of learning logs. A learning log is sort of an all-purpose collection of informal writings that students can use to record their thoughts and see how their understanding changes over time. For example, before reading a passage about atoms and molecules, students might be asked to use their prior knowledge to write a brief explanation of what each one is and how they differ. After reading, they might be asked to write a revised definition or to draw a diagram that shows the basic structure of an atom. Teachers may occasionally check to see that students are completing their learning logs, but they should not grade individual entries or comment on spelling or punctuation since the goal of this writing is to stimulate the writers' thinking rather than to communicate effectively to others.

Formal Writing

"Formal writing" does not need to be a synonym for "boring writing" or for "impossible writing." Writing can be considered formal whenever it follows the conventions for some commonly published genre or *form* of writing. Formal writing assignments ask the writer to try and capture the content, tone, and organization of a genre, which may be a letter, a diary, a story, or an essay. "Real world" products can be written to reach an audience other than the writer or the teacher. Writers can learn a great deal as they reexamine the content of their reading and consider how the information should be organized so that an audience will understand.

Many formal writing assignments call for imaginative products in which students must "reconstruct" information by combining it with their own background knowledge and their knowledge of a particular text form. Figure 11.6 on page 186 provides examples of how students might use poetic forms to express their learning from biographies, from a math book, or from an article in health class.

One way to think about the products that students can create in connection to their reading is the acronym RAFT (Santa, Havens, & Maycumber, 1996), which stands for *role, audience, form,* and *topic.*

- **Role** refers to the imaginary point of view that the student uses to find a perspective for reexamining and reorganizing the material. For example, a student studying the Vietnam War may be given a whole range of options from a U.S. soldier to a South Vietnamese civilian to a member of the Viet Cong, or a particular role might be assigned.
- **Audience** specifies to whom the author is writing. The South Vietnamese civilian, for instance, might be writing to people in the United States or to a child.

- **Form** is the genre that students will produce. Again, this may be specified or students may be given a list of options such as a diary, a letter, a newspaper article, an editorial, or a last will and testament.
- **Topic** is the content of the message. It can also be thought of as the purpose, the effect the message is meant to have. A U.S. serviceman, for instance, might decide to apologize for the damage inflicted on the country or to explain why it was necessary.

Making a good writing assignment requires a careful balance between structure and freedom. If teachers describe the papers they want in minute detail, the result is often boring for both the teacher and the students. The teacher must read a pile of papers that are

FIGURE 11.6   *Poetic Forms for Connecting with Reading*

Cinquains always have five lines with the first line as the title and the last line a synonym for the title. The middle lines are usually feelings, actions, or objects related to the title.

Fitness

Cardiovascular activity
Running walking, pumping iron
Building muscle, losing fat
Health

Parallelograms

Made of lines and angles
Two-dimensional figures
Squares, rectangles, and rhombuses
Symmetrical planes

Biopoems can be adapted for use with fictional or nonfictional characters. The first line is usually the character's first name and the last line is the character's last name.

Benjamin

Inventor, writer, leader, and scientist
Who loved fine food, inventing, making money, and America
Who was famous for "discovering" electricity with a kite
Who was married to a wife he didn't see for almost 20 years
Who was the father of a son who sided with the British
Who succeeded at establishing a post office and library
Who failed at abolishing slavery
Who believed that common people could make themselves better
Who is remembered for Poor Richard's almanac, bifocals, and a stove
Resident of Boston, London, Paris, and Philadelphia
Buried in Philadelphia

Franklin

nearly identical, and the students have all the work of producing text with none of the satisfaction that comes from shaping and communicating ideas. If, on the other hand, an assignment is too vague, students experience a kind of "terrible freedom" that leaves them with no criteria for knowing where to begin or how to judge their progress.

In designing writing assignments, teachers need to draw on their knowledge of their students' skills and experiences to find the Zone of Proximal Development in which students will be able to extend their thinking about the topic without being frustrated. Soven (1998) identifies a list of assignment variables that teachers should carefully consider to be sure that students have the knowledge, skills, and language abilities to do a particular writing task. Even when an assignment is based on a careful assessment of students' interests and abilities, teachers will need to guide the process of completing it in many of the same ways that they guide the writing workshop. See Figure 11.7 for a list of decisions that teachers need to make when planning a writing assignment.

FIGURE 11.7 *Decisions to Make When Planning Writing Assignments*

What is the context for the assignment?
- How does it fit in with previous/current activities?
- How is it like previous assignments? How does it differ from them?
- Who are the students? (Background? Diversity? English language level?)

What is the purpose for the assignment?
- To display knowledge?
- To make applications?
- To synthesize?
- To learn new language forms?

What constraints will you impose? Will you limit:
- Topic?
- Format (e.g, length)?
- Form or genre?
- Audience?

What guidance will you provide?
- Prewriting?
- Guidesheeets?
- Rubric?
- Written response?
- Models?
- Conferences?

What and how will you evaluate?
- What traits count?
- Will you grade content separately from organization or form?
- Will you write comments or use a rubric?

Writing Assignments for English Language Learners

For English language learners who are still trying to grasp the very basics of English, writing assignments may be intimidating. Teacher can help by careful scaffolding and by encouraging collaboration between students. A Language Experience Activity (LEA) is one way to help beginning language learners to learn how to represent their thoughts in English. An LEA generally follows these steps:

1. Students have a common experience. For example, they might have listened to the same book during a teacher read-aloud, viewed a movie together, or performed a science experiment.
2. The teacher invites each student in the group to tell an idea related to the experience. During this process, the teacher can help students with finding the right words, with pronunciation, and with English syntax.
3. The teacher acts as a scribe. On an overhead transparency or large sheet of chart paper, the teacher writes what each student says in language that is as close as possible to what the student said, but in correct form.
4. Students practice reading the finished text in unison with the teacher, in pairs or small groups, and individually.
5. Students write a copy of some or all of the text. They may add to it if they are able, and they make word cards from the text that they can review and use in their future reading and writing.

Slightly more advanced students might do an *interactive writing* activity. This is similar to LEA except that students are called on to do the writing on the chart paper or transparency with the help of their peers and the teacher. Both LEA and interactive writing provide opportunities for English language learners to combine content knowledge with speaking, writing, and reading. They encourage conversational language use and act as a bridge to academic language.

Summary

Teachers have long observed the many similarities between the processes of reading and writing but, until recently, few have capitalized on these similarities by regularly integrating these two processes during instruction. Knowledge of one process appears to reinforce knowledge of the other, and students "derive learning benefits across reading and writing when they understand that connections exist" (Shanahan, 1990, p. 4).

Content teachers tend to take writing skills for granted, yet they expect their students to undertake a considerable amount of writing in their classes. Lab reports in science, answers to questions from textbooks, essays, reports, exams—all mandate student writing proficiency. Writing is an important way to help students formulate ideas about what they are learning and sharpen their thinking. Through a variety of formal and informal writing tasks, including learning logs, reflections, responses to reading, position papers, dramatic recreations, writing from different perspectives, and the like, students of all language abilities use writing to deepen and refine their understanding of course content and learn to use communication skills more effectively.

Responding to Reading

You can review some of the key ideas in this chapter by completing the following RAFT assignment:

Role: Choose from:
- preservice teacher
- teacher completing first year
- 25-year veteran teacher

Audience: Choose from:
- an instructor in a college methods course
- a 20-year veteran colleague
- your former students
- the authors of this book

Form: A friendly letter

Topic: Choose from:
- What helps and what hurts student writers
- The rewards and problems of a writing workshop
- The kinds of writing assignments that work

Key Terms to Know and Use

rehearsal	recursive	interactive writing
publishing	formal writing	editing
informal writing	RAFT	response groups
learning logs	revision	exit slips
Language Experience Activity	freewrites	biopoem
drafting	admit slips	
	cinquain	

Possible Sentences

Use two or three terms in the columns above and write a sentence stating one idea you now know about connecting reading and writing. Write four or five such sentences using different words until you have a nice summary paragraph.

Beyond the Book

- Your own experiences as a writer and a student may give additional insight into the ways that writing is taught and learned. Do a "writing autobiography" in which you reflect on:

- Your memories of "typical" writing in elementary, middle school, high school, and college.
- Stories about writing *triumphs* you remember.
- Stories about writing *traumas* you remember.
- Your skills and attitudes as a writer today and how they have been affected by your past.
- Your conclusions about effective teaching of writing.
- Conduct a web search to locate additional ideas for supporting each aspect of the writing process. You might, for instance, type "teaching writing revision" into a search engine. See if you can find five websites that are worth sharing with your classmates or colleagues.
- The "ReadWriteThink" plans that are available at the IRA and NCTE websites include a number of text engagements that connect reading and writing. Search the site to identify one example of an engagement that uses reading to enhance students' writing and one example where the focus is on writing to extend or reinforce reading.

References

Applebee, A. N. (1984). *Contexts for learning to write: Studies of secondary school instruction.* Norwood, NJ: Ablex.

Atwell, N. (1998). *In the middle: New understandings about writing, reading, and learning.* Portsmouth, NH: Boynton/Cook.

Elbow, P. (1973). *Writing without teachers.* New York: Oxford University Press.

Emig, J. (1971). *The composing process of 12th graders.* Urbana, IL: National Council of Teachers of English.

Fu, D. (1998). Unlock their lonely hearts. *Voices from the Middle, 6*(1), 3–11.

Graves, D. H. (1975). *An examination of the writing processes of seven-year-old children. Research in the Teaching of English, 9*(3), 227–241.

Graves, D. H. (1983). *Writing: Teachers and children at work.* Portsmouth, NH: Heinemann.

Hubbard, R. S. (1998). "The place I will always remember": Drawing on experiences through the quilt project. *Voices from the Middle, 6*(1), 12–16.

Lee, G. (2000). Getting in line to publish online. *Voices from the Middle, 8*(1), 23–34.

McCarrier, A., Pinnell, G. S., & Fountas, I. C. (2000). *Interactive writing: How language and literacy come together, K–2.* Portsmouth, NH: Heinemann.

Murray, D. (1968). *A writer teaches writing: A practical method of teaching comprehension.* Boston: Houghton Mifflin.

Olson, C. B. (2003). *The reading/writing connection: Strategies for teaching and learning in the secondary classroom.* Boston: Allyn and Bacon.

Rubenstein, S. (2000). Words made public/voices made powerful. *Voices from the Middle, 8*(1), 10–15.

Santa, C., Havens, L., & Maycumber, E. (1996). *Project CRISS: Creating independence through student-owned strategies.* Dubuque, IA: Kendall/Hunt.

Schmidt, D. (1985). Writing in math class. In A.G. Gere (Ed.), *Roots in the sawdust: Writing to learn across disciplines* (pp. 104–116). Urbana, IL: National Council of Teachers of English.

Sebranek, P., Kemper, D., & Meyer, V. (1999). *Write source 2000: A guide to writing, thinking, and learning.* Wilmington, MA: Great Source Education Group.

Shanahan, T. (1990). Reading and writing together. What does it really mean? In T. Shanahan (Ed.), *Reading and writing together: New perspectives for the classroom* (pp. 1–18). Norwood, MA: Christopher-Gordon.

Soven, M. I. (1998). *Teaching writing in middle and secondary schools: Theory, research, and practice.* Boston: Allyn and Bacon.

Tierney, R. J., & Pearson, P. D. (1983). Toward a composing model of reading. *Language Arts, 60*(5), 568–580.

12

Integrating Literacy Instruction Through Units

Activating Prior Knowledge and Making Connections

Mr. Jamieson was beginning a unit on Ancient Egypt with his fifth-grade social studies class. He knew that his students differed widely in their reading ability, background knowledge, proficiency with the English language, and interest in history. For these reasons, he decided that he would use informational picture books rather than sticking with the history textbook. Because he was concerned about differences in students' prior knowledge and interest, he decided to use a Problem Situation, a prereading strategy that was suited for this situation (Vacca & Vacca, 1999). This strategy involves students in extensive discussion of a problem as a preview of important ideas in the text. To implement the strategy, Mr. Jamieson divided the class into groups and asked them to do the following exercise:

What Would You Do?

You are an Egyptian priest. The Pharaoh has just died and the new Pharaoh (his son) has ordered you to prepare him for his journey into the afterlife. Doing a bad job could cost you your life.

1. What do you think the Pharaoh would want to have with him? Make a list.
2. The Pharaoh's body needs to be turned into a mummy so it will last forever in the afterlife. Describe step by step how you will accomplish that.

Each group made a list on poster paper to answer one of the two questions. They hung the sheets on the walls and Mr. Jamieson called on the groups to comment on how their ideas were similar to or different from those of other groups. The teacher told students to place a question mark next to ideas on their charts that were in dispute. He then directed them to skim quickly through the picture book *Mummies Made in Egypt* (Aliki, 1979) to determine if their "solution" to the problem situation was accurate.

After they read, the groups made corrections to their posters with different colored markers. The whole class discussed the new information they had acquired and identified what information remained unconfirmed. Then they brainstormed additional questions about mummies, burial practices, pyramids, and the religious beliefs of Ancient Egyptians. For the next two classes, the students were given access to a cart full of informational picture books, other trade books, and reference books on Ancient Egypt to see if they could find answers to their questions.

Before you continue reading this chapter, consider these questions:
1. Besides learning facts about Ancient Egypt, what might students learn about literacy from this activity?
2. What are the advantages of using various trade books, including picture books, as sources of information?
3. How might Mr. Jamieson include additional language arts activities in this social studies project? How might he connect science? art? math?
4. How do these language activities help students to learn content? vocabulary?
5. How do these language activities help beginning, intermediate, and advanced English language learners?

A Model of Integration

Literacy learning in the middle grades does not occur in a vacuum. Learning to read and write needs to connect to young adolescents' development as people and as students. Teachers can help with these tasks by organizing instruction in ways that encourage students to make connections. Although total integration has not been implemented into the middle school curriculum, forms of integrating literacy instruction are fairly common in schools today. Gavelek, Raphael, Biondo, and Wang (2000) conducted a thorough review of the research-based literature on literacy integration and determined that the three components to the integration of thought and language are the integrated language arts, the integrated curriculum, and integration in and out of school.

Distinguishing the forms of integration helps teachers focus on the question "What do I want my students to learn?" Teachers want students to learn a vast amount of content in literature, science, social studies, music, and art. Teachers also want students to master certain language processes such as reading, writing, speaking, listening, thinking, viewing, and representing their ideas visually. In addition, teachers desire for students to acquire a love of reading and writing and to acquire the ability to become lifelong learners. It takes a skillful teacher to incorporate all of these objectives into instructional planning for a day or a week, let alone for an entire school year. The instructional unit is a useful way of organizing learning activities to address these various goals of student learning.

Characteristics of Unit-Centered Reading

Reading, writing, speaking, listening, viewing, and representing are ways of communicating that are inextricably interrelated. Sometimes reading and language arts teachers use one to teach the other. For example, a seventh-grade reading teacher may teach students to recognize text structures in reading so that students can use those structures in their writing. Or, a sixth-grade language arts teacher may have students listen to different dialects while a story is read aloud so that they will be more successful when reading dialect in *The Adventures of Tom Sawyer* (Twain, 1876). A truely integrated language arts unit, however, "involves the coordinated instruction of some combination of the major language processes as tools to achieve a learning goal" (Gavelek, Raphael, Biondo, & Wang, 2000, p. 590). Although there are many different kinds of units, unit-centered reading routines will always include the following characteristics:

1. Students engage with multiple print and nonprint sources, including technology, and are expected to make connections among them.
2. Students have the opportunity to explore a topic or theme long enough to elaborate their schema for the topic by examining it from several perspectives. They can also naturally blend the use of fiction and nonfiction text.
3. Students read, write, speak, listen, and make visual representations to develop new understandings of themselves and the world.
4. In the process of using language to learn, students acquire new vocabulary, learn new language structures, and gain experience with new text structures and genres.

The teacher's roles in unit-centered literacy routines include carefully defining the unit goals, identifying appropriate materials, providing necessary background knowledge, carefully monitoring students' progress, and differentiating instruction to meet the needs of English language learners and other students with special needs. Instruction during units includes posing questions to stimulate new ways of thinking and acting as a "process helper" by modeling strategies for constructing meaning, and supporting students through whole-class, small group, and individual learning activities. Guiding students in the process of making connections between activities is an especially important teacher role in units.

Types of Units

The many kinds of units help students make connections between ideas. Some units are confined to one traditional subject area, such as science or history. Others are interdisciplinary, combining activities from several subjects. Still others focus on a "big idea" such as "invention" or "adaptation" that is not obviously part of any particular subject. Units also differ in their central goals. A short story unit, for instance, could focus on the structure and style of short stories, on finding stories that are fun to read, or on exploring an important theme such as "facing challenges." We will explore the different possibilities by focusing on samples of four kinds of units: topic units, literature focus units, integrated theme units, and inquiry units.

Topic Units

Mr. Jamieson's unit on Ancient Egypt is an example of a topic unit. The unit could be limited to a single discipline, social studies, with a focus on examining how Egyptian society was organized and some important events in its history. Mr. Jamieson was interested, however, in helping his students look at this very different civilization from multiple perspectives, so he created an interdisciplinary unit that included ideas from other subjects such as art, math, and language arts.

Mr. Jamieson teaches in a self-contained classroom, but an interdisciplinary unit (IDU) is often planned and delivered by three to five teachers who serve on a team sharing the same students and usually having a common planning time. Planning for a team interdisciplinary unit takes time and a lot of collaboration. Units, like lessons, should incorporate a framework of preparing students to learn, guiding and supporting students' learning, and reinforcing and extending concepts. In addition, activities that stimulate student interest and motivation are imperative. Mr. Jamieson's planning followed these steps:

1. **Choosing an essential question.** The topic of Ancient Egypt could be studied for many years. Mr. Jamieson elected to narrow the focus of the unit by posing the central question, "What was it like to live in Ancient Egypt if you were not a pharaoh?"
2. **Identifying resources.** Mr. Jamieson decided to confront some of his students' misconceptions head on by showing a few scenes from the film *The Mummy* so they could discuss what in the film might possibly be true. He collected a variety of other materials, and browsed the Internet until he had located a number of WebQuest projects that allowed his students to find interesting information online.
3. **Determining content objectives.** The question about daily life takes in much of the content that would appear in the textbook, so Mr. Jamieson identified some concepts that students should know. These included the role of the Nile river in the economy, artistic and technical achievements, education, and ways in which Egyptian life was similar to and different from American life. He also decided that English language learners could share about their native countries and how they are similar and different from Ancient Egypt.
4. **Determining process objectives.** Finding information relevant to the essential question for the unit required students to decide quickly what parts of a resource were relevant and then to skim for key words to locate the needed information. The unit also presented an opportunity to show how various subtopics were related by constructing a graphic organizer.
5. **Identifying key vocabulary.** Mr. Jamieson realized that his students would confront unfamiliar vocabulary throughout the unit. Table 12.1 on page 196 shows the various vocabulary activities he planned.

Collaboration in Topic Units. It seems logical to most teachers that when students are guided to see connections and relevance across disciplines, they can better understand the topic or theme and can apply ideas to new situations more readily. Sometimes two teachers will create a connection by simply agreeing to do related topics at the same time. An English teacher, for instance, might decide to do a unit on historical novels set during the

TABLE 12.1 *Vocabulary Activities*

Activity	Procedure	Purpose
Knowledge rating	Mark each word to show how familiar it is.	Assessment, introduction.
Graphic overview	Teacher presents a web or other graphic that shows the relationship between words.	Introduce new vocabulary and concepts.
Closed word sorts	Students sort words into categories chosen by the teacher.	Associate words that have related meanings.
Open word sorts	Students sort words into categories they choose.	Assessment, develop schema for the topic.
Concept of definition word maps	Identify category, attributes, and examples for a concept.	Clarify and reinforce meaning of key concepts.
Semantic features analysis	Mark attributes that apply to vocabulary words.	Review and reinforce vocabulary.

Civil War at the same time the students are studying that topic in their social studies class. This type of collaboration is useful for all students, including English language learners. They can learn similar vocabulary and background information that is helpful in both subjects.

The two teachers might also arrange a *multidisciplinary unit* in which students are asked to make some specific connections between the ideas portrayed in fiction and actual historical events. An even greater degree of collaboration is required for an interdisciplinary unit (IDU). This unit may range in length from two to four weeks. Planning an interdisciplinary unit takes time and skill to ensure that each discipline is represented, that all the language modes are included, and that the unit represents a wide variety of activities. Figure 12.1 shows how all the disciplines might be included in the Ancient Egyptians unit.

In summary, topic units such as the Ancient Egypt unit allow students to acquire facts, develop new vocabulary, use a variety of materials on different levels of difficulty, and use all language modes to assist their understanding.

Vocabulary Learning for English Language Learners   Topic units allow English language learners repeated exposures to academic words and the opportunity to use those words in all of the language modes. Herrell and Jordan (2004) suggest creating a word wall to display vocabulary. English language learners and other students who need extra exposure to new words can review these words each day. The teacher might also call on various students to read some of the words aloud. Once English language learners have had the chance to hear and practice the pronunciations, they can also be included in pronouncing them in class.

Herrell and Jordan (2004) also suggest vocabulary role play for English language learners. A group that includes both English language learners and some strong readers

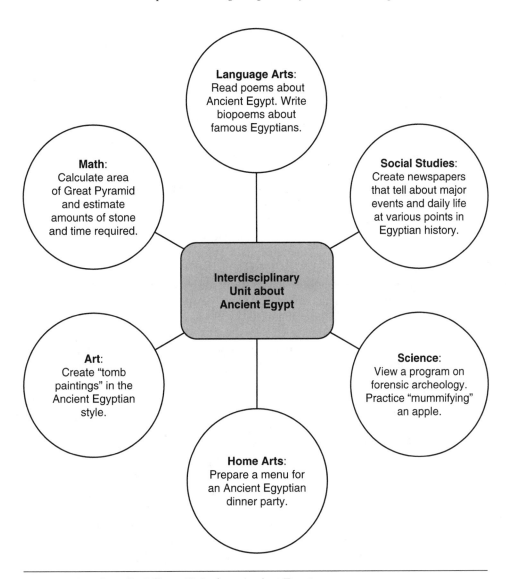

FIGURE 12.1 *Interdisciplinary Unit about Ancient Egypt*

might, for example, dramatize the steps for making a mummy by using props such as bathroom tissue for wrappings, some objects to represent "organs" that were removed, and containers to hold them. The group could then develop a script and various students could act out the steps. English language learners who are involved in the acting must listen carefully to suit their actions to the words. If possible, they should also participate in writing the script and reading part of it aloud.

Literature Focus Units

In this type of unit, reading, writing, speaking, listening, viewing, and representing are used to understand the purpose, structures, and intended affects of a genre, or to focus on a particular aspect of language use. Mr. Hernandez, an eighth-grade language arts teacher, helped students to explore the concept of style by using the books of Walter Dean Myers including *Slam* (1996), *Handbook for Boys* (2002), *Somewhere in the Darkness* (1992), and *Monster* (1999). Students compared and contrasted the character's identity, the setting, the plot line, and recurring themes across the novels.

Mr. Hernandez chose to begin this unit with a read-aloud of the book *Handbook for Boys* (Myers, 2002). As he read his way through the novel, he stopped and modeled how to record key aspects of the story. He could have chosen to examine the setting (Harlem, neighborhood, and barbershop), but he focused instead on describing the main character, Jimmy. Jimmy is an African American teenage boy who has been making poor choices in life so far. As Mr. Hernandez continued through the story, his focus shifted to the relationships Jimmy has with Duke (an elderly gentleman and well-respected businessman) and with Kevin (a peer). At the conclusion of the book, Mr. Hernandez discussed the overriding intent, theme, and plot line (illustrating a perspective on the African American experience, focusing heavily on decision making and what is right, and portraying the development of friendships).

Once his students had the opportunity to listen and discuss Myers's style in *Handbook for Boys,* they then selected another of Myers's books to read either in literature circles, in pairs, or individually. As students read their selected novel, it was important for them to keep a learning log of their observations. Learning logs become a tool to help students organize their thoughts and to provide a support when engaging in discussions or looking for patterns. A student choosing *Slam* or *Somewhere in the Darkness* might record the main character again as being an African American, male, teenager. Again, there is a strong tie to the development of relationships with peers, adults, or even the characters place in the world. Both stories portray the protagonist facing adversity, learning life lessons along the way, and eventually forging new friendships and choosing the "right" path.

Author studies focusing on literary texts allow the teacher to both reinforce learned skills and strategies and introduce new skills and strategies within a meaningful context. Perhaps the greatest strength of a study like this is how it lends itself to writing. Students can begin to identify patterns used by Myers and try out some of his craft as they search for their own voice on the page. English language learners may be asked to write about how they have faced adversity and how they will overcome obstacles in their lives.

Integrated Theme Units

Beane (1990, 1993, 1995, 1997) argues that the middle school curriculum should be based on the personal and social concerns of students. A theme such as "transitions" would, therefore, make an appropriate focus for a unit because it would intersect the young adolescent concern with personal changes and the social concern of living in a changing world. Listening to the hallway chatter about the reality show *Survivor* led Ms. Radcliffe's team to develop a unit around a survival theme.

Notice that the theme is not directly related to any particular school subject. The different kinds of learning that students experience in a theme unit are so thoroughly blended that they are sometimes called "integrated" units. Each teacher on the team may have found a different kind of significance in the theme, but the unit belonged equally to all of them. The following steps, guiding questions, and examples may assist you in the development of a themed unit:

1. **Deciding on a theme.** When considering themes, start with the interests of the students. Current television shows, movies, song lyrics, and fads provide possibilities as well as dramatic events in the news. When considering a potential theme, it is important to ask a few questions regarding its vitality.
   - Does the theme explore the human dimension relative to important understandings (e.g., survival, courage, war, death, friendship)?
   - Is the theme valuable for the particular group of students, providing them the opportunity to think critically about social or cultural issues?
   - Does the theme allow for interconnections within the curriculum framework or scope and sequence?
2. **Identify significant concepts and understandings.** The act of brainstorming or listing generalizations relevant to the theme is crucial. Blending the selection process of literature and resources with this step helps to focus student attention on the most significant concepts. For example, many of the books chosen for this unit clearly had the underlying messages that *challenges make people stronger, resourcefulness of an individual plays a key role in survival,* and *overcoming adversity allows an individual to know his or her inner self.* By narrowing the scope of the theme, students focus their attention on a related set of ideas as they explore different texts and resources.

   Writing, speaking, listening, reading, viewing, and content-related concepts can all be taught within the context of a theme. Themes can provide relevance for students by creating a web of connected relationships and meanings that evoke higher levels of questioning, feeling, and understanding. Because thematic units unfold gradually through a series of experiences, they provide a shared experience for all students regardless of background, prior learning, or reading level.
3. **Locate appropriate resources.** These included *Hatchet* (Paulsen, 1987), *Brian's Winter* (Paulsen, 1996), *Trapped* (Sullivan, 1998), *Between a Rock and a Hard Place* (Carter, 1995), *Escape from Warsaw* (Serraillier, 1963), *The Sign of the Beaver* (Speare, 1983), *Julie of the Wolves* (George, 1974), Island Trilogy: *Shipwreck, Survival, Escape* (Korman, 2001), and *Island of the Blue Dolphins* (O'Dell, 1960). The quality of texts and media selected is as critical as identifying the theme. Some questions to consider include:
   - Does the literature (and other sources) support the theme at a deep and meaningful level or is it a mere superficial integration?
   - Do the texts chosen provide for the varying levels of reading or language ability or do I need a plan for the scaffolding of text (audio books, buddy reading, shared reading)?
   - What additional resources would enrich the study (e.g., videos, lyrics, graphic representations, artifacts, speakers from other cultures)?

4. **Determine what will be assessed and how.** The final consideration when designing a theme unit is to incorporate a variety of ways for students to demonstrate their learning and new understandings about the theme. Learning activities and opportunities must embrace the variety of learning styles of students. Each activity must have a focus that deepens the understanding of the theme, and yet remains meaningful for the students. While not every activity will be graded, it is important to know what students are expected to learn and/or demonstrate (based on theme and communication skills). The assessment will guide the development of learning activities.

5. **Encourage connections.** Theme units are all about students making connections, and sometimes they will make connections other than the ones that teachers plan. In the Survival unit, students were not confined to the stacks of books presented, but were encouraged to find other sources as well. Much discussion came from movies such as *Castaway, John Q, Saving Private Ryan,* and *Titanic.*

   Popular lyrics from different musical artists such as Tupac and Destiny's Child were played and analyzed for references relative to the concepts identified within the theme. One student shared a lyric she thought was relevant, while her peers pointed out what they thought were flaws in her argument. She responded by bringing in a few clips from the music video and arguing that the images were relevant to the conversation; within minutes, she had the support of most the class. The notion that images portray messages sent more students in search of graphic representations. Students began creating PowerPoint presentations and photo essays (through the help of the Internet) on the theme.

   Current events in the media (such as a news story about a wife who had been a coma for a decade) began debates as to whether their first definition of survival, "to stay alive," was really accurate: and others began to question what "alive" meant. One student posed the following question to the class: "If a person overcomes adversity (such as being trapped in an avalanche, digging out, attracting rescuers, and making it to a hospital to get medical help), but in the end dies from complications related to the event (such as hypothermia and frostbite), is he or she still considered a "survivor"?

   Students also developed a wide range of methods for presenting the insights they had gained throughout the unit. From presenting PowerPoints to designing dioramas, writing position statements to acting out relevant scenes, these different exchanges in response to texts and other media provided the opportunity for the students to develop their textual and communicative competences, demonstrating their abilities to comprehend, create, and critique, through such tasks as reading, writing, speaking, listening, and viewing. All levels of English language learners could participate in most of these activities, with minimal scaffolding from the teacher. Students also synthesized all they knew about survival by completing a class concept map as shown in Figure 12.2.

   The power of themed units is that literacy skills and strategies can be taught within a meaningful context. Not only are students gaining a deeper understanding of the theme, but they are developing as readers and writers as well. For example, using anticipation guides not only reinforces strategies such as predicting, but also requires the reader to analyze their thoughts, thus enhancing thematic understanding.

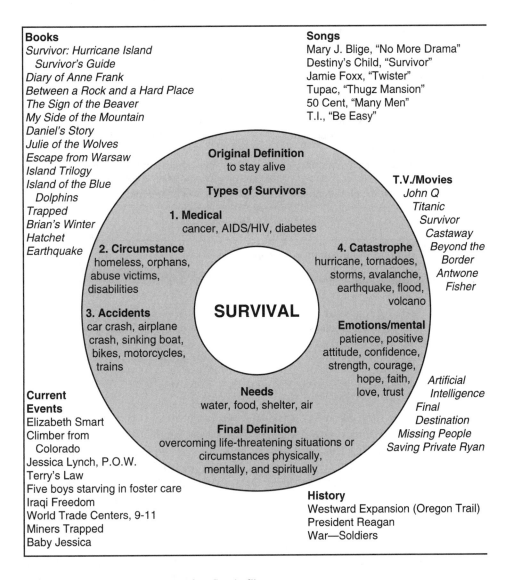

Books
Survivor: Hurricane Island
  Survivor's Guide
Diary of Anne Frank
Between a Rock and a Hard Place
The Sign of the Beaver
My Side of the Mountain
Daniel's Story
Julie of the Wolves
Escape from Warsaw
Island Trilogy
Island of the Blue
  Dolphins
Trapped
Brian's Winter
Hatchet
Earthquake

Songs
Mary J. Blige, "No More Drama"
Destiny's Child, "Survivor"
Jamie Foxx, "Twister"
Tupac, "Thugz Mansion"
50 Cent, "Many Men"
T.I., "Be Easy"

Original Definition
to stay alive

Types of Survivors

1. Medical
cancer, AIDS/HIV, diabetes

2. Circumstance
homeless, orphans,
abuse victims,
disabilities

3. Accidents
car crash, airplane
crash, sinking boat,
bikes, motorcycles,
trains

4. Catastrophe
hurricane, tornadoes,
storms, avalanche,
earthquake, flood,
volcano

Emotions/mental
patience, positive
attitude, confidence,
strength, courage,
hope, faith,
love, trust

SURVIVAL

Needs
water, food, shelter, air

Final Definition
overcoming life-threatening situations or
circumstances physically,
mentally, and spiritually

T.V./Movies
John Q
Titanic
Survivor
Castaway
Beyond the
  Border
Antwone
Fisher

Artificial
Intelligence
Final
Destination
Missing People
Saving Private Ryan

**Current
Events**
Elizabeth Smart
Climber from
  Colorado
Jessica Lynch, P.O.W.
Terry's Law
Five boys starving in foster care
Iraqi Freedom
World Trade Centers, 9-11
Miners Trapped
Baby Jessica

History
Westward Expansion (Oregon Trail)
President Reagan
War—Soldiers

FIGURE 12.2 *Class Concept Map for "Survival"*

Inquiry Units: Searching and Sharing

Most units should include some element of inquiry. A topic unit such as Mr. Jamieson's, for instance, might have begun with the KWL procedure (Ogle, 1986). Students could have been asked to brainstorm a list of what they *know* about Ancient Egypt (the *K*) and then Mr. Jamieson could have asked them what they *want* to know (the *W*). Their prior knowledge and questions would be recorded on either a whole-class or individual version of the KWL sheet shown in Figure 12.3. After their reading, students would fill in the column that

FIGURE 12.3 *KWL Chart for a Unit on Ancient Egypt*

What we KNOW	What we WANT to find out	What we LEARNED
Ancient Egyptains built pyramids. They lived near the Nile. They made dead people into mummies. They had a pharaoh instead of a king. They made slaves of the Jewish people.	Why did they build pyramids? Were the wives or servants of pharaohs buried with them? Did they have pets? Why would a pharaoh want money or a chariot in the afterlife? What kinds of clothes did Egyptians wear? What did they eat?	

Categories of information we expect to see:
   A. Making Mummies
   B. Pyramids
   C. Pharaohs
   D. The Nile River
   E. Jobs and Products
   F. Food and Clothing

shows what they have learned. Notice that the sample sheet shows space for "Categories" of information. This helps students to synthesize their questions into a few central issues for investigation. One variation called KWWL (Bryan, 1998) adds the question "Where can I learn this?" KWL Plus (Carr & Ogle, 1987), adds the step of using the information in the "Learned" column to create a web of information that can, in turn, be used to write a summary of findings.

Ms. Radcliffe's Survival unit also contained an element of inquiry. Students drew from their reading of fiction books, from media, and from current events in order to address questions about what it means to be a survivor. Most thematic units can be thought of as attempts to gather ideas that define and explain a "big idea." Inquiry units make that process more explicit.

Goals and Characteristics of Inquiry Units.   Changes in society are making a focus on inquiry-based learning both easier and more important all the time. An information-rich environment makes it possible for students to find answers to questions by accessing print and nonprint sources from all over the country. On the other hand, the same information-rich culture requires that students learn to sort through the flood of messages that constantly surrounds them and to find information that is reliable and relevant. *The Standards for the Language Arts* (International Reading Association, 1997) developed by IRA and NCTE describe the basic characteristics of inquiry units:

Students conduct research on issues and interests by generating ideas and questions, and by posing problems. They gather, evaluate, and synthesize data from a variety of sources (e.g., print and nonprint texts, artifacts, and people) to communicate their discoveries in ways that suit their purpose and their audience. (p.7)

Searching and sharing are the two engines that drive research units. The activities carried out by students and the procedures that teachers use to guide them are all designed around the twin goals of actively searching for information and becoming part of a community of information users. The process of planning and carrying out inquiry units requires time and close collaboration between teachers and students. The following steps characterize that process:

1. **Introduce a relevant "umbrella topic."** Umbrella topics, like themes, set a broad direction for the unit while allowing as much room as possible for students to pursue their interests. For example, "Going to Court" is an umbrella topic for exploring the ways in which people become involved with the legal system. The investigations that eventually come under this umbrella are likely to relate to such areas of the curriculum as the Constitution, careers, and history, but the umbrella allows plenty of room for students to indulge their curiosity. Some initial reading or other investigation helps students to see the topic from multiple perspectives (Short, Harste, & Burke, 1995). For example, the class could read short newspaper articles about a variety of recent court actions from sentencings to injunctions to damage suits and then hold a class discussion about good and bad reasons to be in court.

2. **Identify compelling questions.** In an inquiry unit, finding the right questions should be given as much attention as finding the answers. Once the umbrella topic has been introduced, students can begin the process of generating, refining, and selecting questions to guide their inquiry. Harvey (1998) points out that inquiry works best when students are directed by a desire to find the answers to compelling questions. She suggests having students post questions on a class bulletin board or work together to create "question webs" around a central question. For the "Courts" inquiry, students in small groups could generate poster-size lists of possible questions. In brainstorming activities such as this, beginning English language learners should be paired with advanced learners so that they can be included in the process. Once the questions are generated, they could examine all the lists and put a tally mark next to the questions they would most like to have answered.

3. **Conduct preliminary investigations.** When students do traditional reports, they are usually assigned a topic or are expected to narrow their inquiry before they begin their investigations. In a true inquiry unit, however, they begin their investigations with a set of focus questions that they may or may not be able to answer. As shown in Figure 12.4 on page 204, an inquiry is determined by a combination of what students want to know, what they can reasonably find out given the available time and resources, and what will meet the expectations of the audience for their inquiry.

   As Short, Harste, and Burke (1995) point out, the process of inquiry is as recursive as the writing process. Students should be encouraged to revise their original ideas as they gain additional insight. Working with a partner or a small group can

Effective Inquiry Units Meet These Criteria

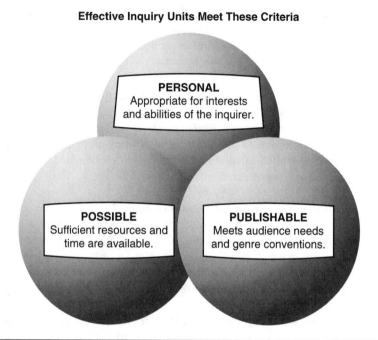

FIGURE 12.4   *Developing an Inquiry*

help students to see additional possibilities and to find out what questions are of interest to their potential audience.

4. **Scaffold the process.** The process of writing is learned by engaging in composition in a community of writers. The research process is learned in a community of researchers in which everyone—including the teacher—is engaged in finding and evaluating information. In such an environment, students can be guided by teacher modeling and whole-class and small-group sharing. Students are quick to share good resources or search strategies they have found.

   Teachers can also provide scaffolds that help students to focus their reading and organize the information they have found. One such scaffold is an Inquiry Chart (Hoffman, 1988). As the example in Figure 12.5 shows, the Inquiry Chart (or I-Chart) encourages students to record their sources and to categorize information according to the question it answers. The relatively small size of the I-Chart boxes discourages copying. The chart often leads students to consider important issues about the reliability of information as they notice contradictions between sources. The I-Chart makes information easier to synthesize when the time comes to create a final product, and students do not have to go back and trace down sources that they forgot to record.

5. **Refine and publish.** The process of sharing and modeling continues as students wind down the gathering of information and begin considering how to reach an audience with the information they have discovered. All of the written products that

FIGURE 12.5 *An Example of an I-Chart*

Topic: Egyptian Food	Q1: What did average Egyptians eat most?	Q2: What did they usually drink?	Q3: How did they preserve their food?	Other Facts	Other Questions
Website 1	Fish, geese, oxen, lentils, grapes.	Beer, wine.	Salting and brining.	Water wasn't safe to drink. Poor people would fish from the Nile and gather fruit.	Did children drink alcohol? Did poor people usually have geese? Why didn't they eat eggs?
Website 2	Ducks, geese, melons, garlic, pomegranates, figs.	Milk, wine, beer.	Salting, drying.	Beer was made from barley. Bread was usually gritty and hard.	Didn't they have chickens?
Website 3	Melons, dates, figs, cucumbers, barley bread, geese, and ducks.	Weak beer.	Salting, drying, smoking over a slow fire.	Olive oil and spices were imported from other countries.	Did they preserve fruit? Did smoke work better than salting?

were discussed in the previous chapter are possible ways of publishing research. Two additional options to consider are WebQuests and Multigenre Papers.

A WebQuest is a an inquiry-oriented activity in which some or all of the information that learners find comes from resources on the Internet (March & Dodge, 2004). As the name implies, a WebQuest sends a learner on some sort of quest to answer a question or solve a problem. Usually the student follows a more or less predetermined path to the specified goal, so WebQuests fit better with topic units than with the type of inquiry unit we have just described. If, however, students collaborate to *create* a WebQuest for others, they will need to synthesize information at a high level, and they will experience the satisfaction of publishing their work in a form where it is likely to be read by thousands of other students. Students should experience several WebQuests before they attempt this option, and you may want to structure a multidisciplinary inquiry that includes a computer science teacher.

The multigenre research paper (Allen, 2001) also requires a high level of synthesis because students are asked to transform the information they have gathered into totally different genres. The products they create might include everything from fictionalized obituaries to poems to narrative stories to internal monologues. As the name implies, they are encouraged to produce a number of different pieces that may be collected into a class book. Students involved in this process must be carefully guided to consider what kinds of writing will best communicate the essence of their findings. For the "Going to Court" unit, students might create imaginary newspaper articles, diary entries, or even legal briefs to illustrate some of the ways in which people experience an encounter with the legal system. Creating these multiple products is an excellent way of helping students to see people and events from multiple perspectives.

Monitoring and Evaluating Inquiry Units.   Rycik (1994) conducted a study of inquiry projects and found that teachers managed the projects by breaking the process down into steps and by setting deadlines for each step. Unfortunately, those procedures interfered with the teachers' goals of supporting independence and exploration.

Teachers can monitor progress by using many of the same procedures that they use in reading and writing workshops. If students work in a peer response group, they can gauge the progress of their inquiry by seeing what their peers have accomplished. Status reports, mini-conferences, self-reports, and observing response groups can help teachers to plan instruction and to provide individual help where it is most needed. The teacher may have regularly scheduled mini-conferences with English language learners and other students with special needs to ensure that they are meeting benchmarks and understanding concepts.

Throughout the unit and, especially, at its end, teachers need to remember that the goal of inquiry is not just to find the "right" answers. During the project, teachers can conduct whole-class meetings in which students share problems they have encountered and strategies for solving them. Students can also keep a "Researcher's Log" in which they can respond to the day's reading, reflect on what they have learned, and record difficulties and successes.

Sometimes the major outcome of an inquiry is to discover that a question cannot yet be answered. The final evaluation process for the unit must take this into account. A sample rubric that reflects process as well as product goals is shown in Figure 12.6. Teachers may want to conduct a conference with individuals or a group of research partners so that

FIGURE 12.6 *Evaluation Rubric for a Research Unit*

Identified appropriate questions related to the topic	adequate good excellent
Explored a variety of information sources	adequate good excellent
Selected useful and reliable information sources	adequate good excellent
Selected information relevant to the inquiry questions	adequate good excellent
Synthesized and organized information	adequate good excellent
Created a unique product	adequate good excellent
Demonstrated learning about the procedures of research	adequate good excellent

they can discuss what they have learned about the process of research, about their topic, and about reading and writing.

Summary

During a unit, ideas are developed though comparison and contrast over several works. The learning activities allow for the exploration of concepts from multiple perspectives through a variety of texts and media: students should not only respond to text but should also create something that connects to their lives. English language learners, for example, may want to choose something culturally relevant to them. Topic units, literature focus units, theme units, and inquiry units all provide opportunities for students to read, write, speak, listen, and visually represent information as they learn about the world around them.

Responding to Reading

- Recall a unit you studied in middle or high school. How would you rate this unit along the continuum presented below?

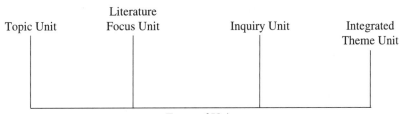

Types of Units

- Here is a list of the ten themes suggested for study by the National Council for the Social Studies. Choose a theme and sketch out how this theme would be developed for each of the points along the continuum.
    1. Culture
    2. Time, Continuity, and Change
    3. People, Places, and Environments
    4. Individual Development and Identity
    5. Individuals, Groups, and Institutions
    6. Power, Authority, and Governance
    7. Production, Distribution, and Consumption
    8. Science, Technology, and Society
    9. Global Connections
    10. Civic Ideals and Practices

A Case to Consider

Ms. Gunn was teaching a social studies unit on the environment and things were moving along well. One day, a seventh grader raised her hand and said, "Is the environment we are studying in social studies the same environment we are studying in science?" Dismayed, Ms. Gunn went next door and inquired about the science curriculum. Sure enough, the science teacher was teaching a unit on the environment.

The middle school Ms. Gunn taught in was not organized into interdisciplinary teams, so teachers shared some but not all students. They did not have a common planning time, so teachers had very few opportunities to coordinate their instructional units. She knew the students were confused, but didn't know exactly what to do about it.

Consider what school organization could improve communication among teachers.

1. How could Ms. Gunn tie her instruction to what was covered in the science class?

2. In what ways could they plan instruction together?

3. What school organizations or schedules can help teachers communicate about curriculum?

Reinforcing Key Ideas

- In this chapter, you have seen examples of four different kinds of units. Discuss the statement "A unit is more than a series of lessons" by using one of those units as an example.
- How do these units involve students in using the language arts? What language skills and strategies might be taught?

Key Terms to Know and Use

topic unit	Literature focus unit	interdisciplinary unit
integrated thematic unit	KWWL	semantic mapping
inquiry chart (I-Chart)	multigenre research paper	WebQuest

Possible Sentences

Use two or three terms in the columns above and write a sentence stating one idea you now know about integrating literacy instruction through units. Write four or five such sentences using different words until you have a nice summary paragraph.

Beyond the Book

- Write or discuss the ways in which the units in this chapter are and are not like those you experienced in the middle grades. You might consider materials, groups, the role of oral language and writing, or evaluation.
- To experience a WebQuest or learn more about how and why they are used, visit the WebQuest page at San Diego State University at http://webquest.sdsu.edu/.
- A web browser will take you to many other sites with samples of WebQuests produced by teachers and students. Try to find one that is multidisciplinary and contains multiple genres.

- James Beane first published *A Middle School Curriculum: From Rhetoric to Reality* in 1990 (the second edition was published in 1993). This book lays out a framework for true integration in the middle school. It is available through the National Middle School Association. You may find this very readable book helpful as you plan units.
- The National Middle School Association has numerous books available on curriculum integration. Some of the most interesting are listed below:
  - Alexander, W.M. (1995). *Student Oriented Curriculum: Asking the Right Questions.*
  - Nesin, G. & Lounsburg, J. (1999). *Curriculum Integration: Twenty Questions with Answers.*
  - Beane, J. A. (1990). *A Middle School Curriculum: From Rhetoric to Reality* (2nd ed.).
  - Brazee, E.N., & Capelluti, J. (1995). *Dissolving Boundaries: Toward an Integrative Curriculum.*
  - Beane, J.A. (1997). *Curriculum Integration: Designing the core of democratic education.*

  You may wish to visit its website at www.nmsa.org. NMSA also has a published position statement on curriculum that you can download free from the website.
- Northwest Regional Educational Laboratory published another good article. You can access their cite at http://www.nwrel.org/scpd/sirs/8/c016.html.

References

Allen, C. A., (2001). *The multigenre research paper: Voice, passion, and discovery in grades 4–6.* Portsmouth, NH: Heinemann.

Beane, J. A. (1990). *A middle school curriculum: From rhetoric to reality.* Columbus, OH: National Middle School Association.

Beane, J. A. (1993). Problems and possibilities for an integrated curriculum. *Middle School Journal, 25*(1), 18–23.

Beane, J. A. (1995). Curriculum integration and the disciplines of knowledge. *Phi Delta Kappan, 76*(8), 616–622.

Beane, J. A. (1997). *Curriculum integration: Designing the core of democratic education.* New York: Teachers College Press.

Bryan, J. (1998). K-W-W-L. Questioning the known. *The Reading Teacher, 51*(7), 618–620.

Carr, E., & Ogle, D., (1987). K-W-L Plus: A strategy for comprehension and summarization. *Journal of Reading, 30(7),* 626–631.

Gavelek, J. R., Raphael, T. E., Biondo, S. M., & Wang, D. (2000). Integrated literacy instruction. In M. L. Kamil, P. B. Mosenthal, P. D. Pearson, & R. Barr (Eds.), *Handbook of reading research,* Vol. III (pp. 587–607). Mahwah, NJ: Lawrence Erlbaum.

Harvey, S. (1998). *Nonfiction matters: Reading, writing and research in grades 3–8.* York, ME: Stenhouse.

Herrell, A., & Jordan, M. (2004). *Fifty strategies for teaching English language learners* (2nd ed.). Upper Saddle River, NJ: Merrill Prentice Hall.

Hoffman, J. V. (1988). *Understanding reading instruction: A guide to field-based experiences in reading education.* Boston: Allyn and Bacon.

International Reading Association. (1997). *Standards for the language arts.* Newark, DE: Author.

March, T., & Dodge, B. (2004). The learning power of WebQuests. *Educational Leadership, 61*(4), 42.

National Education Association. (1984). *Report of the Committee of Ten: On secondary school studies with the reports of the conferences arranged by the committee.* New York: American Books.

Ogle, D. M. (1986). KWL: A teaching model that develops active reading of expository text. *The Reading Teacher, 39*(6), 564–570.

Rycik, J. A. (1994). *An exploration of student library research projects in seventh grade English and Social Studies classes.* Unpublished doctoral dissertation. Kent State University.

Short, K. G., Harste, J. C., & Burke, C. (1995). *Creating classrooms for authors and inquirers.* Portsmouth, NH: Heinemann.

Vacca, R. T., & Vacca, J. L. (1999). *Content area reading: Literacy and learning across the curriculum* (6th ed.). New York: Longman.

Adolescent Literature References

Aliki. (1979). *Mummies made in Egypt.* New York: Harper and Row.

Carter, A. (1995). *Between a rock and a hard place.* New York: Scholastic.

George, J.C. (1974). *Julie of the wolves.* Boston Harper Trophy.

Korman, G. (2001). *Island trilogy: shipwreck, survival, escape.* New York: Scholastic.

Myers, W. D. (1992). *Somewhere in the darkness.* New York: Scholastic.

Myers, W. D. (1996). *Slam.* New York: Scholastic.

Myers, W. D. (1999). *Monster.* New York: HarperCollins.

Myers, W. D. (2002). *Handbook for boys.* New York: Harper Trophy.

O'Dell, S. (1960). *Island of the blue dolphins.* Boston: Houghton Mifflin.

Paulsen, G. (1987). *Hatchet.* New York: Bradbury.

Paulsen, G. (1996). *Brian's winter.* New York: Delacorte.

Serraillier, I. (1963). *Escape from Warsaw.* New York: Scholastic.

Speare, E. G. (1983). *The sign of the beaver.* Boston: Houghton Mifflin.

Sullivan, G. (1998). *Trapped!* New York: Scholastic.

Twain, M. (1876). *The adventures of Tom Sawyer.* Hartford, CT: American Publishing Company.

13

Comprehensive and Collaborative Programs

As we have shown throughout this book, the literacy development of young adolescents is a complex process. Reading and writing must be more than subjects to be studied. Literacy is intricately linked to every aspect of a young adolescent's life inside and outside of school. So, supporting literacy development requires a comprehensive and collaborative effort. In this concluding chapter, we briefly review some of the crucial elements of a comprehensive plan for developing literacy in the middle grades: supportive classroom instruction, school-wide commitment and collaboration, and parent and community involvement. We include a Planning Instrument that teachers can use to create and evaluate their programs.

Supportive Classroom Instruction

In Part 1 of this book, we argued that teachers needed to understand literacy from multiple perspectives: as a thinking activity, a language activity, a way of making sense of one's own life, and a way of relating to others. These multiple perspectives suggest that literacy learning will be most effective in environments that include:

- Using literacy as a means to explore the personal and social issues that challenge adolescents.
- Using literacy to learn new information and new ways of thinking.
- Seeing reading and writing strategies modeled and being encouraged to use and reflect on those strategies.
- Experimenting with language and examining its forms and structures.
- Discussing how and why language is used and engaging in authentic reading and writing.
- Reading a wide range of material including some easy material and some that requires careful scaffolding or other accommodations.

- Learning to make choices about the texts they will read and write, and about what strategies will be most effective for learning from other readers and writers by collaborations in making meaning.

Part 2 of this book presented a range of literacy routines and showed how each of them addresses the issues listed above. Teachers can make decisions about which of these routines will be most effective for meeting the needs of their particular students and how the routines should be combined. Teachers may, for instance, alternate between reading workshops and writing workshops by doing each one for several weeks or by doing each for several days within a week. They might also include both workshops within one large language arts block.

Teachers can also select literacy routines based on their own expertise, beliefs, and comfort levels and the prevailing curriculum and content standards of their schools. One way to do this is to lay the language arts curriculum goals next to the overview of literacy routines in Chapter 6 and ask which routines fit best. Standards help focus the *goals* of instruction and routines help to plan the *means* of instruction. Assessment can play an important role in clarifying both goals and means.

Beyond the Classroom: School-Wide Commitment and Collaboration

Teachers and administrators need to develop a shared vision of proficient literacy in the middle grades and to work together to make that vision a reality. Classroom teachers need to be open to working with reading specialists to examine instructional options and to monitor the progress of all students, including English language learners and those with disabilities. Reading specialists, on the other hand, need to develop their abilities to act as "a partner, not an expert" (Henwood, 2001, p. 146). Teachers in subject areas other than language arts must be willing to model and reinforce strategies that are effective for learning through literacy.

Humphrey (1998) argues, "For middle grades students, libraries and reading are indispensable partners" (p. 122). He notes that research has established a clear link between high achievement in reading and a school library with a large collection of books and a qualified librarian. Librarians can be important partners in selecting books for literature circles and reading workshops and in planning units.

The library can be an important center for drawing attention to reading. Hallways, bulletin boards, and the cafeteria are also spaces that can be used to highlight students' preferences and achievements. The physical environment of a school, its rituals and events, and the interactions among staff members can all become part of what Fiersen (1997) calls a "culture of literacy." He suggests that staff members regularly conduct a "culture audit" (p. 135) to examine how effectively the continued importance of reading has been communicated. He also recommends forming a reading committee within the school that could plan special events related to reading, writing, and public speaking, and to encourage working collaboratively to improve student performance.

Beyond the School Day: Parent and Community Involvement

Supporting literacy development may extend beyond the traditional school day. After-school programs may involve students in activities that are different from those that are typically found in the classroom. After school book clubs, for instance, may provide an opportunity for students to choose and talk about books outside of the usual context of assignments and grades (Alvermann, Young, Green, & Wisenbaker, 1999).

Technology can be another way to extend the literacy program. Girod, Marineau, and Zhao (in press) found that an afterschool "computer clubhouse" that included electronic literacy activities such as authoring web pages and interactive chat was especially effective with those teenagers who had a low appreciation for school as well as low achievement.

Involving Parents and Community Members

During the middle grades, literacy development continues to be affected by the environment at home. Rasinski and Fawcett (2000) note that many teachers in the middle grades have experienced frustration in parent involvement and had come to believe that parents had the ability to help with reading but were not interested in doing so. They argue that the key element for supporting literacy growth at home is "students and parents reading and writing for real purposes: to enjoy a story, to learn about the world, to communicate with others, to refine thinking through note-taking and organizing information, to compose a personal story" (p. 69).

Rasinski and Fawcett (2000) suggest involving parents through literacy activities such as having students interview them about family history or their recollection of historical events. They also describe how parents can be involved through a school-wide event such as a "reading marathon" in which students try to reach of goal based on every student reading at home for 20 minutes a day for a set period. Meaningful involvement is not always easy to achieve, but parents are more likely to make an effort to help their children in the middle grades when home literacy activities are interesting and meaningful to both student and parent.

Community Involvement and Support

Young adolescents are becoming increasingly connected to their communities as they make the transition into adult life. Closing the gap between school and the "real world" makes true engagement with texts more likely. Throughout this book we have suggested ways to bring the world into the classroom including:

- Inviting guest speakers, especially members of cultural minority groups.
- Using the Internet to find information and audiences for student writing.
- Using popular media such as magazines, movies, and television shows as ways to build background information or to consider the uses and forms of language.

- Building lessons or units around current events, especially issues that are creating concern or great interest among students.

We would also like to suggest taking literacy outside of the classroom and into the community. Students can interview community members to investigate a local problem or create a local history. When students are involved in the community as volunteers through service learning programs, reading and writing can be woven throughout their experience from reading rules and instructions, to writing letters of introduction, to doing research, to writing reflective journals (Magner, 2001).

A Final Thought

An old adage says, "What you do speaks so loud that I can't hear what you say." When literacy instruction is focused on easily testable skills students hear that tests matter, not reading and writing. When time is set aside for reading each day and adults routinely carry around books and share their reading and writing strategies, students hear that literacy matters.

We do not believe that the comprehensive view of literacy learning that we have taken in this book is in conflict with the idea of high standards. We believe that high standards are best achieved when literacy instruction is in harmony with the overall development of young adolescents. We also believe that students in the middle grades need literacy programs that go beyond tests. They deserve programs that help them become thoughtful persons and productive citizens.

School-Wide Planning for Supporting Literacy in the Middle Grades

The following questions can be used by a planning group to examine possibilities for extending literacy learning beyond the classroom.

WHO?

How can you involve:

- Content teachers
- Librarians
- Parents and other family members
- Community organizations/businesses
- Special Education and English language learner teachers

WHAT?

How can you include:

- Electronic literacy
- Career-related literacy
- Consumer literacy
- Media literacy

WHERE?

How can you communicate/support students' literacy activities?

- On walls and bulletin boards
- In trophy cases
- In libraries
- In classrooms
- In school publications
- In communities
- At home

WHEN?

How can you support literacy?

- Before school
- During the summer
- After school
- In the evenings and weekends

WHY?

- What literacy demands do students face academically?
- What literacy demands do students face vocationally?
- What literacy demands do students face socially and culturally?
- What would you like students to believe and feel about their own literacy?

HOW?

- How can you mobilize a comprehensive effort?
- How can you create collaboration?

Beyond the Book

The following are some additional resources for planning a comprehensive literacy program:

Berger, A., & Shafran, E. A. (2000). *Teens for literacy: Promoting reading and writing in schools and communities.* Newark, DE: International Reading Association.

Epstein, J.L. (1995). Creating school/family/community partnerships: Caring for the children we share. *Phi Delta Kappan, 76,* 701–712.

Fisher, D. (2001). "We're moving on up": Creating a schoolwide literacy effort in an urban high school. *Journal of Adolescent and Adult Literacy, 45* (2), 92–101.

Humphrey, W. J., Lipsitz, J., Mcgovern, J. T., & Wasser, J. D. (1997). Supporting the development of young adolescent readers. *Phi Delta Kappan, 79*(4), 305–311.

Irvin, J. L. (1998). *Reading and the middle school student: Strategies to enhance literacy.* Boston: Allyn and Bacon.

Moore, D.W., Bean, T.W., Birdyshaw, D., & Rycik, J. A. (1999). *Adolescent literacy: A position statement.* Newark, DE: International Reading Association.

National Middle School Association. (2002). Supporting young adolescents' literacy learning: A position paper jointly adopted by the International Reading Association and the National Middle School Association.

Stowell, L. (2000). Building alliances, building community, building bridges. In K.D. Wood & T.S. Dickerson (Eds.), *Promoting literacy in grades 4–9: A handbook for teachers and administrators* (pp. 77–96). Boston: Allyn and Bacon.

References

Alvermann, D.E. Young, J. P., Green, C., & Wisenbaker, J. M. (1999). Adolescents' perceptions and negotiations of literacy practices in after-school book clubs. *American Educational Research Journal, 36*(2), 221–264.

Fierson, R. F. (1997). Creating a middle school culture of literacy. *Middle School Journal, 28*(3), 10–15.

Girod, M., Marineau, J., & Zhaoy. (in press). After school computer clubhouses and at-risk teens. *American Secondary Education.*

Henwood, G.F. (2001). A new role for the reading specialist: Contributing toward a high school's collaborative educational culture. In J. A. Rycik & J. L. Irvin (Eds), *What adolescents deserve: A commitment to students' literacy learning* (p. 145–159). Newark, DE: International Reading Association.

Humphrey, W. J. (1998). Supporting the development of strong middle grades readers. *NASSP Bulletin, 82*(600), 87–92.

Magner, M. (2001). Reaching beyond yourself: A middle school service learning program. In J. A. Rycik & J. L. Irvin (Eds.), *What adolescents deserve: A commitment to students' literacy learning* (pp. 165–172). Newark, DE: International Reading Association.

Rasinski, T.V., & Fawcett, G. (2000). Encouraging family involvement in the intermediate and middle grades. In K.D. Wood & T.S. Dickerson (Eds.), *Promoting literacy in grades 4–9: A handbook for teachers and administrators* (pp. 63–76). Boston: Allyn and Bacon.

Index